THE NEWSPAPER

An Introduction to Newswriting and Reporting

Ronald P. Lovell
Oregon State University

Wadsworth Publishing Company
Belmont, California
A Division of Wadsworth, Inc.

Communications Editor: Rebecca Hayden
Production Editors: Connie Martin, Jeanne Heise
Designers: Katie Michaels, Detta Penna
Copy Editor: John Feneron
Illustrators: Debra A. Fox, Don Fujimoto, Stephen Osborn

© 1980 by Wadsworth, Inc. All rights reserved. No part of this book may be reproduced, stored in a retrieval system, or transcribed, in any form or by any means, electronic, mechanical, photocopying, recording, or otherwise, without the prior written permission of the publisher, Wadsworth Publishing Company, Belmont, California 94002, a division of Wadsworth, Inc.

Printed in the United States of America

1 2 3 4 5 6 7 8 9 10—84 83 82 81 80

Photo credits: James A. Folts, 2, 278; Chris Johns, 94. Cover photo: James A. Folts.

Library of Congress Cataloging in Publication Data

Lovell, Ronald P
    The newspaper.

    Bibliography: p.
    Includes index.
    1. Journalism. 2. Reporters and reporting.
I. Title.
PN4775.L6   070.1′72   79–13012
ISBN 0-534-00729-5

To Joseph A. Brandt
who taught me how to be a good teacher
and To My Parents
who taught me how to be a good person.

Preface

This is a book about newspapers and writing for newspapers. It is aimed primarily at beginners, but includes material that all good reporters at all levels of accomplishment need to know about.

The book covers its subject, in part, through the words of editors and reporters on three newspapers: a large Eastern daily, the *Washington Star;* a medium-size daily in the Midwest, the *Topeka* (Kansas) *Capital-Journal;* and a small Western daily, the *Corvallis* (Oregon) *Gazette-Times.* Reporters and editors talk about how they carry out their jobs and why they do the things they do. They also talk about the joys and sorrows of their jobs.

At the outset I want to explain something of the structure of the book. Because of my approach, I have used quotations extensively in the "people at work" segments. The people quoted in these sections sometimes talk in the jargon of the newspaper business, a jargon that may not be familiar to the reader. I do not explain this terminology at the point it is first mentioned because that would break the narrative. I do explain it later. Readers are invited to pause and look up unfamiliar terms in the Glossary at the end of this book if they do not want to wait for the explanation.

By telling their stories, the reporters and editors in the "people at work" segments of the book give the "feel" of what it is like to work on a newspaper. Readers accompany a police-beat reporter on his rounds in Oregon and learn from a reporter in Washington, D.C., how she covered a home for the mentally retarded. They hear why reporters write stories as they do and how editors change them to make them read better. They confront the ethics of going on an all-expenses-paid trip to the Caribbean and the worry of keeping notes and source names confidential.

After introducing the various chapter topics in this way, the book turns to a more conventional approach to cover usual introductory journalism material. Part One, "From Newsroom into Type and onto the Street," sets the scene, with chapters on journalism's place in the world, the different definitions of news, and newspaper organization. It also details two subjects not normally included in basic texts but encountered by reporters early in their careers—printing and photography. Part Two, "News, News, and More News," includes chapters on reporters and editors, and the writing of news stories, feature stories, speech stories, obituaries, and service stories. A chapter on interviewing completes the section. The chapters in Part Three, "Preparing for the Unexpected," review two major problems for reporters and editors—ethics and legal problems.

Much of the discussion in Part Two is illustrated by newspaper stories. Not all of them represent the best writing; some have rough edges, as I point out. Readers are invited to improve them. Part of learning, after all, is looking at things in a critical way.

No book of this kind would have been possible without the help and cooperation of the people who allowed me to probe their professional lives. I am very grateful to them for their patience and kindness.

My unlimited access to, and permission to reprint articles from, the *Corvallis Gazette-Times* would not have been possible without the cooperation of editor Tom Jenks, who also discussed editors and editing with me. I owe him my special thanks. Reporter Bill Monroe of that newspaper also willingly gave me hours of his time and allowed me to look over his shoulder during a hectic day, enduring unending questions and not once losing his temper. For this and his friendship, I thank him. City editor Rod Deckert put up with almost as much observation and interviewing, and I thank him gratefully. Special thanks must also go to reporters John Atkins, John Marshall, and George Wisner and to production manager Wally Newton for their time.

My friend Chris Johns set up my visit to the *Topeka Capital-Journal* newspapers, and I thank him for that and for permission to use his excellent photographs. Assistant managing editor Dick King has my gratitude for access to the newspapers and permission to reprint material. Special thanks must also go to reporter Mike Hall for letting me trail him around for a day, and to photography director Rich Clarkson and photographer Jim Richardson for their time in answering my questions.

At the *Washington Star,* public relations representative Joan Anderson arranged my interviews expertly, for which I thank her. She also saw to it that I received the necessary permission to reprint *Star* material, another indispensable help. I am also very grateful to metropolitan editor Dennis Stern, who gave me five hours of his precious time on a busy day. I also want to thank reporter Diane Brockett for her time and thoughtful answers to my questions.

I want to thank Jim Folts, a colleague in the Oregon State University Department of Journalism, for his excellent photographs, and Fred Zwahlen, chairman of that department, for never questioning the time I spent working on the book.

My thanks must also go to the journalism professors around the country who reviewed my manuscript. John Jay Black of Utah State University and Larry Lain of the University of Dayton devoted a great deal of effort to constructive criticism, and I incorporated many of their helpful suggestions into my revision. I also appreciate the comments of William F. Foreman, Jr., Enterprise State Junior College in Alabama; George K. Hinton, Middle

Georgia College; W. A. Kamrath, El Camino College in California; and Tom Reilly, California State University, Northridge. Wadsworth editor Betty Smith also made valuable contributions to my revision, for which I thank her.

Finally, I want to pay special tribute to my editor, Becky Hayden, who has been a source of continuing encouragement and help during the long months of preparation of the manuscript; to Jack Rochester, then a Wadsworth representative, who saw possibilities in my early, rather hazy outline; to production editors Jeanne Heise and Connie Martin, who guided the rough pile of pages into their final form; to manuscript editor John Feneron for excellent suggestions on the original manuscript; and to designers Katie Michels and Detta Penna for the uniquely clean look of the final book.

My main hopes for readers of *The Newspaper: An Introduction to Newswriting and Reporting* is that they will be able to imagine that the reporters and editors quoted within its pages are in the same room with them, looking over their shoulders, telling them about the good and the bad, and helping them get a good start in a useful and exciting career.

Ronald P. Lovell

Contents

Part One   From Newsroom into Type and onto the Street 2

Chapter 1   Journalism and Its Place in the World 4 / Journalism: In on Everything 6 / The Power of Journalism 7 / The Newspaper 7 / Three Newspapers in Depth 8 / Other Aspects of the Press 10 / Summary 13

Chapter 2   The Event: What Is News? 14 / The Elements of News 16 / *News: Something You Didn't Know Yesterday 18* / Gatekeeper Theory 27 / Front-Page Placement 27 / Knowing What Is News 37 / Summary 40 / Suggested Exercises 40

Chapter 3   The Newspaper: How It Is Organized 42 / The Publisher 44 / The News Side 44 / The Business Side 47 / The Production Side 50 / Summary 50 / Suggested Exercises 51

Chapter 4   Printing, Production, and the New Technology 52 / Letterpress Printing 54 / Offset Printing 57 / Glossary of Printing Terms 57 / The New Technology 59 / *The Newspaper Production Process 64* / Summary 74 / Suggested Exercises 74

Chapter 5   Photography 76 / The New Photography 79 / Editor-Reporter-Photographer Interaction 79 / A Photographer's Typical Day 80 / *The Photographer's Day 82* / Summary 90 / Suggested Exercises 92

Part Two News, News, and More News 94

Chapter 6 The Reporter Uncovered 96 / Three Reporters 98 / *The Reporter's Day* 100 / A Reporter's Routine 112 / Characteristics of a Good Reporter 115 / Why Become a Reporter 120 / Summary 121 / Suggested Exercises 122

Chapter 7 The Editor Observed 124 / Two Editors 126 / Characteristics of a Good Editor 132 / The Different Kinds of Editors 137 / Summary 138 / Suggested Exercises 138

Chapter 8 Writing News Stories and Leads 140 / Inverted-Pyramid Style 143 / Leads 145 / How to Approach a News Story 150 / How Reporters Write News Stories 151 / Attribution 165 / Transitional Sentences 167 / Editorializing 169 / Summary 171 / Suggested Exercises 172

Chapter 9 Writing and Rewriting 174 / General Rules of Writing 176 / Rewriting 179 / Rewriting Public-Relations Press Releases 182 / Updating 187 / Summary 189 / Suggested Exercises 190

Chapter 10 Writing Obituaries and Other Service Stories 192 / Obituaries 195 / Weddings and Engagements 197 / Meetings 199 / Births, Birthdays, and Anniversaries 202 / Summary 204 / Suggested Exercises 205

Chapter 11 Beyond News: Writing Speech Stories 206 / Speech Stories: Routine and Frequent 208 / Covering the Speech Story 217

/ Writing the Story 218 / Summary 222 / Suggested Exercises 222

Chapter 12 **Interviewing 224** / Preparing for the Interview 227 / The Interview Begins 228 / Interviewing 229 / Notes, the Tape Recorder, and the Telephone 231 / After the Interview 233 / Summary 235 / Suggested Exercises 235

Chapter 13 **Beyond News: Writing Feature Stories 236** / News Features 242 / Sidebar Features 246 / Short Features 248 / People Features 253 / Investigative Features 259 / Preparing and Writing the Feature 275 / Summary 277 / Suggested Exercises 277

Part Three Preparing for the Unexpected 278

Chapter 14 **Ethics 280** / Code of Ethics 282 / Ethical Problems 286 / Summary 295 / Suggested Exercises 295

Chapter 15 **Libel, Privacy, Contempt, and Other Legal Concerns of the Press 296** / Libel 298 / Invasion of Privacy 305 / Obscenity 309 / Contempt and Confidentiality 309 / Access to Official Information 318 / Summary 319 / Suggested Exercises 322

Appendix Stylebook 325 / Copy-Editing Marks 329 / Copy Preparation 332

Glossary 335
Bibliography 345
Index 349

THE NEWSPAPER

*An Introduction to
Newswriting and Reporting*

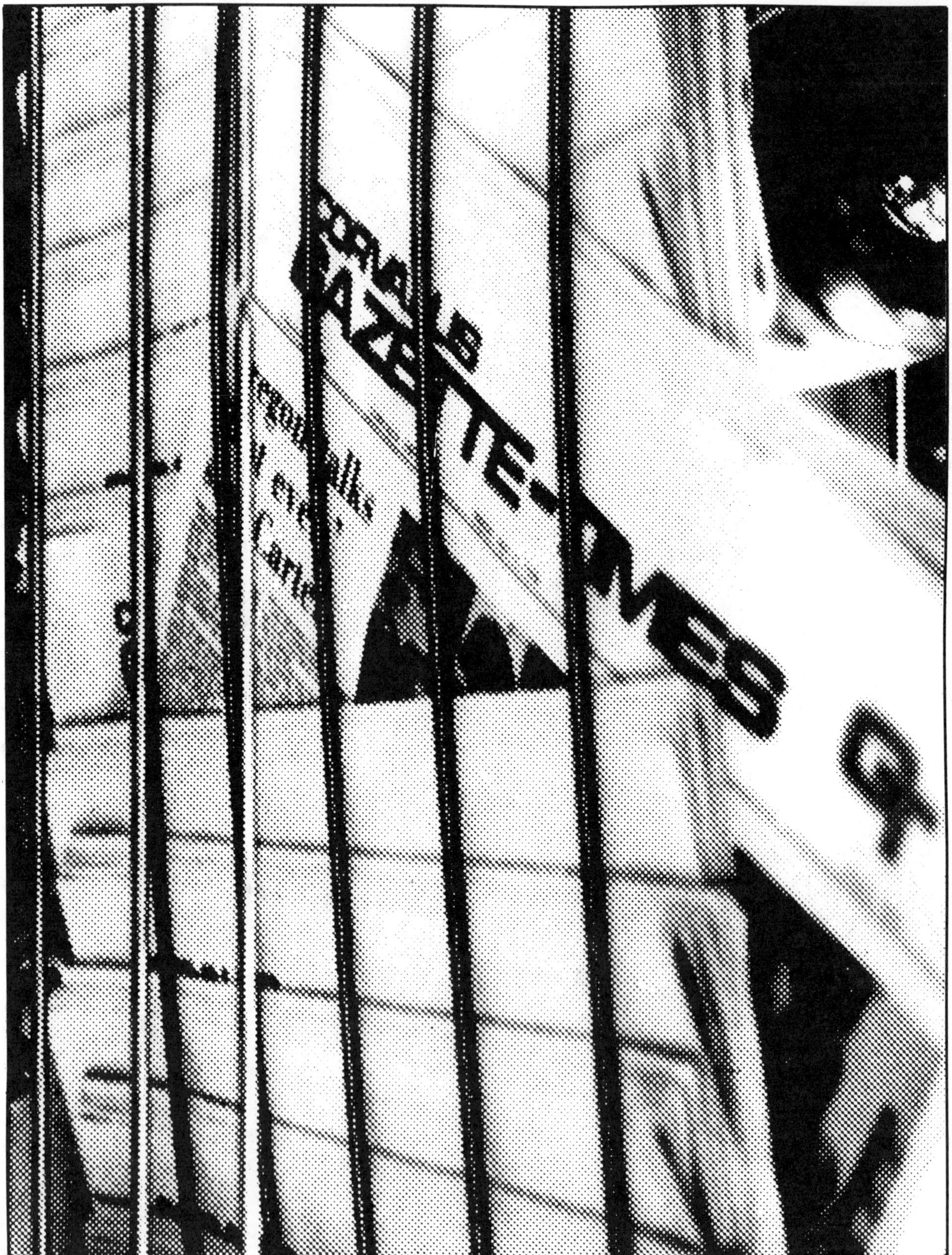

ONE

From Newsroom into Type and onto the Street

"Were it left to me to decide whether we should have a government without newspapers, or newspapers without a government, I should not hesitate a moment to prefer the latter."

Thomas Jefferson

"Responsible journalism is journalism responsible in the last analysis to the editor's own conviction of what, whether interesting or only important, is in the public interest."

Walter Lippmann

1

Journalism and Its Place in the World

Journalism: In on Everything
The Power of Journalism
The Newspaper
Three Newspapers in Depth
Other Aspects of the Press

Journalism in the United States had a beginning as humble as the nation's. It started with almost illegible price lists and shipping news sheets used primarily to spread information about the fledgling nation's commerce. It continued in the form of pamphlets and primitive newspapers whose editors attacked Colonial authorities and risked jail to promote the cause of liberty. In these forms and others that came later, journalistic publications have played an important role in U.S. growth and development.

These publications reported and promoted the expansion of the West, brought details of Civil War battles, and carried stories and advertisements about industrialization. The penny press helped thousands of immigrants learn to read and provided them with facts about their adopted country. When large industrial and business companies acquired too much power, a group of magazine writers called muckrakers exposed their activities to the public, and regulatory legislation resulted.

It was in part because of the press that a war was fought (the Spanish-American) and public morale kept high during national upheaval (World War I, the Great Depression, and World War II). Journalists provided the information that helped turn public opinion against recent wars (in Korea and Vietnam), elected presidents and other politicians, and toppled governments (President Richard Nixon's).

Journalism: In on Everything

To be part of journalism is to be in on many things. Reporters talk to presidents and movie stars and farmers and garage mechanics. They ride in new airplanes that break the sound barrier, and they creep along the bottom of the sea in submarines. They learn secrets and expose wrongdoing. They cover fires, bank robberies, meetings of the city council and the school board. They do good by publishing stories that help people or causes. Sometimes they make mistakes or cause people to lose their jobs or to go to jail. Sometimes they go to jail themselves to protect their sources.

Journalism is an integral part of this country. And people at all levels of society are probably better off after reading or hearing or seeing the news brought to them by the press for one reason: It gives them knowledge, and that knowledge makes them free.

A world without a free and unfettered press would be a world in blinders. How else but through the press are citizens to know enough to vote, pay taxes, or even get mad at their leaders?

Journalism has its faults: People in the press exaggerate and make mistakes in judgment, emphasis, and fact. Without reporters and editors and the work they do, however, the world would be less agreeable because people would be less knowledgeable. What people don't know *can* hurt them. If the press doesn't communicate as much as possible of what citizens need to know, nobody else will.

The Power of Journalism

Journalism has not arrived at its important place in society overnight. Years and events have placed it there. Nowhere is the power of journalism more vividly illustrated than in two recent national traumas, the Vietnam War and the Watergate scandal.

The larger part of the national press turned against the war rather late in its progress. Slowly at first, editorials and news stories presented information that cast doubts on the reasons for U.S. involvement in Vietnam. As these articles appeared, public opinion began to turn against the war. President Lyndon Johnson decided not to run for reelection because of the war, and American society was nearly torn apart when his successor took four years to end it.

In the Watergate scandal, the press revealed much of the information that forced impeachment hearings and President Nixon's eventual resignation. People realized that they could be hurt by what they didn't know. In this case, the press told them what they needed to know.

The press was an important element in society before these two events, but its influence on their outcome brought it new respectability and power—and much criticism. With that heightened respectability and power, however, has come the need for greater responsibility and care in handling news. Readers and viewers do not necessarily like what they read and see any more than they ever did, but they are now more ready to believe it.

Everyone working in journalism must exercise this newly gained power with caution. A trust given by the public can easily be taken away. Abuse, arrogance, and the certainty of always being right—these attitudes can ruin and discredit journalists and betray the ideals and abilities gained from long years of being in on everything that counts.

The Newspaper

From small weeklies produced for audiences of limited size and interests to small, medium, and large dailies, which serve their readers with a more varied and professional content, newspapers constitute a large part of American journalism. In 1977 there were, according to the American Newspaper Publishers Association, 1,764 daily newspapers in the United States, 353 of them published in the morning, 1,433 in the evening, 22 all day, and 665 on Sunday. In the same year, 7,466 weeklies were published. Circulation (the number of subscribers) reached 61.7 million in 1977, with Sunday circulation at 52.8 million.

Employment in the newspaper business—393,000—made it the third largest manufacturing industry, surpassed only by the automobile and steel industries. Advertising revenues for daily newspapers totaled $11.1 billion.

As these statistics indicate, the newspaper business is a significant force in the U.S. economy and a continual source of employment. Newspapers also provide readers with the most complete news coverage available.

In recent years, newspapers have changed considerably. Technological advancements have revolutionized the way news stories are set into type and printed and how the final product looks, for example. But the biggest change is the trend toward consolidated ownership: fewer and fewer companies owning more and more newspapers. This has caused a similarity of content among newspapers, but it has also allowed many to survive when they might otherwise have gone out of business.

Some newspapers have become a profitable and desirable investment. Since 1976, newspapers under single ownership have been purchased so quickly that only 400 dailies remained under separate ownership in 1978.

In large cities, however, afternoon papers (sometimes called PMs) are struggling to survive. Some are losing the battle because their middle-class readers are moving to the suburbs and prefer to get their evening news on television. The delivery trucks are also having increasing difficulty in conveying papers to newsstands and homes over traffic-clogged streets during rush hour.

Morning papers (AMs) are doing better, even in large cities; commuters like to begin the day with a paper, and delivery trucks have fewer traffic problems in the morning. In smaller cities, even PMs are doing well. Indeed, it is the afternoon newspapers that are attracting the attention of the chain owners.

Three Newspapers in Depth

This book will deal with the daily newspaper. It is not the only form of journalism in this country, but it is the oldest and the one that comes to the public's mind when they think of the press. It is also the part of journalism many students enter college planning to join. These days, however, many of them graduate with different ideas and take jobs on general and trade magazines or in television and radio news departments. They also accept employment in such allied fields as public relations, technical writing, and advertising.

This book will deal with the daily newspaper by looking in detail at three of them. The richness of the press in this country derives, of course, from the diversity of publications and television and radio stations that form its substance. But it is not possible to look in depth at all newspapers or at any part of the press in one book. The idea here is to capture the flavor of the daily newspaper business today by considering three of its members: a small Western daily of the type in which most reporters would like to begin their careers, a medium-size daily in the Midwest of the kind that represents a step up in importance and career advancement, and a big-city Eastern daily that epitomizes the best in journalism and for which many reporters would like to work. These three newspapers were selected both for their size and for their geographical location.

The comparison that emerges in the comments of the reporters and editors on these newspapers reveals that the three are not so very different in terms of what it is like to work on a newspaper in the United States today.

The *Washington Star,* located in Washington, D.C., is an afternoon daily of 330,000 readers, and exemplifies the big-city problem outlined earlier. During much of its 125-year existence, the *Star* was owned by three wealthy families. It used to dominate the city but began to lose ground in the 1960s because it failed to keep up with the shift of Washington's population from downtown to the suburbs. Because it lacks regional printing plants, its trucks must fight their way through heavy highway traffic. The *Star* nevertheless reaches many wealthy suburban neighborhoods, but its morning deadlines cause it to miss much of the day's news. The early afternoon edition relies on downtown street sales to workers who are less wealthy than the suburban crowd that advertisers want to reach. Both kinds of readers are tempted to turn to television for their news and entertainment.

Nevertheless, the *Star* has gained ground since its purchase in 1974 by Joe L. Allbritton, a Texas millionaire. He and his first editor, James Bellows, introduced features and kinds of coverage that began to attract new, more affluent readers. In 1978 he sold the paper to Time, Inc., publisher of *Time, Sports Illustrated, Fortune, People,* and *Life* magazines and other allied businesses. That company should have the resources to put the *Star* on a competitive basis with its morning rival, the *Washington Post,* owned by the company that controls *Time* magazine's chief competitor, *Newsweek.*

The morning *Topeka* (Kansas) *Daily Capital* (65,000 circulation) and evening *State Journal* (28,000) are part of the seventeen-newspaper Stauffer chain. The two combine on Sunday as the 75,000 circulation *Topeka Capital-Journal,* the name that shall be used in this book. These newspapers share executives, some editors, some reporters, a photography staff, typesetting equipment, and a printing press. They are typical of the monopoly situation existing elsewhere in the country. These newspapers are so well-entrenched that it would be difficult for another newspaper to get started in Topeka. But citizens are also served by three television stations (one owned by the Stauffers) and a number of radio stations. The newspaper monopoly here is not necessarily bad for readers; it just limits diversity and choice.

The *Corvallis* (Oregon) *Gazette-Times* (14,200 circulation) is part of Lee Enterprises, a fifteen-newspaper chain that also owns broadcasting stations and other allied businesses. The newspaper was privately owned for the first 100 years of its existence before 1971. That year the Ingalls family decided that it could not afford to pay for modernization and new equipment on its own. Lee came in and quickly spent $1.5 million on a new office building and printing plant and purchased modern typesetting and printing equipment. Readers got a better-looking paper and no less diversity; there hasn't been a rival newspaper in town for years. Only three radio stations and a public television outlet operate.

For all three newspapers combination and monopoly meant survival or improvement or both. Some critics deplore this situation in so many daily newspapers. The alternatives are more bleak: no newspaper or a technically inferior one, neither of which benefits readers.

Later chapters will return to these three newspapers, in describing the components of daily-newspaper journalism in detail. The remainder of the present chapter will describe other aspects of the press in this country.

Other Aspects of the Press

Wire services

Associated Press (AP) and United Press International (UPI) are the major wire services in the United States. Every day, reporters for these organizations cover news all around the world, facing what has been called "a deadline every minute." The reporters send their stories by teletype to central locations where they are edited and sent out to those around the country who subscribe to the service. (A similar wire serves television and radio stations and is written in the style of those two forms of journalism.) Each newspaper has in its offices teletype machines, which operate constantly, printing out stories on rolls of paper or perforated tape that can be inserted into computer typesetting machines. The subscribers have the right to use these stories as they wish. Thus, even the smallest newspapers can, in effect, have reporters in Washington, New York, Los Angeles, London, Moscow, or any other place around the world where a news event is taking place. Reporters for wire services perform demanding, pressure-filled jobs that are also challenging and rewarding.

Magazines

For readers who prefer more detail on specific subjects, better packaged and laid out, magazines are the choice, published weekly, biweekly, monthly, bimonthly, or quarterly. Magazines have been in business in the United States for over 200 years. They have undergone a number of changes in the twentieth century. The rise of television as a source of news and light entertainment killed *Life, Look,* and the *Saturday Evening Post* and limited the number of general-interest magazines to a few like *Readers Digest.* (*Life, Look,* and the *Post* have recently been brought back as monthlies.) High postage rates put some magazines out of business and caused others to modify their paper weight and size (and therefore their typographical appearance) so that they would be less expensive to mail. This move away from general-interest magazines caused the industry to turn to more specialized audiences for survival. When editorial material and advertising were more finely focused on specific subjects, like sports, women, city life, hobbies, recreation, photography, self-improvement and countless other subjects, the magazines' chances of survival were greater.

Trade publications

Trade publications look like regular magazines and newspapers at first glance, but their editorial material and advertising are different. These publications are intended for readers in specific fields; they are tailored to contain information exclusively for chemical engineers, construction engineers, factory owners, and people in a hundred other fields. This segment of the press offers many job opportunities and should not be overlooked by those entering journalism.

Television and radio

People are getting more and more of their news from the electronic side of journalism, especially television. The quality of television news may vary, but its popularity is undeniable, and the field is growing rapidly, bringing new local and network television stations to more and more cities, and increased employment opportunities for reporters, writers, editors, and production personnel. The same is true of radio, although few radio stations have television's commitment to news.

News is covered differently in broadcasting than in print. For television, a story is best if it is accompanied by good film footage that portrays the events of the news story accurately and dramatically. Television news coverage therefore requires not only reporters but also camera people, sound technicians, and other specialized personnel. This is an expensive and sometimes cumbersome process that can disrupt the events being covered; but there is no better way for the public to be in on a news event than to be there via the film and sound brought back and broadcast. Radio relies less on recordings of events and people, called "actualities," and is less intrusive in obtaining them.

Stories for television and radio are also written in a different way than are printed stories. For one thing, writers for television and radio make frequent use of the present tense and must write more concisely than for print because of the short amount of broadcast time available to them. They must also be careful to use words and phrases that can be easily understood by their audience.

The biggest difference between print and broadcast is in completeness and depth of coverage. There is no way people can be properly informed if they rely exclusively on television, although more and more of them do so every year. This prime difference is illustrated by Figure 1.1. The 3,881 words of a typical thirty-minute broadcast of "The CBS Evening News with Walter Cronkite" do not fill even one page of the *New York Times*. The

The Forms of Journalism Compared

Newspapers	*Magazines*	*Television and Radio*
Permanent, readers hold in their hands	Permanent, readers hold in their hands	Fleeting, news is broadcast and disappears
Time lag, event to printing, at least three hours	Time lag, event to printing, varies from one week to one month	Instantaneous transmission
Read at leisure	Read at leisure	View and hear, or hear, at set times
Readers and printed page	Readers and printed page	Audience and announcer, film footage
Adequate space allows for complete coverage, but limited time may work against it	Adequate space and time allow for complete coverage	Limited air-time and preparation time may result in limited coverage
News value determines placement	News value determines placement	News value determines placement
Need for pictures and for striking headlines may cause exaggeration	Need for pictures and for striking headings may cause exaggeration	Television's need for visuals may cause exaggeration
Newsprint and short deadline may cause poor quality in photos and bad layout	Good quality paper and adequate time result in good photos and good layout	Film footage enhances understanding of news, as do imaginative graphics
Readers pick what to read	Readers pick what to read	Audience receives highlights of the day's news
Stories are chosen by others	Stories are chosen by others	Stories are chosen by others and must be viewed, or listened to, in a fixed order
Reporters take notes quietly	Reporters take notes quietly	Camera and sound equipment may disrupt events being covered
Reporters must write quickly	Reporters have more time to report and write articles	Reporters must think visually or aurally, condensing material into a few minutes
Rising subscription costs hurt readers	Rising subscription costs hurt readers	Free
Advertisements are easily ignored	Advertisements are easily ignored	Commercials may be obtrusive
Monopoly ownership lessens diversity	Monopoly ownership lessens diversity	Monopoly ownership lessens diversity
Government supervises monopoly ownership	Government sets postal rates	Government licenses broadcast stations

Times on the following morning ran to eighty-four pages and 200,000 words of news.

Figure 1.1. The length of a television news broadcast, measured in a newspaper's terms. (Photo by Dennis Pohl, courtesy of Esquire *magazine, January, 1972.)*

Summary

Journalism has played an important role in the growth and development of the United States from the nation's beginnings. It is still playing that role today. Reporters and editors who work in journalism are constantly in on the events they report. The press in this country ranges from newspapers, wire services, and general magazines, to trade publications and television and radio stations. Although formats vary from one to another, the goal is the same: to present the public with news as accurately, understandably, and quickly as possible.

This book will concentrate on one part of journalism, the daily newspaper. It will aim to acquaint the beginner with what it is like to work for a daily by using the words of people who work on three of them.

"*If a man bites a dog, that is news.*"

> John Bogart

"*A reporter is always concerned with tomorrow. There is nothing tangible with yesterday.*"

> Anonymous

"*To want to know more—that's news.*"

> Dennis Stern, Metropolitan Editor,
> the *Washington Star*

2

The Event: What Is News?

The Elements of News
Gatekeeper Theory
Front-Page Placement
Knowing What Is News

It occurs in thousands of places and happens to thousands of people. Sometimes the people involved in it don't know what they're involved in. At other times, the enormity of the event changes the lives of all it touches, leaving no doubt that something significant has taken place. News is very different from ordinary, everyday events.

Those with enough training and experience recognize it instantly for what it is: an event that will affect the lives of more than one person and be interesting for others to read about or view. An additional element is necessary as well. To be considered news, an event must be reported. The biggest story in the world will not receive that designation if nobody knows about it.

"Starting with school, you build upon your experience," says Tom Jenks, editor of the *Corvallis Gazette-Times*. "You feel it. It's primarily a gut feeling. News is a certain thing you know automatically. Proximity, impact, consequence, unusual aspects, that which has a significant effect on many people—all of these things are news. Death counts in news. If enough people get killed or if enough escape, it's news."

A continent away, Dennis Stern, metropolitan editor of the *Washington Star,* sees it differently: "News is whatever interests me. If I'm bored with stories about cats up a tree and demonstrations, we'll do something like a recent piece about a school teacher who was having her hair done and was killed. We first ran a short item, then went back for more. To want to know more—that's news."

"There is no standard definition of news," says George Wisner, a reporter for the *Gazette-Times*. "Anything that has happened, is happening, may happen. Whatever your editor says."

His colleague Bill Monroe agrees, adding that "sifting it out and sorting it" is what is difficult.

In Topeka, Kansas, *Capital-Journal* reporter Mike Hall lets his readers and sources decide: "You get some help from . . . what people are talking about—any time they talk about taxes, for example. Just from hanging around you get some sense. News is an individual judgment. Everybody in the community has his own ideas."

The Elements of News

Definitions may vary, but it is possible to compile a list of elements that always make news.

Proximity

"News is what's happening here," says Dick King, assistant managing editor of the *Topeka Capital-Journal*. If an event happens close to the newspaper and its readers, it is news. Usually, this means in the same town or on the same campus or in the general area served by the publication. The defeat of a school bond issue during an election is important to citizens of the town affected, but holds little interest for people ten miles away where a similar bond issue may have passed. Conversely, new parking regulations on a campus are important only to people who work there.

Impact on numbers of people

Events that affect a large number of people always make news. The more people involved in a story or affected by it, the more interest there will be in reading about it. Bill Monroe, explaining his coverage of city council meetings, offers the following illustration: "If one person comes to complain about a building that is too close, that may be of interest to two of his neighbors, two building people, two city planners. Six people for a readership of 40,000 is not a judicious use of newsprint. Now if that person had threatened to kill someone if he didn't move that building, that would be different."

"How many people will the story affect, how close to home is it?" says Rod Deckert, city editor of the *Gazette-Times*. "Will the issue affect every property owner or three houses on one street? You can ask, What is valued in the community? Money is valued. Health and safety are valued. Natural resources, clean air and water, open space, bike trails. You can make a long list. If a story has these and a community connection, it's a news or feature story."

Accidents, crime, natural disasters

The horrible side of life is always news. As editor Tom Jenks says earlier in this chapter, "Death counts in news." But so do robberies, airplane crashes, train wrecks, natural disasters like tornadoes, floods, snow storms, rainstorms, hurricanes, and typhoons. Without knowing it, readers of such stories may be comparing their own safe situations with the plight of the victims. At any rate, horrible events have their peculiar fascination and rank high on any list of newsworthy stories.

Unique, bizarre people or events

After observing the events of the 1960s—wars, assassinations, the growth of the counterculture society—few readers are surprised by anything that happens. They never tire of reading about such events, however, though they demand something more than the classic "man bites dog" type of story.

Nostalgic, humorous, sad, or ironic people or events

Readers like to read about "the little guys," the people who become news through no fault of their own. The public can identify with them and view them in a "there but for the grace of God, go I" way. According to Dick King of the Topeka newspapers: "News is a story of a little old grandma who turned 100 today or a guy with a coin collection. That's news. I get so tired of reading, 'The city council did this; the city council did that.' " Important as the latter kinds of stories are, readers often feel a need for more im-

News: Something You Didn't Know Yesterday.
(Photos by Chris Johns.)

Ronald Reagan arrives in Topeka, Kansas.

The Event: What Is News? 19

*The CBS news team after
the 1976 Republican
National Convention.*

A fire in a small Kansas town.

The Event: What Is News?

The first day of school.

A football victory.

In Shawnee County Jail, Kansas.

The most curious dog in the world looks at the biggest rabbit.

The Event: What Is News? 25

A much-maligned pony.

mediate, human-interest stories, tinged with nostalgia, humor, sadness, irony.

Prominent people

Readers always seem fascinated by the activities of a small group of notables with position and money, whom they imagine to have a lot of time on their hands: movie stars, rock groups, European royalty, African tyrants, the Kennedys, and the family of whoever is president of the United States. The list is long, and its composition changes as the public grows tired of one person and looks to another.

Federal and other governments

As daily life in the United States becomes increasingly influenced and controlled by the federal government, information about the people of rank and the actions they take make news. The president, vice-president, cabinet members, congressmen and senators, and Supreme Court justices are always of interest—as are people campaigning for these positions—but so are the laws, new taxes, regulations, hearings, rulings, and budgets they produce. The principle applies to state and local governments, although readers have a lower boredom threshold for information about people and events at the latter two levels.

Wars and threats of wars

No matter how obscure the conflict, it is almost always newsworthy. Readers have more of a stake in the outcome of any Middle East fighting than they do in a border feud between two obscure African states, but both conflicts are news and will be covered by news organizations. The difference is in the number of reporters sent to observe the action. That word—*action*—is the reason for the high interest in war news. Death, destruction of property, displacement of large numbers of people, create a drama that is irresistible to readers.

Timeliness

Any of these elements will cease to be newsworthy if no new details emerge. Readers want to know the latest developments about anything, and they will quickly scan and leave unfinished a story that doesn't offer anything fresh. Today's hot story is tomorrow's candidate for the garbage can. News has to be new to be news. What this means for a story lasting for several days or several weeks is that reporters must offer fresh details at the start of each story and only summarize what readers already know. Putting a "second day" lead on a story means including fresh details in the first and second paragraphs to make it more timely.

Other elements

Other kinds of stories are news some of the time and in certain kinds of newspapers with certain kinds of readers. *International affairs* are always important to the readers of big-city dailies but are sometimes ignored by smaller newspapers. *Local weather*—below the disaster level mentioned earlier—is always news to local readers. *Sports* always has a large following.

Gatekeeper Theory

Reporters and editors use their experience in making judgments about the newsworthiness of stories. Admittedly, what is news to one reporter or editor may not be news to another. Someone has to make the decisions, however, or the newspaper would never come out.

The *gatekeeper theory* helps explain how such decisions are made. A gatekeeper is any person in the newsgathering process with authority to affect the flow of information as it reaches the public.

The phenomenon begins with the reporter at the scene of the event being reported. What happened? The reporter asks the necessary questions to find out. But what about the questions he or she forgets to ask? Or what if the key source of information is not there at the time? By inadvertently neglecting information for reasons like this, the reporter affects the readers' understanding and perception of the final story. In this instance, the reporter is gatekeeping.

As the reporter returns to the newspaper office and moves the information from raw notes into the form of a finished story, the gatekeeping continues. The reporter decides what to feature in the first paragraph (the lead) and what information to place in a later position. The copy editor decides to move another bit of information into the lead and write a headline based on it, completely changing the emphasis of the story. The layout editor puts the story on page 6 instead of page 1, where the reporter hoped to see it run. Because of this decision, many readers may not see it. All of these people are gatekeeping because the decisions they make on one news story affect its perception by readers.

The process goes on for every element in the newspaper: stories, headlines, photographs, and advertisements. The decisions that govern what happens are made quickly, sometimes arbitrarily, but they are made daily, and no better way has been found to make them.

Front-Page Placement

Although a story does not have to appear on the front page of a newspaper to be thought news, its placement there indicates its newsworthiness without question. A look at front pages of the three newspapers serving as examples in this book reveals how the gatekeepers on these newspapers did their work on one day, Monday, March 20, 1978. Using the different categories detailed earlier in the chapter, one sees how different the individual perceptions of editors and reporters can be at newspapers of varying sizes in separate parts of the country.

On a big-city daily like the *Washington Star,* which has four different editions, the news can change throughout a day. What was important to editors in the early morning in the Capital Special (first) edition may have been replaced by the time the Night Final (fourth) edition rolls off the press.

In the Capital Special edition (Figure 2.1), a story on suburban development (proximity, timeliness) sits at the top of the page, above the flag (name), and one about the setting up of a United Nations peace force in Lebanon (wars) rests right below. A piece on campaign financing (federal government) is next down the page, with something on French elections (international affairs) and a congressional election campaign (federal government) rounding out the hard news. The other two articles are standard features appearing every day in the *Star:* "Q and A," a column of questions and answers ("Why Do Birds Suddenly Go North, South?"), and "In Focus" ("What Would Happen if New York City Went Broke?"), an in-depth look at a controversial subject, not necessarily always tied to the day's news but sometimes making news by what it reveals. The page is rounded out by a picture of five children and a puppy made homeless by a fire in Chicago (sad people or events), photo of a boxer (sports) that refers to a story inside, the weather, an expanded index, and races to be run that day at Pimlico.

By the Home Final (second) edition (Figure 2.2), the editors of the *Star* have begun to make changes in the makeup of the front page as they react to the news of the day. The paper's flag has been moved up and the suburban development story moved down near the bottom of the page. The story on the United Nations peace force is still deemed important enough to follow the masthead, but the one on campaign financing has surrendered its prominent position to a new story, on a possible cutback in Social Security taxes, and has been moved down a notch to the place earlier occupied by the expanded index and photo of the boxer. The pieces on suburban development, the congressional campaign, and the French election are still there, but they have been moved around and new headlines written to make them fit their different column arrangements. Both "Q and A" and "In Focus" are in the same place. The index is now smaller.

In the Home Final (third) edition (Figure 2.3)—same name, same intended audience—new stories appear. The lead story, on the United Nations peace force, has been changed, its emphasis now on the Israeli advance into Lebanon. News of the charges against Bert Lance (prominent people) has replaced campaign financing, which in turn has displaced the story on the

Figure 2.1. Front page of the Washington Star, Capital Special (first) edition. (Courtesy of the Washington Star.)

Figure 2.2. Front page of the Washington Star, *Home Final (second) edition. (Courtesy of the Washington Star.)*

Figure 2.3. *Front page of the* Washington Star, *Home Final (third) edition. (Courtesy of the* Washington Star.)

First Day of Spring
Partly cloudy tonight, low 40 to 47. Chance of showers tomorrow, high 64 to 69. Details: B-3.

The Washington Star

HOME FINAL

126th Year. No. 79 — Copyright © 1978 The Evening Star Newspaper Co. — WASHINGTON, D.C., MONDAY, MARCH 20, 1978 — Phone (202) 484-5000 — CIRCULATION 484-3000 CLASSIFIED 484-6000 — 15 Cents

Israelis Claim Control Up to Key Lebanese River

TEL AVIV, Israel (AP) — The Israeli army, driving northward despite a U.N. call for withdrawal, claimed control of southern Lebanon up to the Litani River today. The government declared that any settlement of the conflict must ensure that Palestinians do not return to the area.

In Beirut, the Palestine Liberation Organization denied that all of Lebanon south of the Litani, 15 miles north of the Israeli border, had fallen to the invasion force. The PLO said guerrilla "suicide squads" were counterattacking "in many embattled locations."

The Israeli military command reported no heavy fighting, however. It said its forces had reached positions dominating the slopes of the Litani along a 30-mile front from the coast eastward.

THE ISRAELIS SAID they went around Tyre, the biblical port 12 miles north of the border, and cut it off. They said their line of control extended eastward to a point north of Abasiya and to a position dominating the Akiya Bridge over the Litani.

The Israeli advance indicated Prime Minister Menachem Begin's government wanted to flush out the

Another argument on Saudi plane deal. Page A-3.

guerrillas from the entire region south of the river before any withdrawal in favor of a U.N. force authorized by Security Council resolutions yesterday.

The council had called for an Israeli pullout "forthwith" from the region.

The Cabinet, meeting in special session without Begin, who was in the United States, issued a statement saying any settlement of the Lebanon crisis "must ensure southern Lebanon will no longer serve as a base for the terrorists and their murderous attacks."

The statement reiterated that Israel does not intend to occupy southern Lebanon.

Two more Israeli soldiers were reported killed, bringing the admitted Israeli death toll to 20 in six days as the invasion force expanded the "security belt" to a depth of some 15 miles above the border.

The PLO in Beirut claimed it inflicted "heavy casualties" on the Israeli soldiers. The Lebanese government reported 1,168 Lebanese and Palestinian soldiers and civilians killed in the fighting, which began last Wednesday.

THE GUERRILLAS yesterday said 144 of their fighters had been killed and 450 Israelis had been killed or wounded.

A Palestinian spokesman in Beirut claimed the Israelis made several helicopter raids during the night on guerrilla positions just north of the river. But there was no expectation that the Israelis would cross the Litani in force, since that would constitute a challenge to the 30,000 Syrian troops in central and north Lebanon. The river is the so-called "red line" which the Syrians for nearly two years have been careful to keep north of because the Israelis said they would not permit them south of it.

Beirut Radio and the PLO said waves of Israeli fighter-bombers roared across the border before daybreak to join navy missile boats in pounding guerrilla fallback positions and supply routes.

The Palestinians said Israeli helicopters landed commando units during the night at a string of villages east and south of Tyre. The Christian Voice of Lebanon radio station said

See MIDEAST, A-4

Q and A

Why Do Birds Suddenly Go North, South?

The swallows have returned to the mission of San Juan Capistrano in California. Dr. Eugene Morton, a research ornithologist at the Smithsonian's National Zoo, was interviewed about this annual spring rite and the general phenomenon of seasonal bird migration by Washington Star Staff Writer Cristine Russell.

Question: *This is the time that the swallows traditionally return to Capistrano. Do they really return at precisely the same time every year?*

Morton: Probably not, although I haven't witnessed it myself. Chances are that people simply look for them at that date. They are probably in the area, but not building nests until about that date.

Q: *In the Eastern United States, when do the normal spring migrations begin and when are we normally expected to see them?*

A: There are three divisions in these birds one might make. One are the waterfowl, which are at the peak of their migration right now. The others are blackbirds, which are also at the peak now, or slightly before now, and then there are all the birds we call foliage gleaners because they eat insects off the leaves of trees. And their peak is in late April and May in this area.

Q: *Where are all these migrating birds coming from in general and how do they manage to cover such tremendous distances from the places they spend the winter and get back to their breeding grounds in the summer?*

A: If we're restricted just to the small birds one might see in the trees of one's backyard, many of these birds are coming from the tropics. Most of them winter in Central America and western and northern South America. The factors that answer how they make the flight are simply that they are able to store enough fat to make flights of significant magnitude to get them over, say, the Caribbean Sea. And a small bird, say, that's about 12 grams, like the Blackpoll Warbler can store maybe 15 grams of fat on its 12-gram body and can fly 2,500 miles on that, given the right tailwinds — the right wind direction. And so they store fat and then they choose the right time to migrate, that is when there is a tailwind. They generally stop if they are out of fuel or in a headwind. And, of course, they don't if they are out over water, although they do make mistakes.

Q: *Which birds have the reputation as the longest migrators?*

A: These tend to be the larger birds that can store more fat, and also birds that find their food along coastal areas in the water, like terns and certain shore birds. These birds

See MORTON, A-6

INSIDE TODAY

SAVING THE THINGS THAT COUNT

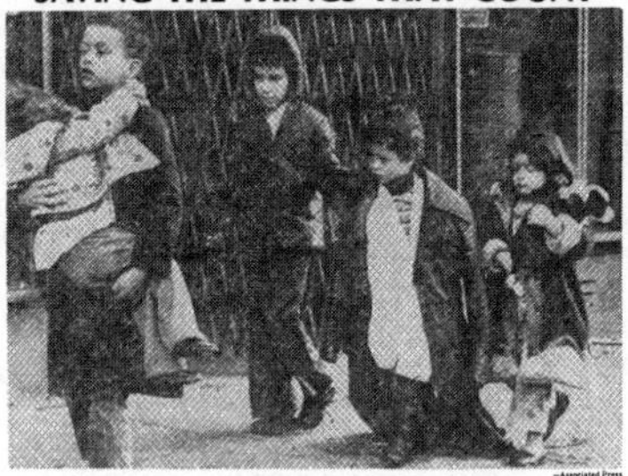

—Associated Press

Children take to the street with some of their belongings and a puppy after a fire displaced them from their apartment building on Chicago's west side over the weekend. A fireman was injured in the blaze.

'The Perils of Abner Mikva'

GOP Tries to Cast Out A Serpent in Its Garden

By James R. Dickenson
Washington Star Staff Writer

EVANSTON, Ill. — John E. Porter, a leading candidate for the Republican nomination in the 10th Congressional District, was speaking at a coffee in one of those upper middle-class Evanston neighborhoods that looks like a Hollywood set of the American Dream.

"John," one earnest GOP matron finally asked with the air of someone who is finally cutting through the froth to get down to the nitty-gritty. "This area used to be *so* Republican. What happened?"

THE RACE FOR THE HOUSE: A PRIMARY

Porter smiled. "Well, what happened is that *he* moved out here so he could be elected," he quipped.

Except that Porter really wasn't joking. Republicans in the 10th don't joke about the "he" Porter was referring to and Porter didn't have to name him. "He" is never far from many Republicans' minds.

"He" is Abner Mikva, the 10th's two-term Democratic congressman who wins with margins so narrow his career is a political version of "The Perils of Pauline."

MIKVA IS A MAN Republicans discuss in the same tones as they might the fallen angel Lucifer. A man they blame for nearly everything from inflation and rising taxes to fallen arches. A man they would like to welcome back to the Midwest. To welcome him to any place but Washington.

Six Republicans are still campaigning to win the right in tomorrow's primary to try to drive this serpent out of their former Eden but they generally ignore each other like ships passing in the night. They keep their eyes on the real target.

The invariable opening statement of each Republican candidate defines the major issue. "The issue in this campaign is, who can beat Ab Mikva," each begins.

"We Republicans have to work and stick together," each concludes and Porter sometimes takes it an Alfonse and Gaston step further.

"I'm proud to be on the ballot with these Republicans," he says. "They're fine human beings. Let's beat Ab Mikva."

It is really a three-man primary, although none has managed to excite his fellow Republicans enough to make a breakthrough. Telephone polls and canvasses indicate that Porter and Daniel Hales, a Winnetka lawyer, are running about even but that a large number of Republican voters, maybe as many as 50 percent, were still undecided in the last week of the campaign.

Porter, 42, is a native of Evanston,

See MIKVA, A-6

Democrats Offer A 'Guarantee' on Election Funding

By Ron Sarro
Washington Star Staff Writer

An influential group of House Democrats today gave Republicans a highly unusual political guarantee in an effort to end the two-week partisan war in Congress over proposed changes in federal campaign financing laws.

The House Democratic Study Group told GOP congressmen today that they have an "ironclad guarantee" of at least 100 Democratic votes to kill proposed changes in the law Republicans say would cripple their party's political comeback this year.

The 100 Democratic votes plus those of the 147 Republicans in the House would be more than enough to kill provisions of the bill which would cut by three-fourths the amount of money national political committees can channel to candidates.

THIS PROPOSAL would reduce from $50,000 to $15,000 the amount of campaign money national committees can contribute to each candidate and more than neutralize a huge lead

See FUNDING, A-4

Tax Rollback Urged On Social Security By Democrats, GOP

By Edmond Le Breton
Associated Press

Democrats on a congressional study committee said today that upcoming Social Security tax increases should be cut by $33 billion even before the tax boost takes effect next year.

Republicans on the Joint Economic Committee agreed that the Social Security tax increase should be moderated to avoid disproportionate burdens on middle-income families.

The Republicans by and large have opposed the Social Security tax increases from the start and now have joined that with criticism of President Carter's proposed income tax cut to offset its effects. Their minority opinion said, "At best, we must expect 1978 and 1979 economic activity to do well in spite of the government and not because of it."

THE CALL BY Democrats for the $33 billion cut in the Social Security tax increases came in the joint committee's annual report on presidential economic programs. The Democrats proposed shifting to general income tax revenues the cost of disability and Medicare benefits — programs now borne by the Social Security system.

Such a move could substitute for Carter's proposed $25 billion income tax cut, the majority members said.

The congressional report comes only five days after House Speaker Thomas P. O'Neill called for Carter to initiate a plan to rescind part of the upcoming increase. He said failure by the White House to propose the cut would force the House to take its own initiative.

O'Neill and many others in Congress say the public will not stand for the increase and that its discontent will show at the polls this November.

Congress is backing away from the law which it passed just last December to prop up the financially troubled system. The measure is designed to raise an additional $227 billion for the program over the next decade.

MAJORITY MEMBERS also said in the report that the Federal Reserve should ease money supplies to counteract growing interest rates. They also called for government spending of at least the $500 billion President Carter has called for in his 1979 budget.

But Republicans on the committee disagreed, saying that easing money supplies would not work to lower interest rates but instead might increase them with heightened fears of growing inflation.

Continuing their criticism, minority members called for Congress to lower individual income tax rates and to review the tax code annually. Those members also suggested that businesses be allowed to deduct depreciation based on current equipment cost rather than on the preinflation price as is now allowed.

"These two steps would go a long way toward guaranteeing rapid increases in jobs and after-tax wages," the Republicans said.

Lance Group Calls Complaint A 'Smokescreen'

By Rudolph A. Pyatt Jr.
Washington Star Staff Writer

A Financial General Bankshares Inc. complaint charging Bert Lance and others with conspiracy to acquire the company is merely a "smokescreen" spread by the company's president and chairman to cover a "palace revolt" and possible violations by the company's top management, according to a memorandum filed in U.S. District Court.

A brief filed over the weekend by attorneys for Lance, Bank of Credit and Commerce International, and Agha Hasan Abedi, a top official in BCCI, also says the real estate investment trust Financial General Chairman B. Francis Saul II heads has loans outstanding from Financial General banks, which may place in him a conflict of interest situation.

The brief describes Financial General as a "company without leadership or direction." Until recently "control of its business has been in the hands of an increasingly deeply divided board of directors," the brief contends.

THE BRIEF WAS FILED in opposition to a Financial General suit seeking a preliminary injunction against Lance and several other defendants. The complaint, which Financial General filed Feb. 17, asks for a preliminary injunction to prohibit the defendants from fraudulently acquiring control of the company.

Arguments which will be based on briefs submitted in the case are scheduled to be heard Wednesday.

See LANCE, A-4

MONTGOMERY TESTS SHOW BLACKS BEHIND WHITES

By Gloria Borger
Washington Star Staff Writer

In what Montgomery County officials say is one of the nation's first publicly released comparisions by a school system of the test performance of black and white students, black students averaged consistently below their white counterparts.

While white county student test results generally averaged above national norms at all grade levels, the scores of black students fell below the same national averages in both achievement and scholastic ability tests.

As part of the county's Black Action Steps schedule and the Title IX action plan — both developed by Board of Education advisory committees to improve the education of minorities and women — county school Superintendent Charles M. Bernardo released the test comparisions this afternoon.

In a county comparision of black and white students' average achievement scores on the Iowa Tests of Basic Skills, the average black pupil score at each grade level — 3rd, 5th, 7th, 9th — registered below the results of white students on every test.

IN 9TH grade on a reading comprehension segment of the ITBS tests, for example, black students averaged one year and nine months behind their white peers. Black students scored an average of 7.7, which is at the 7th grade, 7th month level. The white students scored at the 9.6 — 9th grade, 6th month. The national norm is 9.6.

In a work-study skills segment of the same test at the 9th grade level, black students were about two years and one month behind white students.

In surveying a sample of the county's black student population — which amounts to 9.3 percent of all students enrolled — officials also discovered that achievement scores were directly related to ability scores.

In a scale of test results which divides the total possible scores of the Cognitive Abilities Tests (CAT) into nine categories, or stanines — ranging from a low score in the first group to a high score in the ninth group — about 50 percent more black students scored in groups 1 through 4 — the low end of the scale — than would be expected in a national sample of all students.

The 9th grade distribution, for example, shows that approximately 60 percent of all black students scored in the lowest groups 1 through 4 and about 20 percent tested at the top end of the scale in groups through 9.

The white students, however, had scores that were distributed in an almost identically reversed pattern.

See SCHOOLS, A-4

IN FOCUS ▸ *What Would Happen if New York City Went Broke?*

By Lee M. Cohn
Washington Star Staff Writer

New York City, the banking system and the national economy are in better shape now than in 1975, which creates problems for the city in lobbying for federal financing aid.

Second of two articles

The economy, emerging from a recession, was so shaky in 1975 that Congress feared a New York bankruptcy might set off a national disaster. That fear helped persuade Congress to vote grudgingly for federal loans to New York.

Despite persisting troubles, the economy now is much stronger and steadier as the city approaches a new crisis this summer. A New York bankruptcy this time would cause problems, but many experts believe the damage would be moderate.

Because the risks seem smaller, Congress may be less willing to pass legislation New York says it will need after the 1975 financial rescue program expires June 30. The city wants direct federal loans to cover some of its short-term seasonal needs for money, and federal guarantees of long-term bonds.

OCCASIONALLY, CITY leaders get carried away and issue dramatic warnings of what may happen if federal help is denied. Mayor Edward Koch says the city might "decay and slowly die, becoming a

Bankruptcy could provoke political and social turmoil

ward of the state and federal governments."

But in calm moments, nobody in authority predicts flatly that the city would even go into bankruptcy without federal financing assistance. That's a risk, but there's a chance that New York could scrape by on its own credit, according to most experts. Although reforms have a long way to go, the city has strengthened its finances since 1975.

The Senate Banking Committee is so confident that it opposes extending any federal loans or loan guarantees to the city.

Felix G. Rohatyn, New York's chief financial strategist, says he will not "prophecy the certainty of bankruptcy." That is "not a banner to be unfurled carelessly," he says. "Suffice it to say that the risk is there, and it is most serious. The question we ask of our government is 'why run it?'"

Rohatyn offers few specific predictions of what might happen. Instead, he warns vaguely that "a bankruptcy of New York will be viewed as a bankruptcy of the free enterprise capitalistic system, as proof of the impotence of our system to solve difficult, but nonetheless finite, problems."

The Carter administration also stops short of predicting bankruptcy or severe damage to the economy. Arguing for limited federal financing aid, a key official says: "Bankruptcy is a risk. We have a reasonable alternative. The risk is not worth taking."

No one denies that financial failure by New York would have harmful repercussions. The argument is over how severe those effects would be, how long they would last and how far they would spread. Many analysts believe the impact would be limited, though others fear serious damage.

If New York fails to raise enough money to pay its bills, meet payrolls and redeem debts as they come due, it will go into default, formally or informally. That could happen as soon as July.

THROUGH LAWSUITS by creditors or other processes, the city might then be declared bankrupt. There are no comparable precedents and the new federal bankruptcy law is untested, so it is not possible to predict exactly how bankruptcy would work.

In principle, the courts would protect the city from lawsuits while supervising execution of a plan to provide minimum municipal services and gradually pay off creditors.

See NEW YORK, A-10

French election; that story, and the one on suburban development, having been removed from page 1. An article on the comparative test results of black and white students in a suburban school system (proximity) has replaced the development piece. The rest of the page, including the photograph, is unchanged.

By the Night Final (Figure 2.4), the lead story is still on Lebanon, but it is a new lead story, about the reported cease-fire (wars and threats of wars). The next story is still on the possible Social Security cutback, but a new piece on tuition credit (federal government, impact on people) has replaced the Lance story, which has been moved to the spot occupied by the campaign funding story, displacing it from the front page. The rest of page 1 is the same, except for the addition of Pimlico race results. A new photo appears (international).

The front page of the *Star*'s "Metro" section on the same day shows a similar bow to changing makeup based on the flow of news. This is the section where most local news appears, the front page of the newspaper usually being reserved for national and international stories.

The Capital Special (first) edition (Figure 2.5) leads with a story on D.C. General Hospital (proximity, impact on people). Next on the right comes a piece about the move by the local government to block disability payments for a former city college official sent to prison (prominent people, crime). Three photos and a story on early spring weather (timeliness) come next, along with a piece on alleged police brutality (crime). The page is completed with a story on a new literary magazine that publishes the work of senior citizens (nostalgia).

By the Home Final (third) edition (Figure 2.6), the suburban development story bumped from the front page has displaced the D.C. General story in the lead position. The hospital story has been moved to the position where the weather story used to be. That story has been discarded, although the photos that went with it remain. The rest of the page is unchanged. For the Night Final the "Metro" edition stays the same.

Of the two newspapers that constitute the *Topeka Capital-Journal*, the morning *Daily Capital* serves a wider area and a wider audience than the evening *State Journal;* it therefore gives more prominence to national and international news.

The front page of the *Daily Capital* (Figure 2.7) is dominated on March 20, 1978, by international news—the Israeli advance into Lebanon, a United Nations Security Council call for an Israeli withdrawal, and the arrival of Prime Minister Begin in New York. Another international story, on the defeat of leftists in the French election, completes the space above the fold. A piece on the state senate's plans for the week (impact on people, govern-

Figure 2.4. Front page of the Washington Star, Night Final (fourth) edition. (Courtesy of the Washington Star.)

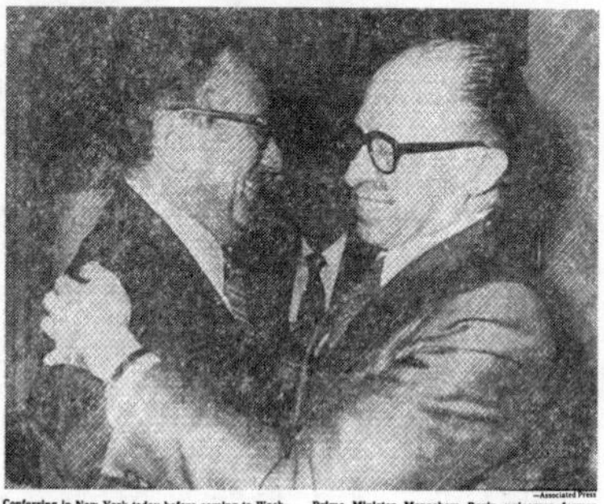

Figure 2.5. Front page of the Washington Star *"Metro" section, Capital Special (first) edition. (Courtesy of the Washington Star.)*

Figure 2.6. Front page of the Washington Star "Metro" section, Home Final (third) edition. (Courtesy of the Washington Star.)

Figure 2.7. Front page of the Topeka Daily Capital. *(Courtesy of the Topeka Daily Capital.)*

ment) comes next, followed by a plane crash (accidents), and a report on the county spelling-bee champion (nostalgia). The page is completed with a sports picture and a large index.

The front page of the *State Journal* (Figure 2.8) carries only one non-local story—a short item on the Equal Rights Amendment. The rest of the stories deal with various levels of government: a pothole relief bill, a tax relief issue, and funding for a civic center (state government); reorganization of a city agency (city government); and the announcement of a candidate (state government). The page is completed with a story on the arrival of spring (weather), a Lenten prayer, an Easter-oriented photograph (timeliness), and a small index.

On the same day, a story on the loss of a water system in a nearby town (timeliness, proximity) leads the front page of the *Corvallis Gazette-Times* (Figure 2.9). A photograph and accompanying story on early spring weather (timeliness, impact on people, weather) share the remainder of the page above the fold. Below the fold, stories on the fighting in Lebanon (wars, international) and Social Security (federal government, impact on people) come next in importance. The page is finished with a piece, accompanied by a picture, on the hiring of a new county official (local government, proximity) and news of defects in auto transmissions (impact on people). A box including weather and an index fills out the rest of the space.

The only stories appearing in all three newspapers are the ones on the Middle East and Social Security. The other stories are chosen for their interest to large numbers of local readers.

Knowing What Is News

The ability to recognize news immediately comes with experience acquired over many years. Making both right and wrong choices helps build the background needed to succeed. Sometimes the policy of a newspaper overrides the normal decision making process. For example, if this policy prohibits the mention of death or illness (the *Christian Science Monitor*'s policy) or candidates from a political party the newspaper opposes, several of the important elements of news noted in this chapter are eliminated. At other times budgetary factors prevail; a newspaper will not spend the money to cover a story if the coverage will be too expensive, no matter how important and newsworthy the story.

In other instances, the readership of a newspaper will dictate the choice. For example, a weekly newspaper seldom tries to present national and international news; its readers are more interested in local happenings. A big-city daily, on the other hand, does not spend much time chronicling church suppers and Boy Scout merit-badge winners. Indeed, the larger the

Figure 2.8. Front page of the Topeka State Journal. *(Courtesy of the Topeka State Journal.)*

Figure 2.9. Front page of the Corvallis Gazette-Times. *(Courtesy of the Corvallis Gazette-Times.)*

daily, the less often this kind of story appears and the more nonlocal news is included. This is true of all but the two dailies in Washington, D.C., where news of the federal government is also local news. Some newspapers also conduct surveys of their readers and use the results to make changes.

In time, reporters and editors acquire a sixth sense for whether a person or event is or is not news. If they do not, they might consider getting into another line of work. Above all, reporters should not be as unaware as the reporter who was sent to cover a wedding but returned without a story. "Why?" his editor asked. "There is no story to report," he replied. "There was no wedding. The church burned down."

As a final test, reporters should ask themselves, Is this something or somebody I didn't know about yesterday? If so, it is news. "I think newspapers ought to work harder at what's news," says Rod Deckert, city editor of the *Corvallis Gazette-Times,* "not just from the time standpoint but telling the community something it didn't know about itself before."

Summary

News is very different from ordinary, everyday events. Those with enough training and experience recognize it instantly for what it is: an event that will affect the lives of more than one person and be interesting to others to read about or view. An event must also be reported to be news. Elements like proximity, impact, accidents, crime, natural disasters, uniqueness, nostalgia, humor, sadness, prominence, government, war, and timeliness help reporters and editors decide what news is. In this selection process they act as gatekeepers, making the decisions that affect the flow of information as it reaches the public. Front-page placement signifies newsworthiness. In deciding what is news, reporters and editors rely upon their training and experience and also take into account the policy of the newspaper and the opinions of readers.

Suggested Exercises

1. Bring to class and be prepared to discuss stories clipped from newspapers. Be sure that the stories fit all the elements of news listed in this chapter.

2. Identify five things, among those observed in a twenty-four-hour period, that constitute news. Jot down details about them and come to class prepared to argue your case to the instructor and other class members who will serve as editors in deciding whether your stories reach page 1.

3. Identify five things, among those observed in a twenty-four-hour period, that are *not* news. Jot down the details and explain why they are not newsworthy, comparing them with the five newsworthy items noted in exercise 2.

4. Analyze the front page of a daily newspaper and classify the stories according to the news elements noted in this chapter.

5. Analyze the front pages of two daily newspapers from different cities on the same day and classify the stories according to the news elements listed in this chapter. Then try to analyze why one newspaper put a story on page 1 and the other one did not. Present your findings to the class.

"*I am bothered at not being able to put out a newspaper every day with the excellence I know we're capable of, because, once in a while, we do it. People don't check facts, the equipment doesn't work. There is no reason yesterday's paper is not as good as today's. An error in a story, a headline, a caption, or bad makeup. When you know you're capable, it's frustrating to put out a newspaper not as good as it ought to be.*"

Tom Jenks, Editor,
Corvallis Gazette-Times

3

The Newspaper: How It Is Organized

The Publisher
The News Side
The Business Side
The Production Side

The goal of the daily newspaper is unusual when compared with that of other money-making ventures. Everyone working in the newspaper building is intent on one thing: the daily deadline and the preparation of a new product, a new edition, every day. Chapter 3 examines the complex organization that makes this possible.

The Publisher

The *publisher* heads the newspaper. In some cases, the publisher owns the paper; in others, the publisher is the local representative of the corporation that owns the paper. Because of the recent trend toward chain ownership discussed in Chapter 1, the latter arrangement is the most common. In either case, the publisher is the boss, the person to whom every department reports, the person who determines budgets and sets overall policy. A publisher often represents the newspaper in the community as well, by serving on boards and committees as a public service. The publisher also mediates disputes between the news department and the advertising staff over allocation of space and occasionally helps the advertising staff by meeting with advertisers and potential advertisers.

Below the publisher, a typical small-to-medium daily is usually divided into three separate areas: the news side, the business side, and the production side. Although not always equal in power and financial support, these three departments need to be strong to produce an effective newspaper.

The News Side

Editors

The *editor* is the top person on the news side, answering only to the publisher and responsible for filling the newspaper with news, features, editorials, and photographs. The editor hires and fires editorial personnel, evaluates the work of the staff, and manages the editorial budgets. The editor may also represent the newspaper on some of the same boards and committees as the publisher.

A *managing editor* manages the daily operation of the newspaper, relieving the editor of some of the budget and personnel responsibilities as well. This post does not exist in some smaller dailies.

The *city editor* directs reporters, photographers, and copy editors as they prepare the stories and pictures that detail the previous twenty-four hours of the city's life. On smaller papers the city editor also writes headlines and edits copy, tasks he or she does not have time to do on big-city dailies, where there are more reporters to manage. (On larger newspapers covering more than one city, this person may be called the *metropolitan editor* and has similar, though expanded, duties because more reporters and a larger geographical area are involved.) The city editor is crucial to the

The Newspaper: How It Is Organized   45

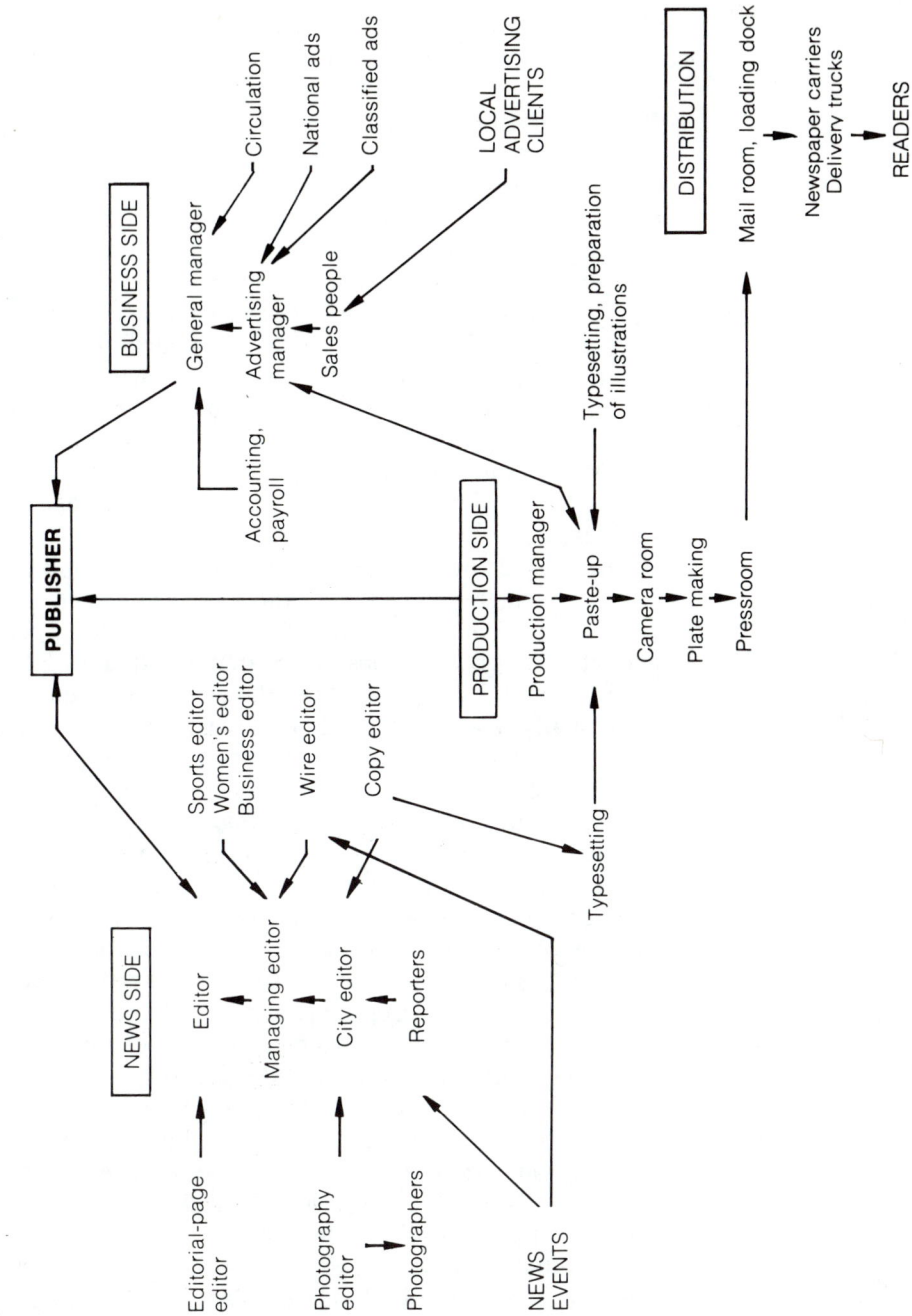

Figure 3.1. The newspaper from start to finish.

success of a newspaper, especially one without a managing editor. The person in this job is the link between the publisher and editor and the reporters.

The number of department editors varies with the goals and financial resources of a newspaper. An average-size daily has a *sports editor,* a *women's editor,* and a *business editor.* Sports and business coverage have remained fairly constant in recent years, but the coverage of women's news has changed greatly. In fact, the traditional women's page of fashion, food, and social events is no longer exclusively a women's page; it has been replaced by a page or whole section with a name like "Modern Living," "Spectrum," "Style," and the like that goes into the problems of men, women, and families in much greater depth than before.

Department editors gather material and write stories just as reporters do, but they also design and lay out the pages in the newspaper devoted to their subject areas. Sometimes reporters are assigned to help them, depending on the willingness and ability of management to provide funds for salaries.

Big-city dailies with budgets to match also employ specialty editors for science, medicine, travel, education, entertainment, gardening, foreign affairs, national affairs, urban affairs, cultural affairs, energy, environment, and other subjects that subscribers are interested in.

In a small subdepartment of the news side is the *editorial-page editor,* who usually reports to the editor, bypassing the news room itself. This editor writes the daily editorials that present the newpaper's point of view on important topics of the day. He or she also selects and edits guest columns and syndicated columnists, and edits and processes letters to the editor. Larger newspapers employ several such editorial writers.

Another small department is photography, usually presided over by a *photography editor* or *photography director* and employing *photographers.* The people in this department assist the editors and reporters by taking photographs to accompany local stories. They also prepare photo essays and picture pages. They take the photos, develop the film, print contact sheets, and select and print the photographs to be used in the newspaper. The managing editor or copy editor, at times assisted by the photography editor, selects the wire-service photographs to be used.

The *copy editor* reads most of the editorial material for errors in grammar, spelling, style, and readability before it is set into type. This person also writes headlines and designs the layout of many of the pages. Since the advent of the video-display terminal (VDT), copy editors on smaller newspapers often work without copyreaders because reporters act in this capacity themselves at their own VDT consoles. In newspapers without VDTs, copy editors are assisted by copyreaders in catching mistakes before stories are set into type.

The *wire editor* handles the AP, UPI, or other wire-service material about state, national, and international subjects, tearing it off the constantly clattering teletype machines or pulling it from computer storage, and organizing it for selection and placement. This editor must keep up with late-breaking developments and be ready to add information to important stories just before deadline.

Reporters

Reporters gather facts and write news and feature stories about the part of the city—the beat—they cover every day. A few of them on general assignment handle whatever story comes up on a given day at the direction of the city editor. Reporters are the solid base of a good newspaper. Without good reporters to write stories about the area covered by the newspaper—or about national and international news handled by wire services—the newspaper could not function. There would be no stories for readers to read.

The number of reporters varies with the size of the newspaper and the willingness and ability of management to spend money for salaries. The *Corvallis Gazette-Times* has nine, the *Topeka Capital-Journal* fifty shared by the two newspapers, and the *Washington Star* thirty-three on the city side and a similar, but varying, number on its national desk. It is a rare editor who is satisfied with the number of reporters. Only short-sighted publishers limit the number an editor can hire; the better ones are realistic in making the assessment, and a better, more complete newspaper is the result.

The Business Side

Advertising

The second part of a newspaper organization is the business side. In essence, this department fills the newspaper with something to go between the stories and photographs—at least that is the view of the editorial staff. In the view of the business staff, the stories merely fill the space not taken up by their advertisements.

The rivalry is an old one. In reality, one part cannot function without the other. Subscribers would not read a newspaper containing only advertisements (except for "throwaway" shopping guides), but editors and reporters would not get their paychecks without the revenue generated by the selling of ads. The friendly rivalry will no doubt go on forever.

On the best newspapers, the two sides are managed separately. The practice of publishing news stories because a person buys an ad is a cheap, shoddy, unethical kind of journalism to be avoided at any cost. Compromise of this kind can ruin a newspaper and make it unworthy of the designation *news*paper. That does not mean that compromises do not have to be made occasionally. If the news department is planning an exposé on all the supermarkets in a town and the newspaper gets all of its advertising revenue from these same supermarkets, it would be foolish for the editorial and advertising departments not to consult one another and consider the consequences of the story. A newspaper might have performed a public service by such an act, but it might also be out of business.

Another factor is the part advertising plays in determining the size of a given issue of the newspaper. There must be a proper editorial-to-advertising ratio, and it affects size in this way: A newspaper must devote a certain percentage of its space to advertising to earn the revenue it needs to stay in business. Typically, this is 60 to 65 percent. The remainder of the space is reserved for stories, headlines, and photographs and is called the "news hole." The U.S. Postal Service prohibits newspapers from being mailed if they contain more than 75 percent advertising. Readers, too, would object to such a high advertising percentage, which would overwhelm the editorial material.

This means that the number of pages of a newspaper varies from day to day and so does the size of the news hole. It all depends on how much advertising was sold for a particular issue.

The amount of money advertising generates affects the quality of the overall newspaper product. It determines editorial budgets and the kind of production equipment the newspaper can afford to buy. These factors, in turn, affect the paper's readability and the quality of its coverage. Readers will not continue to subscribe to a newspaper that does not adequately cover their region and is not technically competent enough to be legible. And because they are exposed to national publications and television programming of high quality, even readers on a local level are becoming increasingly sophisticated and are demanding a better quality of product.

The *general manager* or *business manager* heads the business side of things, directing a staff that sells advertisements and does the bookkeeping and payroll tasks necessary in any business. This person reports to the publisher.

Next in line of responsibility is the *advertising manager*. The main task of this person is to see that the newspaper sells as much of its space as possible at rates that are high enough to ensure a profit, yet not so high as to discourage advertisers.

This manager directs a sales staff trained to bring in three different kinds of advertisements: local, national, and classified.

Local ads are sought by the *sales people,* who call on businesses, or accounts, in their area. The sales staffs on smaller newspapers in smaller towns also help their accounts design ads and write the copy. In larger cities this job is usually handled by either an advertising agency or the company's own advertising department.

National advertisements come to a smaller daily newspaper via a national sales representative or advertising agencies. Small newspapers rarely solicit this advertising directly but wait for national companies to request use of their pages. If, for example, an automobile manufacturer decides to advertise its new models in a certain part of the country, it has its advertising agency check the statistics of newspapers in that area for such features as size and frequency. That agency then sends the completed ad with an insertion order to the newspaper ready to be pasted up. The agency has designed the ad and written the copy, and its commission is usually 15 percent. The local newspaper merely runs the ad and collects its fee. On a larger newspaper, an advertising sales person might seek out the same auto company to sell space for an entire year, not just for introducing new models.

Local department stores that are part of larger chains submit ads prepared by their own advertising departments. This retail advertising is profitable and, with supermarket ads, forms the backbone of the advertising business of many newspapers.

For classified ads, the newspaper sales staff plays the role of order taker from people who want to buy or sell everything from houses to baby cribs. The newspapers often solicit customers for their classified ads, finding this very lucrative because the ads are small and charges are based on every square inch of space sold.

Circulation

No newspaper can function properly on subscription money alone, for to attempt to do so in these days of spiraling production costs and salary increases would be a break-even proposition at best. Yet neither can a newspaper survive without an adequate number of subscribers. Advertising rates are based on this figure, and so is the prestige of the newspaper. If a newspaper is the only publication in town but fails to reach many potential readers, something may be wrong. In a two-newspaper town—increasingly rare in the United States—both publications will be vying constantly for the number-one position in circulation.

The *circulation manager* is responsible for getting new readers for the newspaper and keeping them happy with the product they receive. He or she may run campaigns to gain new subscribers from time to time and also to increase the efficiency of the *carriers* who every day deliver the newspapers to the readers' doorsteps. In a big city where many readers buy their newspapers at newsstands instead of having them delivered at home, the circulation manager spends more time organizing the routes of delivery trucks and worrying about traffic jams.

The remaining personnel on the business side prepare payroll, keep books, order supplies—perform all the operations essential to any business.

The Production Side

The third part of the newspaper puts together the products of the other two—editorial material and advertisements—and brings out the completed newspaper. It is in this department that the words of reporters and headlines of the editors are set into type and ultimately printed (see Chapter 4). The production department sets the deadlines around which the rest of the newspaper's operation revolves. Everything is worked backwards from that time—anywhere from a half hour for a late-breaking story to one and a half to two hours for a normal day's flow of news.

The *production manager* heads the department, presiding over people who operate computer typesetting machines; paste up copy, headlines, and advertisements; run copy cameras and platemaking equipment; and operate the press.

From the press room, the finished newspapers run on a conveyor belt to a sorting area where they are picked up by employees of the circulation department. Route managers then deliver them to carriers on corners or to newsstands around the city in a pattern worked out in advance to ensure that copies of the newspaper are in the hands of readers as quickly as possible. A few are addressed for mailing out of town.

At this point, the day is over.

Back in the news room, however, reporters and editors have already begun the next day's newspaper.

Summary

Most newspapers have three departments, or sides. On the news side, reporters gather information and write stories. The stories are turned in to editors, who make changes, write headlines, and decide where the stories, and any accompanying photographs, are to be placed in the newspaper. On the business side, salesmen sell the advertising space that keeps the newspaper financially healthy. Other employees undertake to increase readership, or circulation, and to see that the newspaper is delivered as quickly as possible. Employees of the production side take the output of the two other sides—editorial material and advertising—and set it into type, paste it into page form, prepare it for printing, and print it to meet the deadline.

Suggested Exercises

1. Examine the structure of the newspaper in your town to see how it is organized. Draw a chart of the different jobs and departments and present it to the class.

2. Examine the structure of a large newspaper. Draw a chart of the different jobs and departments as determined by reading the paper and looking at its listing in the *Editor and Publisher* directory.

3. Compare and contrast the organizational structure of the newspapers researched in exercises 1 and 2.

4. Using the newspaper organization chart in Chapter 3, trace a story through the news side and identify the gatekeepers.

5. Analyze the content of your local newspaper. What percentage of it (by number of column inches) contains editorial material, and what percentage contains advertising? Do the same thing with one of the big-city daily newspapers. Compare and contrast the two in terms of the percentage of advertising and the resulting "news hole."

"Initially, we got the paper out in spite of the new technology. It took a while to settle down. Now, I wouldn't want to go back to paper and pencil, gluepot and scissors. . . . It takes longer to bleed, tighten, and tidy up with a pencil. You can't go too fast. You get sloppy in adding lines typesetters can't read. There are still problems, and the machines are not perfect because human beings are not perfect. It's just so much faster."

Rod Deckert, city editor,
Corvallis Gazette-Times

"It's better with machines than without. It only has one drawback: It takes longer to edit than it did with a paper and pencil. You have to insert a lot of codes; the reporter becomes a bit of a typesetter. It also does away with proofreaders, which you suffer for. It has advantages. The primary one is greatly reduced production costs. . . . Money has been shifted to editorial salaries, staff, and other resources. Neatness and tidiness are other advantages. . . . There has been no effect on reporters; it's simple to learn."

Tom Jenks, editor,
Corvallis Gazette-Times

4

Printing, Production, and the New Technology

Letterpress Printing
Offset Printing
The New Technology

After struggling for centuries with cumbersome, slow, and costly "hot type" typesetting sytems and letterpress printing, newspaper editors and reporters are now able to use fast and efficient "cold type" methods of computer typesetting and offset printing. The new systems are called the new technology and have revolutionized the newspaper business.

Letterpress Printing

Letterpress incorporates a technique from the oldest form of printing: raised surface (the type) pressed against flat surface (the paper). It was derived from the old art of woodcutting, in which artists gouged out the surface areas of wood blocks not meant to print, leaving the printing design raised in relief. The Chinese began printing books from such wood blocks as early as A.D. 868.

But in Europe printing was still unknown, and monks copied the books of the time by hand. A German, Johann Gutenberg, changed all of this with his invention of movable type in about 1448. Although his letter forms resembled those used by the monks, they could be used again and again, a real breakthrough for printers and readers alike. Individual letters, made first of wood and later of lead for permanence, could be formed into words and the words into lines. When the printing was finished, the lines and words could be broken up and the type sorted alphabetically, ready to reuse.

Printers arranged the type on a flatbed, or tray, inked it, laid paper on it, and screwed down the platen, a wooden (later iron) plate, which pressed the page against the type. When they removed the paper, it contained the image. (See Figure 4.1.)

This approach satisfied printers for several centuries until they decided it took too much time to unscrew the platen after each impression. In 1822, steam was added to Gutenberg-style presses. This equipment was faster and served book publishers well, but was still not good enough for newspaper editors, who found it took too much time to lift the platen away from the type.

Their solution was to substitute a cylinder for the platen, and it worked well. The cylinder picked up the paper and carried it over a moving type bed. Later a press with two cylinders was invented, to allow printing on both sides of the paper. Soon a continuous web of paper was also used, to avoid the need to insert it one piece at a time.

By the mid-nineteenth century, a revolving press was perfected, on which type could be rotated instead of being held in one place. This development led to stereotyping and the more modern rotary presses of recent years. In stereotyping, the pages of type are formed into metal facsimiles that can be placed on the press. This is done by placing a page-sized papier-mâché sheet over the flat bed of type and running it through a

Figure 4.1 *The flatbed press. (Sketch by Debra A. Fox.)*

stereotyping machine that rolls it under great pressure. A papier-mâché sheet, called a mat, or mold, emerges from this machine as a perfect facsimile of the page. The mat is dried and then curved into a half-cylinder shape.

The mat is placed in an autoplate machine, where it is filled with hot lead. The page emerges as a cylindrical metal plate, a curved duplicate of the original flat bed of type. After it has been removed from the machine and cooled, this plate and others like it for other pages are placed on the press.

In spite of these improvements in press design and operation, however, type was still being set by hand even in the late nineteenth century in much the same way it had been set in Gutenberg's time. This method was slow, time-consuming, and costly because each line had to be set up—letters, spaces, and punctuation marks—and taken apart. Newspaper publishers especially began to look for a faster, more economical way.

A group of them in New York financed Ottmar Mergenthaler, a German watchmaker then working in the United States, as he tried to develop an automatic typesetting machine. His invention of a new machine in 1886 was another milestone in printing history. His Linotype—literally "lines of type"—injected hot metal into brass letter molds. (See Figure 4.2.) Operators put the molds in place, and set the copy by hitting a keyboard similar to, but more complicated than, that of a typewriter; within seconds, the Linotype turned molten metal from a heated container on the back of the machine into a line of type evenly spaced and cool enough to touch. The lines would not have to be broken up and rearranged, as the handset type had been; they could be melted and formed into lead bars, ready to be remelted and to be formed into new lines. The new process was used for regular textual matter, but headlines were still set by hand for many years.

With slight variations, the Linotype has remained in constant use, only recently being replaced by computer typesetting equipment. It was a machine that revolutionized printing. It is still a marvel of sight and sound, a fascinating assembly of moving belts and pulleys, of jangling brass molds and clanging iron arms.

Figure 4.2 The Linotype. (Sketch by Debra A. Fox.)

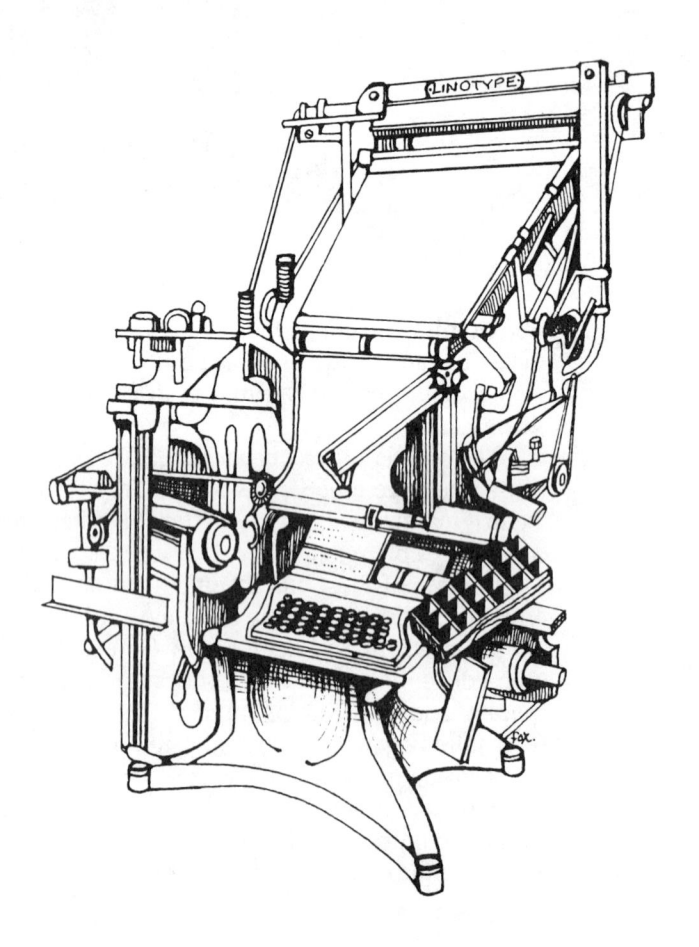

Offset Printing

Until recent years, letterpress dominated the industry. During the past decade, however, offset has replaced letterpress on all but a few big-city dailies and small weeklies. In 1977, 45 morning newspapers and 44 afternoon newspapers were still using letterpress, according to the American Newspaper Publishers Association, while 220 morning and 502 afternoon newspapers had turned to offset. Printing companies, however, still produce books, magazines, and other kinds of publications with letterpress.

Offset, also called photo-offset lithography, differs from letterpress in that it prints from a flat surface rather than a raised one, involves a chemical process rather than a mechanical one, and makes an indirect impression rather than a direct one.

Copy for offset is prepared for printing by a photographic means. Thus, material is not restricted, as it is in letterpress, to that cast from hot metal. In fact, various cold-type methods can be used for type composition.

The development of offset is another significant event in the history of printing. Offset was discovered as early as 1796, when Aloys Senefelder, a Bavarian actor and playwright, worked out a way to print from the flat surface of a stone. He could not afford to have his plays printed and was trying to reproduce them himself by writing backwards on the stone. He used a flat stone instead of engraver's copper because the stone could be used again. One day, he wrote something on the stone with a greasy substance and discovered later that water would not wash it away. He had inadvertently discovered the basic principle of offset printing: Greasy surfaces accept only ink and reject water.

Early in the twentieth century, an American printer noticed that a precise image would sometimes show up on the back of a sheet as he fed paper into his press. When a sheet did not feed correctly, the image was transferred onto the impression cylinder and would appear clearly on the back of the next sheet. He later incorporated the idea into a press he developed; a special rubber-covered cylinder received the image from the plate and "offset" it onto the paper.

Glossary of Printing Terms

Cold Type Typesetting by computer or photographic means; used in offset printing.

Column The vertical arrangement of type on a newspaper page at varying widths.

Dummy A plan of how a newspaper page is to be arranged.

Galley Proof The first printing of a story after it has been set into type.

Hard-Copy Printer A machine that gives a printed version of a story set electronically on a VDT and stored in the Computer; this version is not used for editing, but for later analysis of the writing and as a record for the reporter.

Hot Type Type set by Linotype or a similar machine using molten metal to cast lines of type; used in letterpress printing.

Letterpress A printing method in which the raised surface image is pressed directly against the paper.

Linotype A machine that casts lines of type from hot lead; used in letterpress printing.

Makeup The arrangement of all elements of a newspaper page: headlines, text, photographs, advertisements.

Mat A papier-mâché mold from which type is cast in letterpress printing.

Offset An indirect printing method based on the principle that grease and water do not mix; the image goes from the plate to a rubber blanket to the paper.

Paste-up The process of preparing a complete newspaper page; when the headlines, stories, and advertisements have been set into type, and the photographs prepared, they are attached, with wax, to a special measured sheet, ready to be photographed.

Pica A printer's way of measuring line width (6 picas to one inch, 12 points).

Plate Metal from which newspapers' pages are printed; formed to fit the press.

Point A printer's way of measuring type size (72 points to one inch).

Production Manager The manager responsible for seeing that stories and advertisements are set into type, pages pasted up, negatives and plates made, and the newspaper printed on the press.

Production That part of the newspaper where stories and advertisements are set into type, pasted up, prepared for the press, and printed.

Reproduction Proof A final printed proof ready to be pasted up and photographed for final printing; also called repro proof.

Stereotyping The process, used in letterpress printing, of making a duplicate metal plate of a newspaper page from a mat; the duplicate plate is flat or curved to fit the press.

Type Printed letters and characters of various sizes and styles.

VDT Video-display terminal, a kind of electronic typewriter consisting of a keyboard and video screen; reporters use the keyboard to type their stories, and an electronic "cursor" to make editorial changes.

The New Technology

Despite its early development, offset was slow to win wide acceptance. The letterpress equipment worked well, and its quick replacement could not be justified easily. Enormous financial considerations came into play; many newspapers, especially those in larger cities, had a great deal of money invested in Linotype machines and letterpress printing equipment that could not be replaced quickly. Furthermore, newspaper-production labor unions on these same papers resisted the change for fear their members would be put out of work because they did not know how to run the machines of the new technology. (See Figure 4.3 for a general comparison of hot and cold type systems.)

Smaller newspapers did not have such problems, however, and began to turn to offset in the late 1950s and early 1960s. By the early 1970s more and more large newspapers were joining them and installing offset systems.

The new technology at the *Corvallis Gazette-Times*

The *Corvallis Gazette-Times*'s conversion to the new system is a good example of what happened throughout the country.

"The change to the new technology was purely economic," says Wally Newton, production manager. "Under the old system [hot type, letterpress] printing was more of a craft. But the law of supply and demand appeared, and the increased volume required by newspapers to survive could not be handled by the old equipment. On the big papers there were rows and rows of Linotypes to set type—as far as the eye could see. It took a massive volume of people to operate them. Ten people now produce double the volume that it used to take twenty-seven people to set."

But the change was not easy. When the *Gazette-Times* sought to modernize its printing plant in the late 1960s, its owners realized that the expense would be great. Not only was the early equipment expensive and cumbersome, but its purchase would also require the newspaper to raise the ceiling of its press room by six feet to meet fire codes.

The family that owned the *Gazette-Times* soon decided that the only way it could afford the high costs was to allow the newspaper to be purchased by a chain. After 116 years as a privately owned newspaper under various names, the *Gazette-Times* became part of Lee Enterprises in 1971. Soon after, Lee purchased a new offset press for $750,000 and paid for construction of a new building to house it and the entire staff for another $750,000. The doors of the new building opened later that year.

Figure 4.3. *The two major printing systems compared.*

COLD TYPE

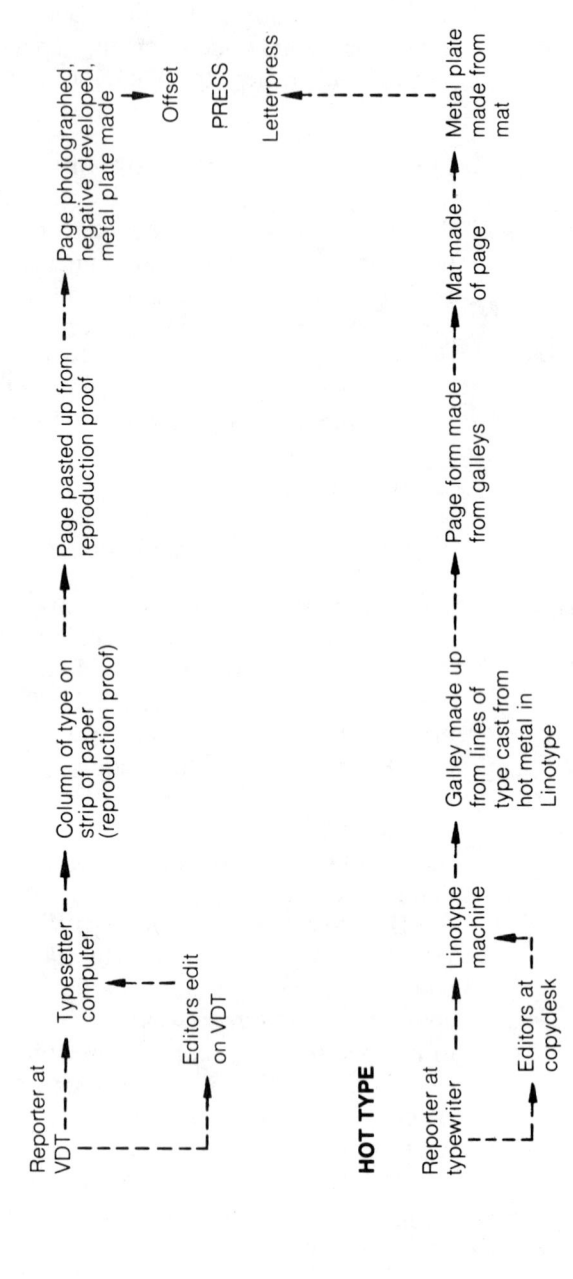

Reporter at VDT ---▶ Typesetter computer ---▶ Column of type on strip of paper (reproduction proof) ---▶ Page pasted up from reproduction proof ---▶ Page photographed, negative developed, metal plate made ---▶ Offset PRESS

Editors edit on VDT

HOT TYPE

Reporter at typewriter ---▶ Linotype machine ---▶ Galley made up from lines of type cast from hot metal in Linotype ---▶ Page form made from galleys ---▶ Mat made of page ---▶ Metal plate made from mat ---▶ Letterpress PRESS

Editors at copydesk

Wally Newton was instrumental in helping the newspaper make the massive conversion to the new system. His career has spanned much of the period of greatest advancement in the technology of newspaper production. He began as a hot-type newspaper printer in the nearby town of Albany, where he "did everything" from page makeup to Linotype operation.

He has worked for the *Gazette-Times* for sixteen years and was foreman in 1971, the year the paper went corporate and began using offset printing. Since then he has supervised the purchase and installation of all the new equipment and trained the staff to operate it. He became production manager in 1976.

"I knew the new technology had to come," he says. "The labor unions were forcing it. Because of the massive volume being produced, a newspaper could no longer be effective with the old methods. A lot of places were forced into converting before they were ready because of competition."

After the newspaper was purchased by Lee, Newton was given a free hand to learn about new equipment and decide what the newspaper should buy. He bought two typesetting units, operated manually by employees who punch out reporters' stories on keyboards. A tape emerges from each machine and is fed through a tape reader, a process that results in a reproduction proof.

The main advantage of this system was that the two machines produced as much output as would six Linotypes. Linotypes can turn out six lines of type a minute; each of these typesetters produced fifty-eight lines a minute. A new Linotype costs $25,000; this typesetter, $8,000. A smaller labor force resulted, even though there was more composition. News and classified ads were set on these new machines.

At the same time, the *Gazette-Times* purchased a $42,000 machine to set advertisements, driven by a $105,000 computer rented for $1,300 a month. The system was the same, in principle, as recent, more sophisticated systems, but the computer was more bulky. These two systems served well for four years.

Then Newton took computer equipment from several sister papers that had been unsuccessful. This allowed him to eliminate all the other equipment, including the big computer, and also resulted in a large cost saving. The new equipment was no faster than the earlier machines (sixty lines a minute), but it could be completely programed without manual typesetting. It has fifteen type sizes and eight type faces available, while the others had one of each.

In June, 1976, the *Gazette-Times* purchased a video-display terminal (VDT) for each reporter and editor in the newsroom. Only two old-style typewriters remain. The VDTs, electronic typewriters with copy displayed on a television screen, eliminate what Newton considers a redundancy. "There is no redundancy of retyping," he says. "There was also a big cost saving. You do not have to retype every bit of information that goes into the newspaper. It also gives the newsroom complete control of the editorial product. No one else revises or misinterprets names, dates, figures, or facts; misplaces commas or adds extra adverbs that change the meaning. One hundred percent of what comes from the newsroom is set by the newsroom."

As a reporter types a story, the lines of the story appear on the television-like screen of the VDT. After finishing the story, the reporter can go back to its beginning and read it again, changing errors electronically with a cursor. When the cursor, a small, oblong device, is moved over the error, it eliminates it by the push of a button on the keyboard.

How the system at the *Gazette-Times* works

Once the format (vertical spacing, or leading, line length, typeface, point size) has been specified, it is stored in the computer of the typesetting machine so that it can be called up and used without manual intervention. Formerly all such changes had to be made by an operator. This limited flexibility. For example, without manual intervention, news copy could only be one column wide.

Reporters write their stories on VDTs at their desks. After the editors have told them the column width of their stories, they type the call for format at the top of the page: six, seven, eight, or nine columns wide. The different column-width and type combinations are retained in fifty-six "addresses," a place in the computer memory from which information can be retrieved automatically. This avoids the delays in production that resulted when manual settings were made for each story.

The VDTs are connected by cable to a central storage device that is connected to two hard-copy printers. These produce carbons for editors to work with in upgrading the writing by showing reporters later why changes were made. These copies are not used by editors to prepare stories for the newspaper.

Once a reporter writes a story on the VDT, he or she activates the hard-copy printer and also sends the story to disc storage at this time. From then on, the news editor and copy editor can also call the story to their own VDT screens for editing and writing headlines.

On newspapers still using typewriters, reporters type their stories and turn them in at the copydesk, where the editors make changes and write headlines before giving the typewritten copy to the operators of perforator machines. The tapes punched in these machines are then fed into a typesetting device like the computer already mentioned. The proofs that result are corrected by proofreaders.

After the editor has conferred with the reporter about changes to the story, and headlines have been written and typed into the VDT, the editor punches buttons on his or her VDT that send the story and the headline to the typesetting machine.

When the stories have been set into type in this machine, they emerge as reproduction proofs. These proofs are dried on a special heated table and excess paper trimmed off. They are put through a waxing machine. Wax is used to fasten copy and headlines to special lined paste-up sheets. With waxed copy, the people doing paste-up can lift stories and headlines and move them around without rewaxing because the wax retains its adhesiveness.

If the headline is with the story at this point, both are sent to page makeup. If it is an advance story planned for another day's edition, it is marked "HTK," for "headline to come," and sent back to the appropriate editor.

Dummying, the process of deciding what is to go where on each page of the newspaper, is done by page editors. For example, sports plans its own page, editorial its own, and so on. The dummying begins the day before the date of publication, when one person in the advertising department designates the placement of ads on each page of the newspaper except the front page and the editorial page, neither of which has ads. This person also takes into consideration early requests by the news department for other "open" pages—those without ads because of a special report or other long article—or open section-fronts. Full-color photography or advertisements are also noted the day before.

The city editor looks at the dummy for every page and makes sure there is enough of a news hole to accommodate the news. When he is satisfied, he routes the dummies to the responsible section editors, and they dummy-in their stories.

These dummies are due in the production area at various times: 3:00 P.M. the day before publication for the relatively timeless "Spectrum" section, noon on the day of publication for community or any other late-breaking news.

Production personnel then use the dummies to paste up the stories and headlines as they come from the typesetting machine, the ads having already been pasted into place. These people communicate directly with the newsroom if stories are too long to fit their pages or contain obvious errors. The various editors then check their pages before they are sent to the camera room.

The paste-ups of the pages are then taken to the camera room and photographed, and the resulting negative developed and dried. Next the

The Newspaper Production Process.

(Photos by James Folts.)

A reporter writes a story on a video-display terminal.

Printing, Production, and the New Technology 65

After it has been edited, the story goes to the typesetting machine, from which emerges a reproduction proof.

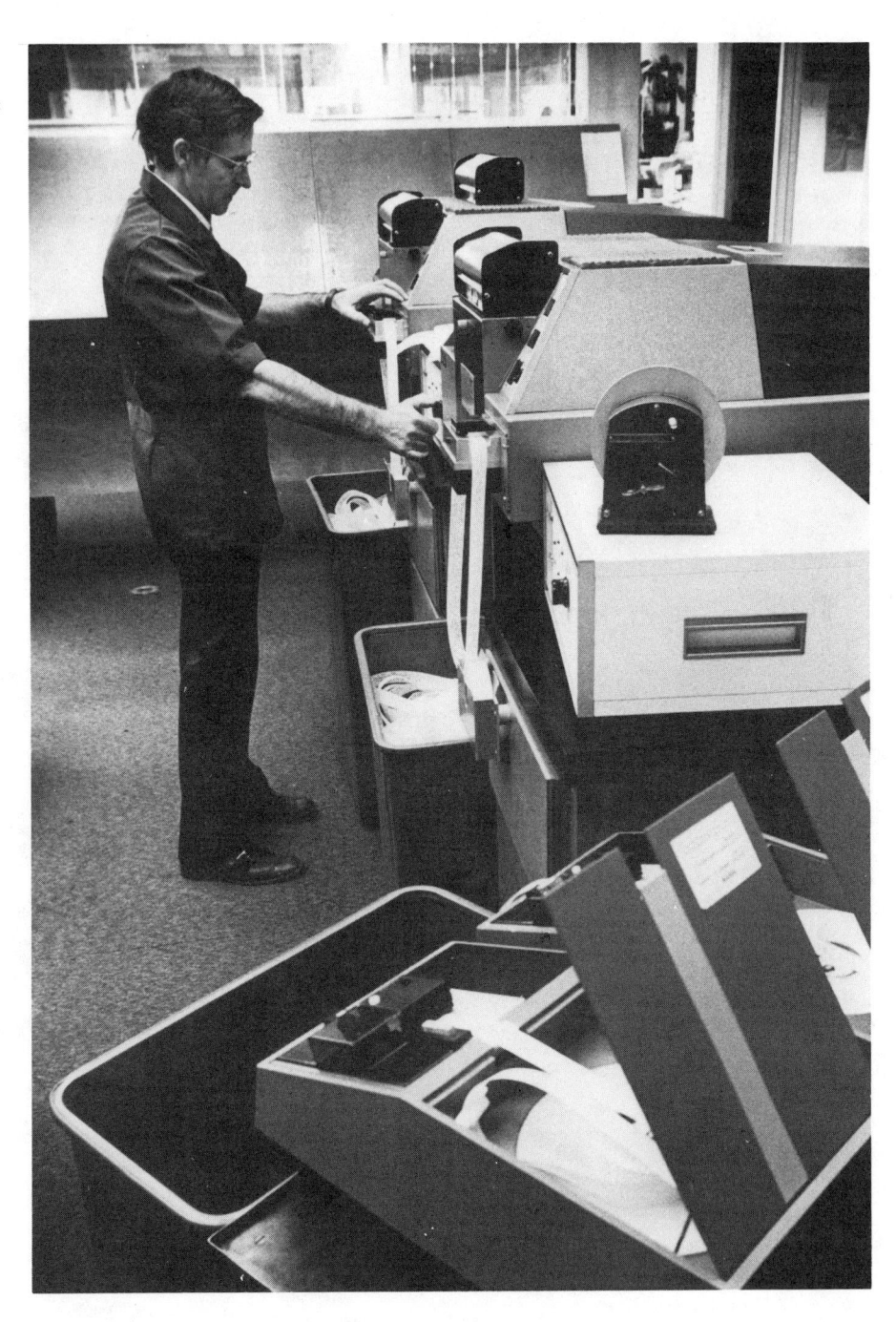

The reproduction proof is pasted onto layout sheets in page size.

Printing, Production, and the New Technology 67

The pages are photographed and the resulting negative checked for dust spots.

The image of the pages is "burned" onto a metal plate and rubbed with chemicals that cause the image to emerge.

The plate is locked onto the press.

The press runs.

Newspapers emerge from the press.

The delivery van is loaded — a different product every day.

negatives of two pages at a time are placed over flat metal plates seven-thousandths of an inch thick. The plates have already been made light sensitive. The plate is then burned, that is, exposed to light through the negative. The plate is developed like a photograph by rubbing chemicals on it to harden the emulsion in the exposed areas, causing the image to emerge.

After the image has been developed, the plate is gummed to prevent oxidation, bent to fit the press lock-up, and placed on the press with other plates. Once the plate is on the press, its surface is moistened with water plus an additive. The water sticks to the nonimage area. When ink is added, it adheres to the image area.

The indirect or "offset" aspect of this process comes when the press is revolving. The plate doesn't touch the paper as it would in letterpress. Rather, it leaves an inked image on a rubber-blanket cylinder. As the paper speeds through the press, the rubber blanket transfers the image to it from the plate.

The paper is trimmed and folded before it emerges in a form ready for delivery on the street.

And what of the total impact of the new technology?

"It has been a boon to news people because it has gotten them more directly involved," says Newton. "It gives them complete control and can provide so much more so much faster. The newspaper is newsier."

A few of the reporters resisted the changes at first, but Newton conducted classes for them, and all of them have accepted it now. "I was trying to put the monkey on their backs," he continues. "By the time we went with the system, only one person resisted it and three were scared to death. I had told them it was coming; they knew it had to be done.

"I've worked in papers that have problems with the new technology. They are people problems. In these papers, management fears strong union resistance, so they keep the new system quiet until the day the VDTs are placed on reporters' desks. The employees aren't involved in decisions and they don't get training. They are told, 'This is the way it is going to be from now on.' "

Despite the best planning, however, the system has problems from time to time. "When the machine blows its top at 11:30 A.M. and loses everything, it gets a little tedious," says reporter Bill Monroe. Newton adds that power failures, too, wipe out material stored in the terminals. "Then there is human error. But the amount we've lost in thirteen months I can count on one hand."

Summary

There are two kinds of printing processes in use on newspapers today: offset (cold type) and letterpress (hot type). Type for offset is set in a variety of ways, the most widely used system one in which reporters at desk-top video-display terminals write and edit their stories and feed them directly into a central computer. Offset is an indirect system, which follows the principle that greasy printing surfaces accept only ink and reject water. This is the direct opposite of letterpress, in which type is set from hot lead on a Linotype or similar machine and printed from a raised surface. Offset differs from letterpress in that it prints from a flat surface rather than a raised one, involves a chemical process rather than a mechanical one, and makes an indirect impression rather than a direct one. Offset is the newer process and has come into wider and wider use on newspapers because it is faster and more economical than the centuries-old letterpress.

Suggested Exercises

1. Prepare a research paper on five major technological advances in the history of printing since the fifteenth century.

2. Prepare a research paper on the advantages and disadvantages of the new technology on newspaper production.

3. Prepare a research paper on the link between labor union resistance and the spread of the new technology on big-city newspapers.

4. Analyze and compare the front page of a newspaper printed in a letterpress (hot type) method with one printed on an offset (cold type) press. Which newspaper looks better? Why?

5. Interview a reporter and an editor on the local newspaper and ask them their experiences with, and opinions about, the new technology.

"*Photographs do all kinds of different things. First and obvious: Any kind of decent pictures are going to have high readership, good pictures even higher readership. They are going to be read first. Pictures are actually like headlines. They get attention. If they do it well and provocatively, they will hold readers and get them into the story.*

Finally, you have to be committed to make pictures talk, not something as a typographical device. You commit yourself: I want this picture to say this about that situation. You get the reader to read. You pull a little movement out of the situation that really has something to say."

Rich Clarkson,
Director of Photography,
Topeka Capital-Journal

5

Photography

The New Photography
Editor-Reporter-Photographer Interaction
A Photographer's Typical Day

Rich Clarkson knows what he is talking about. For twenty years he has been director of photography at the *Topeka Capital-Journal*. From this unlikely spot in the center of the country, he has come to have great influence upon newspaper photojournalism elsewhere.

Many photographers have left the "Rich Clarkson School of Photography" and gone on to the staffs of big-city newspapers and magazines to excel in what they do. Benefiting from his example and from the training he has given them, his staff members and former staff members have won many national awards, among them a Pulitzer Prize, as well as regional and local awards, for their photographs.

"Photographers get a way of working and thinking here," he says. "They don't get it from me. The way we work right now is different than three years ago. It's a constantly changing thing, a freedom and responsibility. If I would edit all of their film and constantly supervise them, they wouldn't get that. One of the things that benefits them, I allow them to make mistakes. I do general critiques of their work with specific examples. I try to give them more of a total direction."

Clarkson's influence derives from his early espousal of the use of photographs, not just as decoration or as dull accompaniment to stories, but as important elements of the newspaper, standing alone and with meaning, often in color and larger than newspapers ran in the past. Many other photo directors and photographers do this today, but Clarkson did it first. Indeed, his photography operation in Topeka is the envy of his counterparts at many larger newspapers around the country. Many follow his approach as much as their budgets allow. His is still an atypical but excellent model.

In developing his style, he was influenced heavily by magazine photojournalism. He began to dabble in magazine photography while he was still a student at the University of Kansas, and went on to do freelance assignments for the *Saturday Evening Post, Life,* and *Time.* He is still a contract photographer for *Sports Illustrated.* "It was good exposure for me," he says. "I was dealing with magazine editors. I got plugged in."

Clarkson happened along at a time when the rather conservative management of the Topeka newspapers was willing to give him a free hand to reach the excellence to which he has always aspired. "I was hired by the general manager," he recalls. "So the general intent at the time was to establish what we're doing now with pictures. Since then, except for the quality of reproduction [plagued by the fact that the newspapers are still printed on a letterpress style press], they've gone along with whatever we've wanted to do."

The New Photography

Clarkson carried his magazine approach to photography with him to the *Capital-Journal*. He explains the approach: "You cover things as they really are, not posed or set up. *Life* was doing stories at the time where they'd put a photographer and a reporter somewhere for two days or eight months. Candid, spontaneous, believable, honest photographs were the result. Now we've swung around—few magazines that run picture stories, but newspapers that do."

The influence of the new photography at the national level has been dramatic. Jim Richardson, one of the photographers on Clarkson's staff, explains it this way: "There are things that come across in pictures—like Vietnam War coverage. The great thing is that they changed people's minds about that war. I can think of the police chief shooting the man in the head and the little girl running naked down the road. Day after day the association with headlines, of how many killed. My opinions were vastly changed by the photographs."

But what does the immediacy of the new photography mean for regional coverage, such as that by the two Topeka newspapers? Richardson continues: "In the *Life* era, it was a national thing. Now photographers can legitimately aspire to that kind of level on a regional basis. We do the kinds of stories *Life* and *Look* did about life in a particular area on an informative level that may not be news, such as a photo essay on a high school. It's not news at all; it's more sociology than journalism. But it's also useful in keeping people in touch with themselves."

Editor-Reporter-Photographer Interaction

On newspapers like the *Topeka Capital-Journal*, good photography results from a good relationship between editors, reporters, and photographers. The news department should keep photographers informed about upcoming assignments, as far in advance as possible. A photographer can take better photographs by knowing as much as possible about the subject in advance.

This approach works well on features and planned news events like press conferences and meetings. It is not possible in spot-news situations like fires and accidents.

Photographers should also be given the chance to select the photos to be used with the story. Too often an editor will make the choice for reasons of time and space, and the best photographs get lost in the process. This will not happen if the photographer is consulted.

Reporters and photographers can work together to maximum advantage if they trust one another and do not interfere with one another as they work. This is especially true on assignments they cover together. A reporter can suggest a photo possibility—and a photographer can ask a source a question—but only in moderation.

From his first day on the newspapers in Topeka, Clarkson has pushed for maximum cooperation among photographer and editor and photographer and reporter, a factor missing on many newspapers, where one hand doesn't know what the other is doing and bad pictures, no pictures, or badly placed pictures diminish quality.

"There is maximum communication between the assignment editor and the photographer," explains Clarkson. "The assignment editor and photographer talk over the photograph. When the photographer is driving back from the assignment, he might talk to the editor on his two-way radio and describe how the picture-taking went, even suggesting size. The editor can then dummy a hole for it."

Although he tends to stay behind the scenes as his eight photographers deal with the editors and reporters, Clarkson long ago paved the way for a smooth interaction between the departments. He and those who work for him seem to have a certain aura of untouchability around the newspapers, but Clarkson denies that his department receives any special treatment or that he overly dominates or influences editors to accept his approach unquestioningly. "If you know what you want done and it will work, there is nothing wrong with a con job. If not a day-to-day respect, we have an overall commitment to use photos well."

Clarkson describes the situation at the *Capital-Journal:* "It is very important that everything is done well—the pictures, the text in combination. Our happiest people get a great deal of satisfaction from the chance they get here to work on an effective team. Photographers and reporters spend half their time together, always on major stories. This is so they each understand the most significant thing they're covering. Four eyes are better than two.

"Our writers get as many helpful tips from photographers. The key to covering a good story is to know what is significant. Sometimes photographers have more background on the subject than writers. Reporters seldom take their own photos. We don't encourage it, but we don't try to stop it. If it seems that not many photos will develop [on a story], the reporters might do it. But we do have photographers writing stories, not just text blocks for photo pages."

A Photographer's Typical Day

Chris Johns is a photographer at the *Topeka Capital-Journal;* his approach to a typical day and to his job is illustrative of the Clarkson style and of the new photography in general. His activities during a typical assignment are illustrated in the photo essay of this chapter. Here the assignment is to photograph a teenager who has bicycled from Kansas to Oregon. At page 83, Johns chats with the subject, building up rapport; he learns where the cyclist rode while training, and he chooses that spot as the place for the photo. The photographer carries all his equipment in his car, which has a two-way radio for constant communication with the office.

After shooting the assignment, Johns returns to the office, where he develops the film and looks at it quickly to see what he has. (If he is pushing deadline, he can tell the city editor what to expect; the two of them can then decide where the picture will run and in what size.) After the film is dry, he cuts it and puts it into cellophane "sleeves" to protect it. He then makes his final "edit" and prints the picture to size. Photographers often try to vary the size of photographs, sometimes making shallow six-column photos (as in this assignment) or deep two-column photos in order to vary the look of the page and increase reader interest. The finished product, as it ran in the newspaper, is shown on the final page of the photo essay.

Commenting on the way in which he works, Johns says, "The first thing I have to do is to determine exactly what the assignment is trying to say. Then I try to capture a moment with some people that says what I have to say to fulfill that assignment. For example, the first day of school, one of the old standbys every photographer has to do. I can take a cute, humorous picture of kids upside down on the monkey bars. I can bring back that hack, grabber picture of kids doing something cute, but it doesn't say back to school." The picture that does convey what Johns wants to express in this case is reproduced in the photo essay in Chapter 2, page 21. For photos like this one, Johns was named 1978 national photographer of the year by the National Press Photographers Association and the University of Missouri.

"When the city editor gives me an assignment, I've got to have something that goes pretty closely with the words of that story. The first thing is to fulfill that assignment. I sometimes pass up a picture because it doesn't fulfill the assignment.

"Then I say that assignment as eloquently as I can, as revealing as I can about that community; for example, a warm nice moment between two people. If the picture really works well and is not just a gallery-type shot designed to win a contest, it is a vehicle to convey information about the community, whether it be local, state, or world. Every now and then you'll convey what needs to be said in that assignment. The picture will stand alone without words. I wish it happened more often."

Johns continues by saying that a story need not be exciting to suggest a good news photograph: "In a town like Topeka, there is not that much hard news. As a photographer on a mundane assignment, you establish some kind

The Photographer's Day.

(Photos by Chris Johns.)

The photographer picks up the day's assignments.

The photo order form tells the photographer the time and location of the assignment.

Topeka Capital-Journal	PHOTO ORDER	Time: 9:30 am	Date: Aug. 22 Tuesday
For: ☐ Capital ☒ Journal ☐ Sunday —Desk	Subject: Teenager who rode his bicycle from Kansas to Oregon this summer.	Where: 3206 SW MacVicar St.	
Size Needed: ?	When and where picture will be used: First edition State Journal	Identifications: yes	
Special Instructions: He will be at home with the bike he made the trip on. Kathy Thomas will be interviewing him.			
Ordered by: Stannie Anderson		Photographer: Johns	

The photographer chats with the subject to build up rapport.

The photographer looks at the developed film while it is washing.

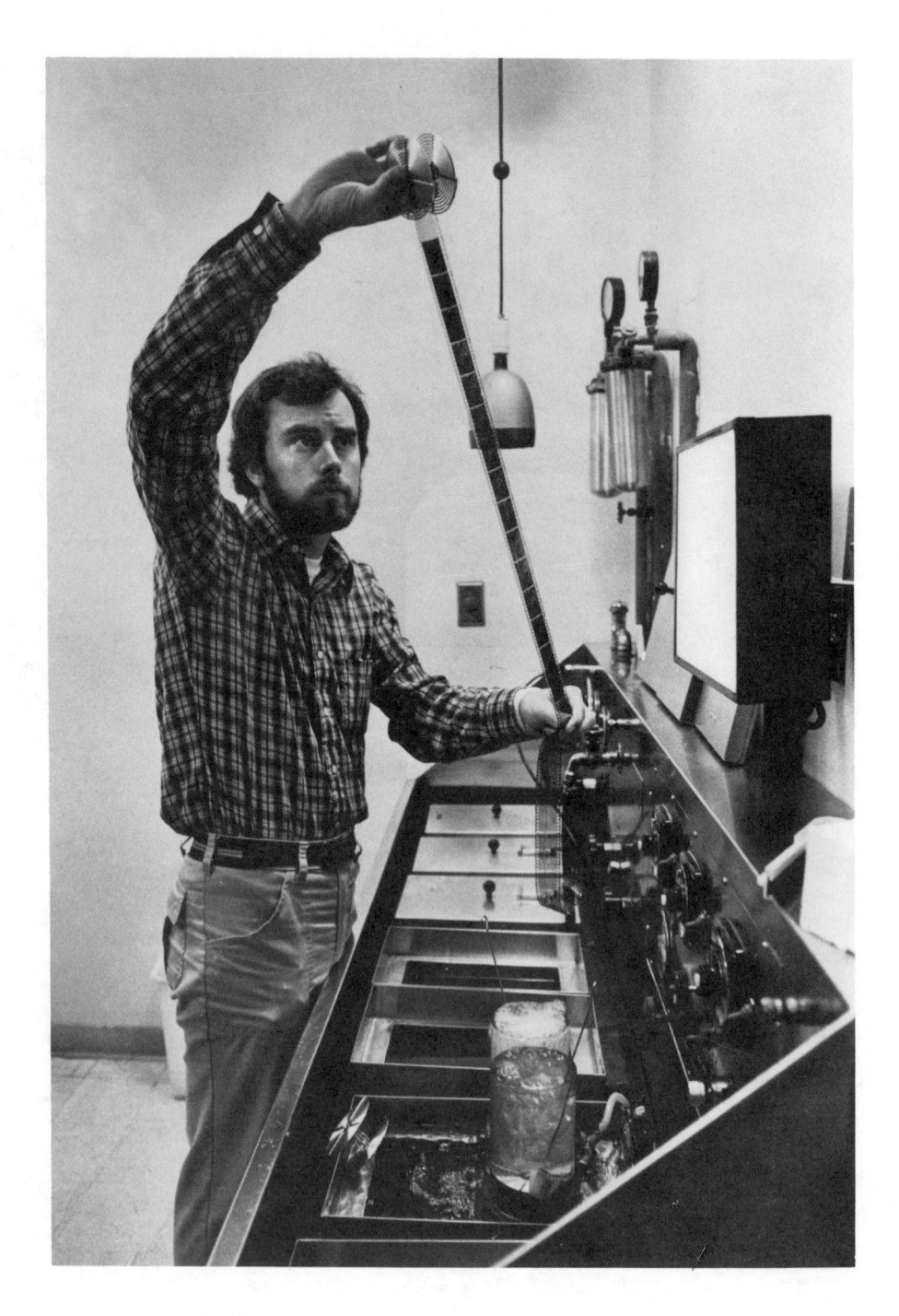

The photographer cuts the dried film, then puts it into cellophane sleeves.

*The photographer prints
the picture to size.*

The photo of the cyclist, as it appeared in the Topeka Capital-Journal.

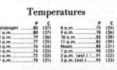

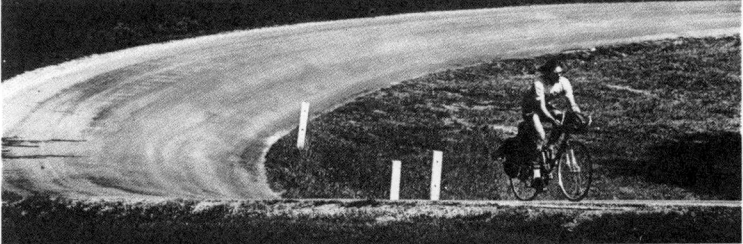

of rapport with the person and appear to be interested in what they are doing. For example, cook of the week: You walk in the door and here's this lady with her hair all combed, the house spotless. She is very nervous. Quite often you make comments about how nice the house is. What's her main dish? I've somehow got to take a picture of this woman in her kitchen, of this woman while she works. If you stop and look, you can get a lot of information into a photo like this—the way people are dressed, the house, little mannerisms.

"The first thing you've got to remember, you're being paid for your time. But when you're working with someone on a big assignment, their time is valuable. There is no time to mess around. Planning is important. You've got to make sure you've got press credentials, that cameras are ready, and that you've got plenty of film. You want to be dressed for it—a three-piece suit or blue jeans. When I get there I want things to be as simple as possible. I want to concentrate on being able to take a good picture. I'll really make people in the shot apprehensive if I'm not decisive, if I run around, shooting photos up and down. You've also got to be on time. If you're late, you're always behind. I have to win a person's trust and they have to have faith in me."

In short, the photographer must be well prepared: "For example, I recently had to shoot out at the home of Alf Landon, the former governor and presidential candidate. I just can't spend a day wandering around. I know what film to use, what light to use, and where I want to take the picture. I remember what I need from previous visits. I know what he likes to talk about too."

As Johns admits, the ideal photograph may not always be obtainable, and the photographer should anticipate that possibility: "Another really important thing is to be covered, to get the picture you can use if all else fails. For Alf Landon, it was him in his study with a fire and his wife. You arrange the room, have camera and lights set up before. I use Polaroid test exposures first. You go for that picture to get it out of the way. Then I push him a bit to do something he may not want to do. I wanted him to let me photograph him behind his bulletproof lectern with his portrait on one side, flags on the other. I ask and he refuses. That was that.

"I tell him, 'I'm going to take more pictures of you than have been taken in years.' I do that for insurance. Film's the cheapest thing I work with."

Johns urges that it is also important that the photographer exercise tact: "Oftentimes people have a picture they think you should take. I'll take it, although I know I won't use it. I feel strongly about this. People are very nice to me. They let me into their homes. They don't have to let me in. I let them know I appreciate it. I never move anything without asking them. They don't want people barging in and barging out."

Beyond simple tact, the photographer must pursue high principles and daily be prepared to face problems of ethics. "The most trying thing about being a photographer," Johns continues, "is the trauma situation—a fatal fire, a fatal wreck. You're very delicately treading a thin wire between the public's right to know and being a voyeur in people's lives. You have to evaluate honestly, Is the picture worth it?

"Once, at a fire at a vacant house in town I took a few shots—which you have to do in case there's a body inside. I was shooting when a black woman knocked me down. A policeman had to subdue her. At a murder scene, the victim's friend came by to ask what I was doing. . . . I had to put a lot of information in, like showing the house, a policeman standing guard, all the trauma taking place. Another friend of the victim took a swing at me, and a policeman subdued him. I let people know where I'm from; I'm not sneaky."

Johns worries about fairness in the photos he takes: "Do the ends justify the means?" he asks. "You may see a 'fine' emotional shot, someone distraught over the loss of a loved one. Your presence may add to the trauma, so much so that taking the picture may not be worth the trauma you put them through. I don't always buy the line 'It's my job,' or the feeling that people have to know everything. I don't have a ticket to barge into people's lives. If someone says I can't go in there, I'm going to think about it."

Johns tries to prepare for the unexpected moments of intrusion by being as inconspicuous as possible. Although he and the other photographers have from $4,000 to $6,000 invested in camera equipment, he travels light. "I take a minimum of equipment," he says, "three lenses, two camera bodies. The important thing for me is to move quickly and not make any noise."

Once the photographs are taken, other duties remain for the photographer. Johns and the other photographers edit their own film. He talks to the reporter and editor to find out how much space the photo will have and then prints the picture to exact size. "We do two prints, one with the identification of the people on the back, the other for screening," he says. "We are responsible for spelling, addresses, ages, and, if a child, the parents' name. I ask people their names on the spot. If it is a large group, I'll line them up and ask their names and then I'll circle people on the print and draw lines to their names."

The number of his assignments varies from day to day. If he is working on a photo essay, he will do only that. If he is covering spot news, he might work on three or four stories. It depends on the day.

"I feel being a photojournalist is a very legitimate kind of journalism," he says. "Photographers are able to make people look at themselves, to look at good things and be aware of bad things, and to show readers some things they need to see. I almost touch too much, enter too quickly, exit too quickly, dart in and out of things too much, become a bit too callous toward the everyday routine and how people live."

It does not seem, however, that Johns needs to worry. He has remained humane and can still be deeply moved by the stories he does—like the one about Allie Neuman (Figure 5.1).

"I was doing a story on hay haulers about thirty miles north of Topeka one day, and I saw a little old man driving his tractor down the road," Johns recalls. "He kind of waved at me. I pulled over, and we talked. I asked him if I could take a few pictures. 'Why don't you drop by?' he said.

"I dropped by several weeks later and gave him a couple of the pictures. He gave me a piece of cantaloupe and told me about his family and showed me his antiques. He was an old bachelor who had had brothers. None of them had ever married, and now they were all dead.

"I came back nine months later and asked if I could do a photo feature on him. He said he wasn't important enough. I was afraid he wasn't eating well, so I brought some cookies my wife had made. We talked for a while, and he said he thought it would be OK for me to spend the day with him. I had twenty-five rolls of film when I left. I narrowed that down to four pictures.

"I thought the angle of the story was a man who lived totally in the past. In order to bring that point over, I took a shot of a shed he had built that was falling down. The house was the same way it had been all his life. He was an old farmer, so I took a picture of him with a pitchfork as he walked around bent over. I used a tighter picture because he had such a neat face—a pleasant guy who had probably never done anyone any harm in his life, a man who was very gentle and nice.

"The photos ran in the Sunday paper. Monday I called him. He was really pleased. He'd seen old friends he hadn't seen in years because of the story. He was very happy, and so was I.

"Two days after that he died in his sleep, at seventy-eight.

"It was pretty hard for me. In a news event, you are an observer and you document what happens. There are other times, like this one, when it is important to become involved, to relate to people. This is one of the most satisfying things about being a journalist. I participated in Allie Neuman's life, and he participated in mine; it helped me as a journalist."

Summary

Photography has grown in importance on newspapers in recent years. Following the lead of many national magazines, newspapers have begun to use photographs as illustrations for individual stories and as separate photo

Photography 91

Figure 5.1 Photographs that tell their own story. *(Courtesy of the* Topeka Capital-Journal.*)*

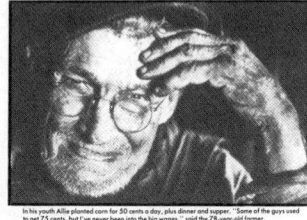

essays with little text material—in short, a new photography. Newspapers have also begun to run photographs in color and in larger sizes than they did in the past. All of these factors have increased reader interest and improved newspaper layout and design. As the use of photographs increases, it is important for editors and reporters to work closely with photography directors and photographers so that assignments are coordinated and story goals made clear. Better photos are the result. Photographers must also remember the moral and ethical problems involved in taking their photographs, especially of traumatic human situations. The best photos result when the photographer involved displays a humane feeling toward the subject.

Suggested Exercises

1. Select five photos that illustrate a news story and write an analysis of their good and bad points.

2. Select five photos to illustrate feature stories and write an analysis of their good and bad points.

3. Select a photo essay and analyze its impact on you as a reader. What is its apparent aim? How well do the text and the photos reach that goal?

4. Select three photos from a newspaper and three from a national news magazine on the same subject and compare and contrast the approaches of the two kinds of publications.

5. Interview a photographer from a local newspaper and find out how that photographer carries out his or her job. What is a typical day in terms of hours, routine, and kinds of assignments? How well does the photographer interact with the news department?

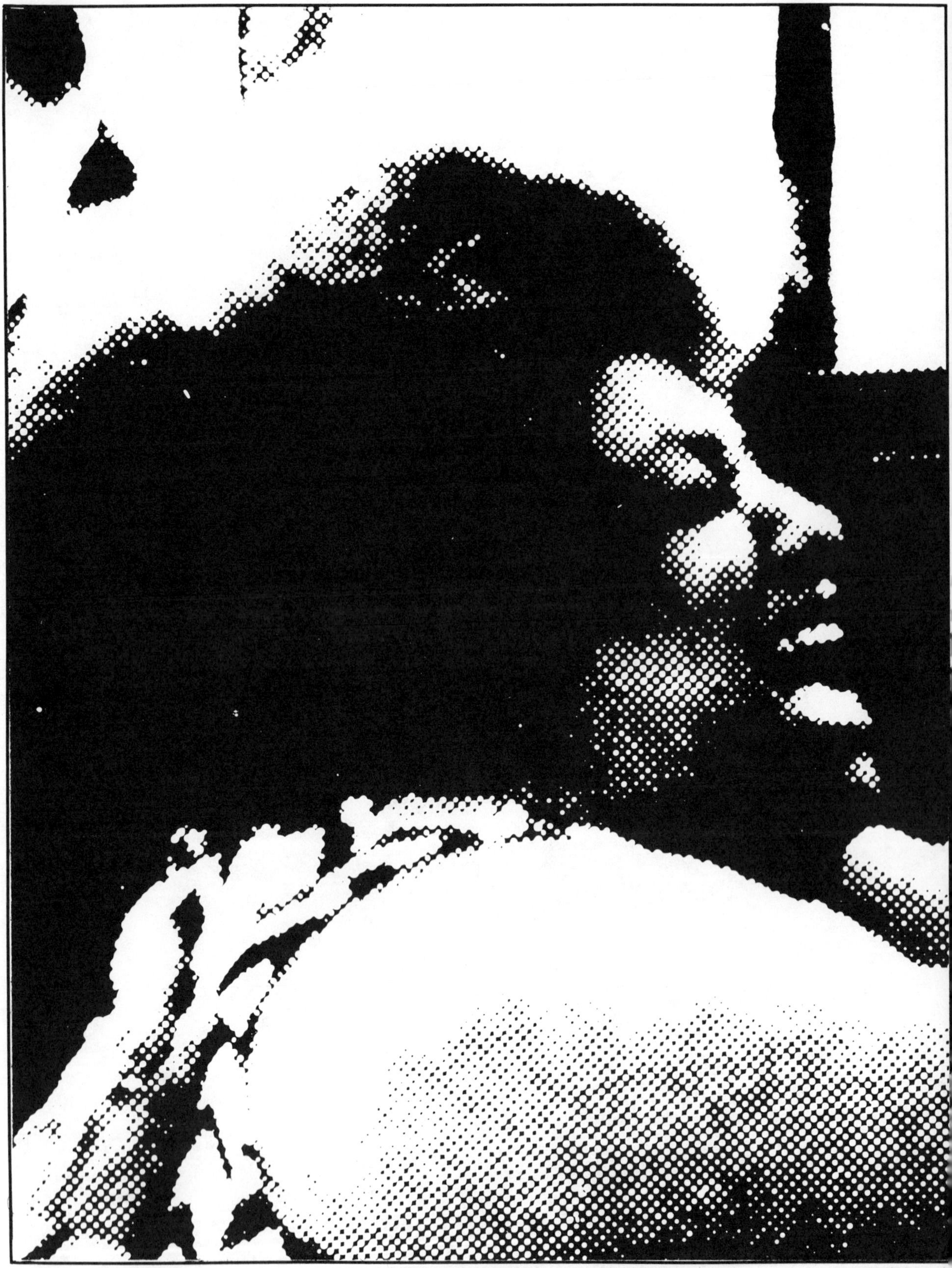

TWO

News, News, and More News

"If people can't read their news and assume it's correct, there's not much use of having it. You can't be a reporter without the ability to be accurate about everything you write. The power is great. The responsibility is great."

Bill Monroe, Reporter,
Corvallis Gazette-Times

"You go in there and you are 39,000 people. All those people are in there in your pencil and notepad."

Bill Monroe, Reporter,
Corvallis Gazette-Times

6

The Reporter Uncovered

Three Reporters
A Reporter's Routine
Characteristics of a Good Reporter
Why Become a Reporter

Three Reporters

"I spend five or six hours a day making lists, the other three worrying about not doing what's on them."

It is 7:15 A.M. on a Tuesday, and reporter Bill Monroe is already at his desk in the newsroom of the *Corvallis Gazette-Times* making a list.

"It's notes of things to do today," he tells a visitor, "like notes of what to tell Rod Deckert," the city editor and his boss in the hierarchy of the newspaper.

His list complete, Monroe looks at the clock hanging on the rear wall of the newsroom. It is 7:25 A.M., and he has to go to the first stop on his beat, the police and sheriff's offices. As a beat reporter, he has the responsibility to gather police news, as well as news of the court system and the city government. To carry out this task, he makes the rounds of key offices daily to find out if anything newsworthy has taken place.

It takes him about two minutes to drive to the nearby Law Enforcement Building, which houses both the Corvallis Police Department and the Benton County Sheriff's Office. He has covered this beat for several years. Since the building opened several months before, Monroe has done several stories critical of its operation. He is proudest of one that revealed that the new facility was open only on weekdays. If citizens needed to report crimes or do business in the building at night or over the weekend, they could not get in. Since his article appeared, the building has been open twenty-four hours every day.

For this and other stories, police and sheriff's personnel are not always happy to see him on his morning visits. "I burn them all the time," says Monroe. "It's a problem for a week or two, then it blows over. When the building opened, there were so many adverse stories, the sheriff put out an edict that he would fire my source if he found out who it was." He never did, but the source was not in that department anyway.

"It's taken me four years to build up trust. It takes a week or so for them to simmer down and the hard feelings to blow over. I can predict now when there will be a complaint. I used to wonder every day when I walked in here. But it doesn't worry me. If you worry about that, you might not do something you should do. You've got to cope with it when it comes."

He opens the door and calls a good morning to two uniformed clerks working at the reception desk as he heads for the police side of the building. At the sound of his voice, both women look up, but only one of them smiles and speaks in return. "She says I misquoted her several years ago," says Monroe of the silent woman. "Like an elephant, she never forgets."

The Corvallis police chief is ready for the reporter.

"Morning, chief."

The police chief nods, smiles, and pushes two stacks of reports toward Monroe. The two men begin to discuss local fishing conditions as Monroe starts to take notes on "Traffic Accident Reports" and "Police Incident Reports."

The incidents explained on the documents range from misdemeanors like the report of a vicious dog, criminal mischief, possession of illegal fireworks, and a dog bite to major misdemeanors and felonies like burglary, assault, disorderly conduct, and a bomb threat at the local offices of Pacific Northwest Bell.

"After four years you see a lot of these names times after time," says Monroe as he finishes going through the second stack of reports; he thanks the chief and walks to the sheriff's side of the building, a few steps away. Once there, he looks through a smaller stack of reports written on forms similar to those used by the police. Finding he has already learned much of the information from the police, Monroe leaves the building. He is back at the newspaper by 8:15 A.M.

He goes immediately to the city desk, where he tells the editor in charge about what he has picked up at the Law Enforcement Building. Soon Monroe is sitting at his desk, which is L-shaped. The main portion holds two wire baskets stacked one on top of the other (one containing contact sheets and negatives of photographs he has taken recently, the other notes from recent stories and other materials he wants to save), various personal pictures and mementoes, and a jar of stubby and dull pencils. He never uses the pencils because he prefers felt-tipped pens to take his notes in spiral notebooks narrow enough to fit into his pocket.

Across the rear of the desk sit copies of *The Solid Gold Copy Editor,* the Corvallis telephone book, a recent *Gazette-Times* readership survey, *The Dictionary of Usage and Style, Webster's Seventh New Collegiate Dictionary,* a city-county telephone directory, the Oregon State University staff directory, and the *Oregon Wildlife Code.*

To his left on the shorter part of the "L" is his video-display terminal. A stack of copy paper sits beyond it, although he grabs paper only for note-taking because he doesn't have a typewriter any more. In fact, there are only two typewriters in the whole newsroom; every reporter writes stories on one of the VDTs.

He calls across two desks to ask the city editor who will be covering the county commissioner's meeting. Informed that the summer intern will be going, he pauses briefly to tell the college student several things to watch for. Monroe takes off his coat and loosens his tie at 8:27 A.M. He begins to return calls from the previous week. In one of the calls he verifies the reservation

The Reporter's Day.

(Photos by James Folts.)

The reporter interviews the chief of police.

The Reporter Uncovered 101

Searching for background information to a story, the reporter scans official records.

The reporter talks with a source over the telephone.

The reporter argues with an editor who makes changes to his story on the VDT.

for a sack lunch he will eat at the noon meeting of the city council and also sets a time for an interview the next day with the city finance director about details of the new city budget.

"We already ran a three part series on the budget," he says, "but that was before the last election, and it was defeated. This time we'll run one or two stories emphasizing what they've cut."

He loads his camera, a Nikon, and again dials the phone.

"Hi. This is Bill Monroe."

Without further explanation, he begins to write down information. He has called the local office of the Oregon State Police to get highway accident reports. He depresses the buttons and dials the local hospital for patient reports.

"Was that *CA* or *CO*?" he asks, to verify the spelling of a name.

The city editor walks over and inquires about the status of land-use hearings Monroe will be writing about soon. The editor tells him to work up an outline later that week and start his research later in the month. Monroe agrees and makes a note on his calendar to turn in the outline a week from now.

He calls the hospital in Eugene, forty-five miles away, to ask about the condition of a man injured in a traffic accident on the southern edge of the county.

He hangs up and turns to face the empty screen of his VDT. He punches several buttons and soon his "file" appears on the flickering screen. It is the portion of the computer's memory that contains everything he writes every day. This morning it holds yesterday's stories, headed "Monroe—Cop Shop."

"I notice on Monday I don't type very well," he says as he begins to press the keys. "Thursday and Friday, I'm better. I never learned to type very well, so the *Gazette-Times* sent me to typing class a year or so ago. It has helped my typing."

He begins to write, "Corvallis Police are looking for the owner of a small dog that bit a girl in the face on a downtown Corvallis sidewalk Thursday. . . ."

He pauses to double-check the spelling of *Pekinese* in the dictionary.

Monroe spends the next forty minutes writing the short items he picked up at the Law Enforcement Building. Several times he stops to verify the spelling of names and addresses in the telephone book and, once, the exact name of the service station that had been robbed. He also instinctively uses the newspaper's style as he writes, making sure that abbreviations, capitalization, and other things are handled as required by the stylebook.

At 10:30 A.M. another editor asks him to find out the necessary facts to write a short copy block to go on a photo page about the Timber Carnival, an event held each Fourth of July in Albany, a town ten miles away.

Monroe has finished the police news at this time. The items will appear as five separate stories that day: "Youth Beaten by Robber of Gas Station," "Cops Seek Owner of Biting Dog," "Three Injured in Accidents," "Deputies Scratch Reported Theft," and "Manager's Note Was Invitation to Timely Thief."

He again consults the telephone book and dials the number of the Albany Chamber of Commerce information booth. The secretary who answers refers him to the main chamber's number.

"The big run-around starts," he says as he dials again. He restates his need for basic facts about results from the various contests held at the carnival as well as attendance figures. This time, he is given the number of the carnival's temporary office at the fairgrounds. He dials, but no one answers.

He then gets up from his desk and walks over to a machine at the side of the newsroom, where he tears off a print-out of his earlier stories. He scans them quickly, circling the item about the apartment manager for possible use in a box, to make it stand out because it contains some humor and irony (an apartment manager has been robbed because he was required to post a note indicating that he would be away for the weekend).

Monroe tries to reach the Timber Carnival people again, with no success. This quest is interrupted by a shouted question from a copy editor at the desk. He wants to know if the police are still looking for the dog that bit the little girl.

"Yes, they are, and I'd like to run the story as a public service," he answers.

While waiting for the telephone to be answered, he scans a routine release of information from the U.S. Army Corps of Engineers about proposed dredging in the Willamette River, which flows by Corvallis. It has rekindled his interest in a story he placed on his list earlier in the morning. He remembers a controversy two years before about the proposed site.

"I want to see if someone is trying to sneak one through," he says as he calls the city's utilities engineer. He spends ten minutes on the telephone and writes down, on the press release itself, the information he gets. Hanging up, he puts the material aside for future use. "The dredging won't begin until fall. I might do a story later."

At 11:15 A.M. he gets a call about a story he did the previous week. It was about a shopping center to be built in town on the site of a demolished cannery by a wealthy Portland industrialist. It is the industrialist himself on the line, and Monroe becomes a bit nervous. The man had been unavailable when Monroe called for a comment earlier, but now wants to make his position clear. He is upset because the story seemed to depict him as playing hard to get; he was certainly not hard to get for the people of Corvallis, he tells Monroe, who now relaxes.

Monroe listens and thanks the man for the call, relieved that it wasn't to complain about an error in his story. Monroe gets up from his desk to tell both the editor and the city editor about the call.

He returns and calls the Timber Carnival number again. At 11:38 A.M. someone finally answers. He asks a few questions to find out what he needs and hangs up. At 11:43 A.M. he begins to write a copy block for the photo page, a copy block the editors on the desk are now waiting for because the deadline is near.

"I don't like this," he mutters. "Now I've got five minutes to write this stupid thing."

He writes it in ten minutes on his VDT and leaves for the city-council lunch meeting the minute he has finished.

He walks the three blocks to the city hall. Once there, he goes directly to the council chambers. Council members and city officials are standing around, and they greet him by name as he makes his way to the far right side of a long table that separates the audience from the council's U-shaped table. He sits in front of a sign marked "Press."

His sack lunch is sitting on the table, and he opens it and begins to eat a sandwich while he scans the agenda for the meeting. He has picked up a packet earlier that includes both the agenda and the background information of the various matters to be covered in the meeting.

The council began these lunchtime meetings several months before, in an effort to shorten the night sessions, which sometimes lasted until as late as 2:00 A.M. Members now meet until about 2:00 P.M., then adjourn until 7:00 P.M. the same day hoping to get a head start on their business.

The meeting begins at 12:15 P.M. The acoustics of the old building are bad, and Monroe leans forward at times trying to hear council members, particularly those with their backs to him.

As the meeting progresses, he relaxes and sits half-turned toward the audience so he can see both the council and how the people react to it.

How does he stand it?

"I don't, always. I fell asleep once. I'm usually pretty interested. Things I don't think anyone will report on, like transit, I probably won't report. So I allow myself the luxury of not listening. I wonder sometimes about my being the one to translate what is done here, to the people affected by it."

Has he ever made mistakes?

"Several times last year I got something wrong. That causes me a great deal of consternation and a lot of trouble. I misspelled a name. I said people would vote on a $3-million bond issue to build a sewage-treatment plant when they were really voting on one-fourth of it, $750,000. It has since wound up at $2.1 million, so we weren't really that far off; but it whacked our credibility. A correction that follows a major story doesn't look good. Newspapers are supposed to be right. To the average man, a newspaper is a monument to the day."

The meeting is adjourned at 1:22 P.M. Monroe pauses on the way out, to ask the city engineer about the availability of the plans for the resurfacing of streets.

He returns to the office and makes another list of things he has to do. He reads the council agenda and background packet in preparation for tonight's meeting and makes a few more telephone calls. He leaves the newspaper for home at 4:15 P.M., a bit earlier than usual because he will be working that night. (The newspaper pays no overtime but grants its reporters time off on other days to compensate for work after hours.)

After dinner Monroe drives directly to city hall, arriving at 6:50 P.M. He has brought the packet and his notes from the earlier session and again takes his seat in front of the "Press" sign.

At 7:00 P.M. "citizen hours" begin, a time when anyone wanting to address the council may do so for a set period. Monroe sits back, again half-turned toward the audience, and listening as people walk one by one to a table in the middle of the aisle. Once there, they sit in front of a microphone and address the members of the council.

The meeting itself starts at 7:30 P.M., and Monroe begins to pay more attention and take more notes as the council members continue their agenda. At 9:10 P.M. the council chairman calls a recess, and Monroe walks out with the audience, trying to get more information on a pending vote from the council members standing in the hall. They are friendly but noncommittal.

He wants to start writing but feels he can't leave early. "I don't trust them," he says of the council members. "We've got the responsibility of doing the whole story."

The meeting resumes and continues until the council finishes its business, at 10:30 P.M., a bit earlier than usual. Monroe returns to the office and enters a locked side door marked "Employees Only," using a passkey. He works until after midnight rearranging lists, rearranging notes, and rewriting material that will appear on the outdoor page he edits each week.

"I've been geared up all week to suffer through this meeting," he says as he looks over his council notes. "I'll make a list of what they did, then lop off everything else. Once that's done, it takes little time to write."

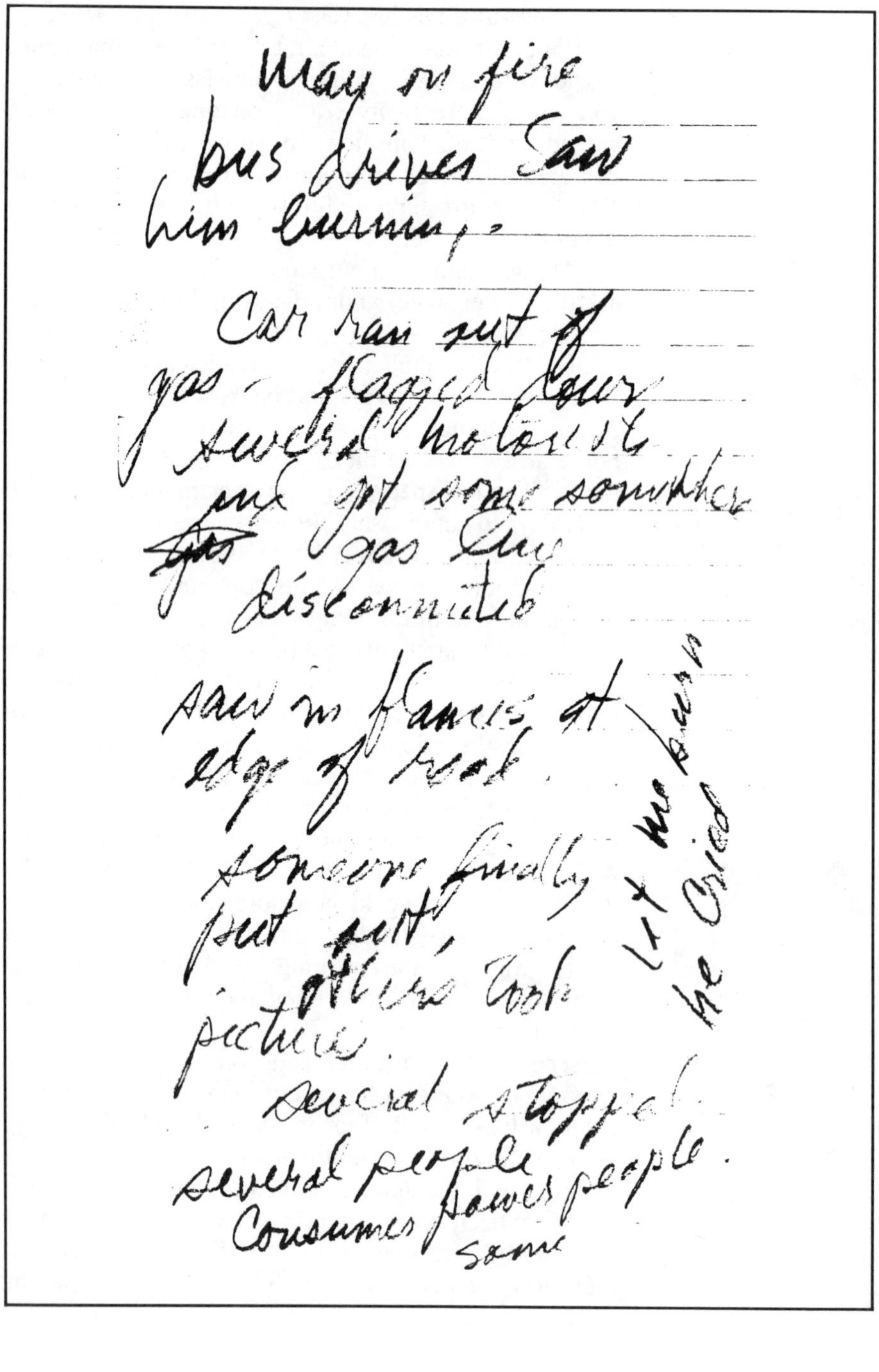

Figure 6.1 Examples of a reporter's notes.

```
                    Acting Mgr?
                      McA    No
    McN.

    Bradley              ?     1
    not decided yet

    Triska              1
    never any trouble  unsure where things.

    Schmidt —    no say


    Barker      ~~~~~~~~~     1


    Berg —                    1


    Tucker


    Patz.



         reluctant to talk
    privately about it.
         Acknowledge problem —
    no 2 jobs work out
```

From 8:00 A.M. to 11:00 A.M. the next morning, he will write three stories about the meeting: "City Puts Federal Money into Walnut Job," "Council Rejects Plan for Use of $190,000 Windfall," and "Council Sets Sights on Plan."

On what is to be reported, his judgment will prevail: "The desk relies on my judgment as to how many stories. They're depending on the reporters to tell them what happened."

But it is almost 12:30 A.M., and he will have to get in early to get over to the Law Enforcement Building and make it back in time to write the items he picks up there and the stories from the council meeting. For now, he decides he had better go home.

Seventeen hours after it began, Bill Monroe's day is over.

Several hours earlier, and sixteen-hundred miles away from Monroe and the *Corvallis Gazette-Times,* Mike Hall's day has begun somewhat in the same way.

The city-hall reporter for the *Topeka* (Kansas) *Capital-Journal* walks into city hall as though he owns it, the result of the easy camaraderie he has developed with the government staff members during his four years on this beat. A tall man, Hall lopes into the city clerk's office, breezing by her to hang up his raincoat in her closet. He exchanges gossip and banter with the clerk and her secretary before he is off into the maze of offices beyond.

"City hall is like a little town," he says. "It has its own grapevine." Hall replenishes the content of his own "vine" by these daily visits.

"On a typical day I get to city hall at nine or nine-thirty. I call the office and converse with the city editor. I check with the clerk's office first. I make my rounds and drop into each commissioner's office. It's pretty casual. I won't interrupt. I stick my head in the door, and if they're busy, I'll come back.

"The office sometimes gives me assignments and asks me to check something out. I don't have a story every day. I've gone three days without a major story. There are always little announcements. It's up to me to ask about things, keep track of issues."

On this day, Hall must cover a city commission's hearing on a community-development agency. Some months before, he wrote a story that exposed irregularities in the agency's use of funds and led to the dismissal of its director; the agency itself, which was set up to rehabilitate housing for poor people, is now being phased out. Feelings about the issue and against the commissioners and Hall are expressed by some of the people in the room as the hearing takes place.

Nevertheless, Hall sits unperturbed at a table marked "Press" in the front of the chamber, quietly taking notes for his story. "You've got to have the self-confidence not to be intimidated by anybody you are dealing with," Hall says later. "You've got to keep in mind who you represent. All those folks who read the newspaper—you are acting on their behalf. You are asking questions readers would ask if they had time to hang around city hall."

As soon as the meeting is over, Hall drives back to the newspaper office, where he writes his story to meet a noon deadline. It appears in that afternoon's edition under the headline "Probe of SCCAA Phaseout Costs Ordered."

For the rest of the day, he calls some of his sources at city hall for information on several stories he will write soon.

"Sometimes I enjoy the job so much, I marvel someone is paying me," he says as he looks around the newsroom. "I've had jobs I've dreaded to get up for. I never know what's going to happen here. You're dealing with the most interesting people because that's the kind of people other people want to read about."

Diane Brockett is already thinking of lunch when Bill Monroe begins his day, and has already met her first deadline when Mike Hall strides into Topeka City Hall. The "Metro" reporter covers District of Columbia affairs in Congress for the *Washington Star,* where she has worked for eight years.

She arrives at her desk near the rear of the *Star*'s long, dingy newsroom earlier than many other reporters on the staff. Almost immediately, she is on the telephone, probing her many sources for story leads.

"The key to covering a beat is getting to know key people and keeping up with what's going on," she says. "I religiously make checks of these people. I call every office on my beat to see what's going on."

One key group is the hundreds of public-relations people who work for members of Congress and congressional committees. Both houses have what she calls a "highly sophisticated PR machine" that prepares documentation like hearing schedules and makes members of Congress and senators available for interviews.

"You quickly learn where the good stories are, what kind of people will be good sources," she continues. "Once I find somebody who is a good source, I contact that person regularly. Usually, those higher up turn out to be sources of good stories. Typically, I hear in one office about what's going on in another office."

She gives the metropolitan editor a list of stories she is working on for the week. She is usually working on more than one, as well as the longer articles known as "projects" at the *Star*.

Now, for example, she has her eye on the ranking Republican on the House District Committee as a possible profile subject. He is spending so much time on district business, she hears, that his own reelection campaign is in some trouble. She wonders why.

She has also been told that a modest emergency clinic in the Capitol building has raised its number of doctors from one to six and has a large budget. What has caused the great increase? "I want to play with that," she says.

Although she shuns meetings unless she thinks there is a story there, she goes to them from time to time. "I feel good when I capture the atmosphere of a meeting," she says.

She is under no pressure to produce a story a day. She can go to an event—like a meeting—and decide that there is nothing newsworthy going on and return to the office without writing a story. "That's the biggest difference between big and small papers," she says. "There's no pressure to write a story unless there is a story."

Her days are more varied than those of most reporters because she can pick and choose the things she wants to write about. When Congress is not in session, she covers other subjects. She wrote two articles on the deplorable conditions at Forest Haven, the District of Columbia institution for the mentally retarded. With two other reporters, she had several months to do a series of articles on pornography.

"I enjoy the sense of dealing with events and people in a significant way," she says. "I find it very challenging. I do enjoy being involved in a removed way from what's going on; I don't enjoy being a chronicler nearly as much. My skills are not writing skills, although they've improved a lot. It's in reporting. My boss says I can get anybody to give me anything. Maybe it's the way I look. I don't look intelligent, but I am. I relate to people very easily. I'm careful. I'm very accurate. I blush easily. I could never lie."

A Reporter's Routine

Although the details of a reporter's work will vary from story to story, it is possible to construct a step-by-step account of how to cover a beat and how to report the stories found there. The account focuses on reporters' coverage of beats because that is where so much of their work takes place. Reporters on general assignment follow the same principles; they just cover a story from a different part of the city every day.

The beat

From the day a reporter is first assigned to a beat, he or she must find out all there is to know about that beat and the people on it. "You've got to stay on top of everything, so you'll know exactly what is going on," says reporter George Wisner. "This means constant daily contact with people—and you can't do it by phone. On my beat—schools—this means I talk to everyone from the janitors to the superintendent and also keep my ear to the ground."

Sources

After a reporter has learned the way around a beat, he or she works constantly at keeping up with what is going on. This means coverage of all the set events taking place on the beat: regular meetings, press conferences, the distribution of official information through reports and press releases. It also means the careful cultivation of sources, both official and unofficial, who provide tips about potential stories and can verify information before it is included in a story. Wisner continues: "Once you become familiar with what is going on, people will say things they might not otherwise say. But this requires constant contact with sources, like sitting down with them for coffee or going out for a beer and general, chatty conversation. You also have to let everybody know you can be contacted by anyone, any time day or night." Sometimes, the best sources on a beat are people who don't have powerful jobs. The good reporter learns fairly early that power and knowledge do not rest in high-sounding titles. No one knows more about the operation of an office, for example, than the secretary. Another key source is the disgruntled person who has just been fired or who did not get a raise.

When covering stories on a beat, reporters need to protect their sources. More than one story is at stake: Day-to-day coverage of a whole segment of a city depends upon good sources. If sources on the beat are alienated, they may well refuse to talk to reporters. "You cultivate sound, accurate sources," says Wisner, "and then you be fair and honest in dealing with them and make sure you quote them accurately. When uncovering scandal, you use anything you can get—but be very accurate with it, and fair."

Once these preparations have been made, reporters will find the coverage itself almost easy.

Coverage

The police beat. For those covering the police beat, access to official sources and information is the key element. Without them it is impossible to learn even the names and addresses of those involved in an accident or crime. The accuracy of this information needs to be verified in telephone books and city directories, however, because the police may not have verified the correct spelling of names and correct addresses in their initial, handwritten reports. Most lawsuits against newspapers result from careless police-beat reporting.

Unexpected events: accidents, robberies, fires. Confusion generally prevails at the time of an accident, bank robbery, or fire. Everyone is reliving his or her part in the event and talking about it at the same time. It is best for reporters to rely on police officials for details of what happened and the amount of damage. The information can be augmented later by conducting interviews with the people involved. It is a good idea, however, to compare details carefully. What do the sources say, and how does this relate to what the police say? Stories about fires, too, are best based upon official information supplemented by eyewitness accounts. If the fire is still burning, a reporter can observe the fire fighters and occupants of the building and give readers the "feel" of being there. The more people a reporter interviews the better, because first-person quotes are more colorful and interesting than dull reports. It is important to stay out of the way of the fire fighters, but hard to get important details from a point safely across the street. A balance between these extremes is best. If possible, two reporters should be sent to cover a big fire; one to detail the actual damage to the structure, the other to do an accompanying piece that deals with human-interest aspects of the story, such as the loss of a home, the narrow escapes, the acts of heroism.

The amount of the loss is important in fire stories but should be learned from fire officials and not the owner of the building, who might inflate the amount for insurance purposes. The same reliance on official sources is necessary if there is any question of arson. Reporters need to be careful in using that word unless officially told to do so; indeed, it should be left out of the first day's story about a fire unless it is certain that arson occurred.

Meetings of governmental organizations.   Most beats include at least one regular meeting a week—often, to the dismay of most reporters, taking place at night. Usually, an agenda and an information packet are made available before the meeting. This helps reporters write their stories, but it is also a good idea for them to keep their own files on the various organizations they cover regularly; the files should include such background information as their own stories on the subject, official information, clippings from other publications, unpublished interview material.

The important thing for reporters to remember in covering a meeting is to keep an accurate record of what decisions were made and who said what. "I keep my notes chronologically," says Bill Monroe. "Some things I don't keep notes on; I remember. Some of the background I know. It boils down to this: I go back and start looking at my notes; I make a separate list of what I think is reportable; I figure out what to do and refer to the notes and the council packet as I go along; I choose what to include in the story." Sometimes, numbering the story possibilities or the items covered in the meeting helps. Reporters can also take notes about the different subjects on separate pages or in separate notebooks.

Miscellaneous: spot news, stories involving people.   The "everything else" of news reporting needs to be emphasized. It is difficult to categorize all the kinds of stories that reporters encounter. This is especially true of a general-assignment reporter; on a beat the news is usually more predictable. In either case, it is important for reporters to gather as many details of a story as possible. They should also seek information from more than one person and get as many different perspectives on the story as possible; this approach enables reporters to compare the details of the story, source by source, and improves accuracy.

Preliminaries to writing the story

After the details of the news event are safely inside the pages of a reporter's notebook, a final step before writing is to make sure that the notes are understandable and complete. This may require no more than a glance back over one's notebook before leaving the news scene; if something is missed there, it may be necessary to call sources from the office for clarification.

Even after the primary sources have been interviewed, the story may not yet be completely covered. Reporters may still need to interview other, secondary sources in order to gather further information or to confirm that obtained in the earlier interviews. Sometimes reporters also have to conduct research on official documents or unofficial information, like letters and notes, for additional story material.

Characteristics of a Good Reporter

What makes a good reporter? Conclusions can be drawn from the typical days of the three reporters described earlier in this chapter, and supplemented by the opinions of these and other reporters.

Productivity and dedication

A willingness to work long hours is a factor that sets a dedicated reporter apart. Diane Brockett works such long hours that she seldom sees the movies she wants to see or reads the books she wants to read. Although Bill Monroe's seventeen-hour day is extraordinary even for him, it is not unusual for a reporter to work ten hours at a time, especially if there is a governmental meeting to be covered; in fact, it is the rare beat reporter who does not have to cover at least one night meeting a week related to his or her beat and, thus, wind up working long hours.

"You've got to have a willingness to produce: to sit down and make yourself put it out," says Monroe. "After doing something good, you can't sit back and coast. After that paper goes to bed and people read it, you've got to give them something new the next day." His colleague John Atkins thinks good reporters need to do a job "for the sake of doing it because it's important, not because it's well paid. You get compensated in ways money can't offer."

Good journalists, Atkins continues, should have a keen sense of the history of their profession, and of its mission. "You have to want to be part of the mystique stretching back to sensational journalism, to Hearst and all the rest of it. All reporters attempt to be defenders of the weak and powerless and to be conduits of information the public needs to survive and to have responsible government."

For another *Gazette-Times* reporter, George Wisner, dedication also involves being your own person. "Although the paper pays me," he says, "I work for myself. One of the freedoms of the job is that I have the freedom to do what ought to be done. There are flexible hours, but at the same time, I've got to be on call twenty-four hours a day and go anywhere on a moment's notice at 3:00 A.M. You can't get an unlisted number, which may mean you get crank calls."

Integrity, skepticism, commitment to truth

A commitment to truth must be made, regardless of how that truth offends sources. One of a reporter's prime duties is to gather the facts and report stories that make other people uncomfortable or angry. If reporters do not make someone mad at them at least once a month, they may not be doing their jobs.

Reporters' constant search for the truth can get them into trouble, of course, especially if they have to return to sources on their beats day after day; and they must be careful not to be unnecessarily abrasive. If a fact is reported accurately and a source gets angry, a reporter can take the criticism as a part of doing the job, and can hope that the relationship between reporter and source will survive the momentary rupture. In Monroe's case, his long coverage of the police beat has built up a mutual trust between himself and his sources that survives momentary arguments. Mike Hall has accomplished the same thing. Reporting that is arbitrary or careless, on the other hand, will deserve the criticism it draws, and may damage the credibility of the reporter, the newspaper, and journalism in general.

Accuracy

A commitment to reporting facts accurately, especially in stories of crime or other police-related matters is crucial. Precise details of the event and the correct spelling of names and exact addresses of the people involved are important to the credibility of the story. A mistake here can lead to a lawsuit and end a reporter's career. The extra time it takes to make calls of verification and to consult telephone books, city directories, and other sources of information pays off in improved stories. Monroe takes careful notes of the details in the police reports he uses as his primary source of information. He asks officials about anything he does not understand at the time; if he does not grasp its meaning now, he will not understand it later as he sits down before a blank VDT screen ready to write his story. Then he would waste valuable time calling to get information or, worse, risk inaccuracy by including it erroneously.

"If people can't read their news and assume it's correct, there's not much use of having it," says Bill Monroe. "You can't be a reporter without the ability to be accurate about everything you write. The power is great.

The responsibility is great." Adds his city editor, Rod Deckert: "You've got to be able to spell right or be able to reach for the dictionary instinctively and automatically as you would reach up and scratch your head if it itches. I don't understand why it's so hard to pick up and open a dictionary or look at a city directory for a name."

Gazette-Times reporter John Marshall found out about accuracy the hard way, during a summer internship at *Sports Illustrated*. "My main job was to check facts in other reporters' stories. Everything had to be checked with two independent sources. I made an error. I spelled the French racetrack Longchamp like the New York restaurant chain (Longchamps). The managing editor called me in and excoriated me for the error. A whole summer spent doing that checking convinced me of the importance of accuracy. I strongly believe I have never misquoted anybody. That's one of the most grievous errors a reporter can make."

"It was tough for me to ask people how to spell things like names," says Mike Hall. *"John Smith* sounds easy so you spell it the conventional way, and the story appears and he says to you, 'I forgot to tell you, I spell it *Jon Smythe.'* It's a matter of dropping your pride and asking questions. I think one of the hardest things to overcome was to force myself to ask dumb questions. There are questions I have a pretty good idea of what the answer is, but I need to ask them so sources can respond in their own words."

Persistence and patience

A persistence to keep after a story, no matter how difficult the quest becomes, is a good quality for a reporter to have. The best stories are often the ones most difficult to obtain information about. Few good stories come easily to reporters. The best reporters are those who step up their efforts when they encounter difficulty. Monroe kept after the elusive officials at the Timber Carnival long after a lesser reporter would have given up. He had been given the assignment and was determined to get the facts and write the story, no matter how unimportant the story might be to many of the newspaper's readers. "You got to be able to hit a dead end and find another avenue," he says.

Ability to plan ahead

Planning ahead and beginning future stories while on a current assignment is crucial. During a lull in his telephone calls on one story, Monroe made an inquiry about another one (river dredging) and made tentative plans to work on another (a series on land use). Diane Brockett is already planning stories she will do during the congressional recess when her regular beat will be in a lull. There are slow periods in any reporting process when a reporter must wait. A good reporter won't sit idly by while waiting for a telephone call to be returned but will use that time to begin planning and gathering material for future assignments.

Writing on deadline The skill to write quickly and accurately, even under the stinging whip of an approaching deadline, separates the good reporters from the bad ones. Nothing is so final as the hands of a clock as they move toward the daily deadline. Everything in the newspaper office has been calculated with that time in mind, for there is no flexibility where deadlines are concerned; delays that take the newspaper beyond that time are counterproductive and intolerable. A reporter who constantly misses deadlines will not remain a reporter for very long. Hall had less than an hour to write his story on the city commission. Monroe had no more than ten minutes to write the photo-page copy block. These stories and thousands of others every day have to be ready on time so that they can be edited and set into type. A long delay will bump the story to the next day, when the material in it may cease to be newsworthy.

Fondness for people A reporter who dislikes talking to people will not do well in journalism. "It's different for different kinds of stories," says John Marshall. "For a feature, you've got to be somebody who genuinely likes people and wants to submerge themselves below the surface so you make that person think you understand their problems, hopes, experiences." George Wisner, another *Gazette-Times* reporter, adds that "you have to have a desire to work with people, explore the human condition, and to like people in general."

Curiosity A good reporter, says Rod Deckert, should "be eternally curious about damn near everything, especially people and issues." Wisner puts it this way: "You should have the desire to know more than the people doing the job you're covering; you are practically half-sociologist, half-psychiatrist, all varieties of things."

Decisiveness, aggressiveness, courage "A reporter has to be able to make decisions quickly," says Tom Jenks. "Reporters decide right now whether to write down what someone says. You have to be confident. And you'd better be right more than wrong, or you'll be doing something else for a living. At the same time, a reporter has to be courteously aggressive and not be put off by hierarchy or office or people in power." Rod Deckert feels the same way: "Reporters have to be courageous, gutsy, even fearless, not in the physical sense but in the face of psychological and political pressures."

An interest in writing "You've got to have an interest in, and gain some feeling of satisfaction from, writing, not just reporting; that is, putting one word after the other, having it make sense and be clear." John Atkins undoubtedly speaks for many reporters. "Even better," he continues, "you hope it will be readable—not just make sense, but make even *you* want to read it."

This list of the qualities of a good reporter could continue, with as many variations as there are reporters. All the qualities noted above—and many more—make up the ideal person to represent a newspaper in the first encounter it will have with the people and events that make the news that will later fill its pages.

The reporter is a kind of front-line figure, whose importance cannot be underestimated. No one else is there at the meeting or the fire or the speech or the interview to ask the questions and write down the answers that will eventually be turned into sentences and paragraphs and become stories. In short, the reporter is the most important part of the newspaper. He or she is there to represent readers at the small and great events of the world. If the newspaper is small, that "world" will be small; the size of that world varies with the size of the newspaper and the resources the newspaper can allow for coverage.

There are flaws, of course, in any system that must place great reliance on the perceptions of individual reporters; no two people watching or reporting a news event perceive the event in the same way. In comparing accounts of the same news event in rival publications, readers often find differences in factual and descriptive details; if they themselves have attended the news event in question, they may even wonder, Is this the same event?

The problem is a basic one of recognition and perception. Is the glass half-full or half-empty? Did the speaker use the exact words written in the story, or did the reporter paraphrase them? Did smoke from the fire in the tall building obscure the scene for the reporter forced to wait below? Was the bank robber wearing a brown jacket or a green one?

Sometimes the problem begins with the people a reporter interviews for a story. Unintentionally they may misrepresent the facts to suit their perceptions. If the reporter and editor make a change or two as well, the printed story is the truth three times revised.

This element of subjectivity is what makes newspapers and the whole reporting process an imperfect one. No better system has been devised, however, and until it is, the reporter, observing the news and recording the facts as accurately and honestly as possible, will continue to play a fundamental role.

Of the characteristics of good reporting that could be added to those discussed earlier, two are particularly noteworthy. "Intelligence," says Mike Hall. "There are journalists who are not intelligent. Generally, they're not good journalists." The other characteristic is training and experience, both classroom training and internship. Things learned well then will get most reporters off to a good start.

Why Become a Reporter

It *is* exciting to cover events, take notes, turn the notes into a finished story, and see the story in print later in the day or the next under a by-line. That same excitement can turn to chagrin, however, if a reporter gets a call from an angry source because of an error of fact.

It *is* fun to be in on things and know first what no one else knows. That "insider" status, however, has its perils, too. Reporters have gone to jail in recent years to protect their sources and their notes from the prying eyes of zealous district attorneys and police officials. Sometimes, being in on the news can put a reporter out of business for a time.

Brockett, Monroe, and Hall sum up the pains and pleasures of their profession.

"You are dealing with something different all the time," says Brockett. "You are dealing with a wide range of people. I enjoy the digging, the ferreting out on my own. But the lack of steady hours is a bad aspect—not having a nine-to-five day. I'm beginning to find the long hours are really taking a toll, but that's the way to make it. I'm given my choice of assignments."

"Being in journalism makes other people respect you," says Monroe. "It's also an ego trip. No one can deny that is good. The salary is so low [Monroe started at $185 a week and now makes $250 a week], part of the payment is the 'trip.' It's rewarding to serve the community and try to help people, although you don't always succeed. Another satisfaction: You don't have to be in awe of anybody. You go in there and you are 39,000 people. All those people are in there in your pencil and notepad.

"Organic chemistry got me into journalism," he continues. "I got out of the navy and planned to become a fisheries biologist. I like to fish, so I came to Corvallis and Oregon State University and got into the major and found out I'd have to take organic chemistry, and I decided I'd better not do that. In high school I liked to write short stories and essays. Why not try journalism? I switched to journalism and kept a minor in fisheries and wildlife. I got a part-time job at the *G-T* doing the police beat. Editors changed, and the police beat became more important. I competed with others from the outside for a full-time job and was hired six months before I graduated."

Diane Brockett had never wanted to go into any other field than journalism. She graduated from Iowa State and worked for a suburban daily and a weekly, both near Washington, D.C., before coming to the *Star* as an intern in 1970. Since then she has covered a suburban county and the District of Columbia education beat and is now in the newsroom. "I got here by happenstance, not by plan," she says. "To be a good reporter you have to be careful, complete, intelligent, thoughtful, and enjoy working through issues and events with people. You have to have a certain amount of aggression. I'm very aggressive; I'm just not overwhelming."

After a brief time as an engineering major, Mike Hall of the Topeka *Capital-Journal* began a career in journalism as a photographer. He was an intern on a small newspaper in Kansas while he was still attending Kansas State University. After time in the army, he returned to the same newspaper, this time as a reporter.

"When I was hired by the *Capital-Journal* newspapers it was for bureau work where I did both reporting and photography," he says. Transferred to the main office, he was assigned to cover education and the state senate before going on to his present beat.

He says the variety keeps him in journalism. "Every day is interesting. That's one thing that got me in. As an engineering major, I went on field trips. I'd see guys in the labs surrounded by test tubes and computers. They'd only see two or three other people for days. I got the feeling I didn't want to do that. If you stay a reporter, it means getting out of the office into the real world, mingling with real people."

Summary

The reporter is the most important person on the newspaper, a kind of front-line figure, whose value cannot be underestimated. Good reporters must be willing to work long hours; must like to write; have integrity, skepticism, and a commitment to truth; must possess a strong desire to be accurate; must be persistent, dedicated, curious, and aggressive; must be able to plan ahead and write on deadline; must like people; and, of course, must have intelligence and training and experience.

Good reporters routinely become familiar with the beat and cultivate and deal fairly with the sources on the beat. They are well prepared and attentive in covering news events; in the case of unexpected news events, they rely foremost on official sources but also seek as wide a perspective as possible, from a variety of other sources, and take pains to verify all details of the story. It is these challenges, together with the excitement of covering the news, that make journalism an attractive profession to enter.

Suggested Exercises

1. Interview a reporter from a local newspaper. What are that reporter's daily tasks and responsibilities? What does he or she believe to be the most important qualities of a good reporter? Present the information to the class.

2. Select a newspaper story that best exemplifies five of the qualities of good reporting mentioned in this chapter. Report to the class.

3. Select a major news story of recent years and analyze how the reporters covering it seem to fit (or not to fit) the qualities of reporting noted in this chapter.

4. Interview key news sources in town (for example, city-government officials, school officials) and ask them what they believe to be the most important qualities of a good reporter. How well do the reporters they encounter fulfill these qualities? Report your findings to the class, comparing them with the findings from exercise 1.

5. Read *All the President's Men* and analyze the various reporting methods used by Bob Woodward and Carl Bernstein in covering the Watergate story.

6. Write a paper on the topic "Why I would make a good reporter."

7. Interview a reporter, an editor, and a news source frequently angry at the press on the topic "The qualities of a good reporter." Present your findings to the class.

"*On a daily basis, city editors have to be able to put themselves in the shoes of The Reader, capital T, capital R. They are the last checkpoint between the reporter and reader. If the reporter is confused, the city editor is the only one to straighten it out. How do you do that for 60,000 people in a county with varying levels of education and sophistication? It might sound farfetched, but you have to try to do it. I find myself saying to reporters, 'Look, you might understand this, but the reader won't if you say it this way. The reader needs more information.'*"

Rod Deckert, City Editor,
Corvallis Gazette-Times

7

The Editor Observed

Two Editors
Characteristics of a Good Editor
The Different Kinds of Editors

Two Editors

It has been Rod Deckert's job to step into the shoes of the reader for four years. As city editor of the *Corvallis Gazette-Times* he presides over a newsroom of eight reporters and is responsible for all the local stories that go into the newspaper. If the stories are inaccurate and unreadable, the editor and publisher blame him. If stories are not covered properly, or not covered at all, the readers blame him. Except for wire copy, sports stories, and the material on the editorial page, Rod Deckert has the final word on what the reporters will write and the readers will read.

From the moment he slides into the chair at his desk at eight in the morning until shortly after noon, when the last page has been closed and readied for the press, Deckert is under pressure.

"When I first took this job," he says, "I'd glance at the clock and say, 'It's moving.' I'd want to jump up and stop the hands some way. I used to come close to panicking, but not any more. As time goes on you realize it doesn't do any good. But when you first start out, it doesn't do any good to tell yourself that."

This day for Deckert begins with a telephone call at 8:06 A.M. The caller tells him all about a teeter-totter marathon some students at a grade school are organizing, "to set a city record." Deckert doesn't commit the newspaper to cover the event but as soon as he hangs up the telephone, he calls over one of the photographers. He sends him out to the playground, cautioning him not to make the photo look staged. At the same time, he asks another photographer to return to the scene of a hotel fire, covered by the newspaper the day before.

He next meets with one of the reporters to ask about the margin of defeat for the city budget in yesterday's election. The reporter hands him a list of stories gleaned from his police and court beat, together with a list of future personality profiles he plans to write. Deckert selects one, and the reporter goes back to his desk.

The city editor keeps a large ledger-calendar on the edge of his desk, the newspaper's daybook, which he uses to keep track of all meetings, town events, and anything else the newspaper must remember to cover. He updates the book each afternoon, when the pace is less hectic, and makes notes for it as he reads the newspaper at home at night.

At 8:55 A.M. Deckert joins the copy editor and the wire editor in the office of editor Tom Jenks. The four have gathered to decide what news will appear on page 1 of that day's newspaper. The copy editor is responsible for state and regional news but says the only thing he has to offer is a wire story about the return of the state energy chief from a trip to Washington. The wire editor suggests President Carter's news conference, abortion, the neutron bomb, and the economy as possibilities. Also, she says, Gordon Liddy has just been released from prison, and the Nazis and Black Muslims are fighting at San Quentin prison.

After the group has discussed the choices, Jenks makes the final selections. (See Figure 7.1.) That day's front page will feature the neutron bomb, the racial clashes at San Quentin, a decline in consumer spending, and a state report about the desire of welfare recipients to work. The lead local story will deal with the budget election, and another one will talk about the tightening of health standards for restaurants. The teeter-totter marathon will be the subject of the only photograph.

Returning to his desk at 9:30 A.M., Deckert listens for a few seconds to the police scanner; he has it turned on all the time, to keep up with reports on fires, accidents, and other breaking news stories. He summons the summer intern to his desk and asks him to attend the Benton County Board of Health meeting that noon.

As the two confer, the newspaper's librarian walks by to announce, "There are no records on teeter-totters," much to the amusement of everyone within earshot.

After brief chats with a photographer, another reporter, and the copy editor, Deckert turns his attention to the mail. Like newspapers all over the country, the *Gazette-Times* is flooded daily with press releases issued by organizations that have news to make known, perhaps positions to defend. As his counterparts elsewhere in the country may be doing at the same time, Deckert discards more of the releases in the large wastebasket next to his desk than he ever allows to appear in the newspaper.

He pauses at one headed, *NEW SCHOOL TO OPEN IN CORVALLIS*. After reading it, he writes across the top, "Is it a nonprofit organization? Does the school district or school board know about it and approve?" He puts the release on the desk of the school-beat reporter who is on vacation.

Resuming his seat, Deckert turns his chair to the left and faces the empty screen of his VDT. He presses the appropriate buttons and calls a story onto the monitor. It was written by the business/agriculture reporter the day before and deals with how the cattle owners in the county are reacting to the long drought in the region. Deckert had assigned the story after reading a similar one on the Associated Press wire.

At this point the photographer returns from the hotel to report that because the damage is less than $1,000, he hasn't taken a picture. The reporter who went with him will write a story, however.

"I counted on that picture, but I've got a backup photo," Deckert tells a visitor. He will try to use the teeter-totter picture, although the other photographer has not yet returned with it. He assigns a reporter to do a long caption to accompany that photo, if it indeed develops into a usable photo.

At 10:50 A.M. Deckert brings a story about personnel changes in county government onto the screen. He looks at it, making minor changes as the lines roll by. As he edits, he is also making sure that the reporter has followed the newspaper's stylebook.

Figure 7.1. Front page of the Corvallis Gazette-Times. *(Courtesy of the Corvallis Gazette-Times.)*

He calls the reporter over. "Don't you think Van Eck should be at the top, because he's probably of more significance?" he asks. The reporter agrees.

Deckert adds a line to the lead and calls the official "controversial."

"Oh my God, he's become controversial," he says to himself. He stops to look up the proper spelling of *record keeping* in the dictionary on his desk. (The reporter had added a hyphen, but it is two words.)

He finishes that story and goes on to one about the previous night's meeting of the planning commission. As he works at the VDT, various people walk by to tell him what they are doing ("Going to lunch") or give him things ("Here's that note"), without his necessarily hearing or assenting.

At 11:40 A.M. he glances at the clock. For the first time all morning, he has become a bit harried.

He edits the caption for the teeter-totter picture; not finding the word *endurers* in his dictionary, he changes it to *enduring*. He also notices that the reporter has spelled a name two different ways (*Marc* and *Mark*). He finds several other names inconsistently spelled. But neither the reporter nor photographer is then in the building.

"I won't use this picture unless I can get the correct spelling," he announces to those sitting around him. "I'd yank the photo before I'd run it. We never knowingly gamble that a particular piece of information is correct, particularly a name spelled correctly. When in doubt I take it out. I put myself in the shoes of the person whose name is misspelled. If once a week the paper misspelled my name, I'd put up with that one time, then I'd be furious. There ought not to be an excuse for that. It gets repetitive, redundant, and tiresome to ask people how to spell their names, but you've got to do it. When you strip it all away, there's no good alibi for not asking."

After another reporter has checked for the proper spelling of the names, the photographer returns with the correct answer and a usable picture. Two of Deckert's problems have been solved.

He edits a few more stories on his machine and sends them to be set into type. He then walks to the production department at the rear of the building and checks page one in paste-up before going to lunch at 1:20 P.M.

He will spend the afternoon making assignments, reading his mail, editing stories, and getting ready for tomorrow, when he will repeat the daily process.

"It's the hardest job I've ever had," Deckert says. "It's the best job I've ever had. There's a lot of excitement some days. It's a privileged position news people are in. They can make a difference. They can count. I get a lot of satisfaction in knowing that. Most good news people are comfortable with the privilege and the responsibility and the power. I know reporters don't think in those terms. I think that element is defined in subtle and not so subtle ways. We have a lot of clout. Anybody who is uncomfortable with this is going to have some trouble."

The responsibilities are still greater and the pace faster in Dennis Stern's job; the metropolitan editor of the *Washington Star* has more to worry about than the swiftly moving hands of the clock.

For one thing, the readership served by the newspaper is large and complex, 3.5 million people in six political jurisdictions. Furthermore the *Star* is a PM newspaper with a morning rival, the *Washington Post*. Historically, news breaks to better advantage for morning newspapers than for evening ones. The staff of a morning paper has the previous afternoon and evening in which to gather news; their counterparts in the afternoon have only the morning.

From the moment Stern enters the newsroom, he and the thirty-three reporters he supervises are in intense competition with the editors and reporters of the *Washington Post*. What the staff of the *Star* cannot do is run the same story the *Post* ran and write it in the same way. "There is tremendous competition," says Stern. "If the *Post* beats us, we can do a second-day lead. If there is nothing newsworthy there, we'll do a small item. Sometimes we gamble that the *Post* will do a story, and they don't. Or we assign a better writer and hope the story will be better."

Stern continues by referring to the longer articles the paper runs, which are geared less to what happened than to why it happened. "As a PM paper, we have to be oriented toward projects. This is because we're scooped so much by the *Post* and TV. If a traffic accident happens at 1:10 P.M. [with the *Star*'s last deadline at 1:15 P.M.], the story will be twenty hours old before we can run anything about it. We don't send out a reporter, but we might send out a photographer and get information over the phone. If the same thing happened at 9:00 A.M., it could make two editions."

Stern has already read the *Post* carefully before he arrives at the office. He refuses to compete with the *Post* on every story, however. For example, he says he is tired of running big stories on the various protest groups who descend regularly on Washington: "I am bored with the subject. We have groups here all the time." In such cases he is gatekeeping, determining which stories will and will not reach his readers.

His day begins at 9:00 A.M., when he arrives at the shabby third-floor newsroom of the *Star*. His desk sits in the middle of the long room, next to one occupied by his deputy and across from one for a copy editor. Each of the three has VDT upon which to call reporters' stories for editing.

"I know what I want," he says, and he and his deputy immediately begin to assign the work that will appear in the "Metro," the second section of the newspaper, covering the metropolitan area. Several times a week, local stories are important enough to be on page 1, but that page is usually reserved for the work of the national desk, a group of reporters and editors who regularly cover the White House, Pentagon, energy, economics, justice, labor, and Congress. Occasionally, because *local* in Washington may mean the federal government, the national desk and metro desks have jurisdictional disputes; at other times, Stern says, a story may even fall "between the cracks" and not be covered at all. But editors on the two desks usually keep one another informed, so that such duplications or oversights do not occur. The *Star* has three other sections: sports, finance, and portfolio, the latter featuring subjects like food, home, fashion, entertainment, and the popular gossip column "Ear."

The "Metro" section's reporters work both in the newsroom and from the pressrooms of the buildings of the government agencies they cover. Those working outside telephone their stories to "dictationists," who take them down on VDTs for later editing.

In determining the daily assignments, Stern and his deputy refer to a "futures" file, handled by the deputy, which contains a folder for each day of the current month and one for each month of the year. In these folders they place memos, clippings, and other reminders of events that need to be covered on a fixed day. Whichever man arrives first looks into this file to make sure everything has been assigned for coverage.

Stern and his deputy keep up with what is going on in the city in a variety of ways. The newspaper subscribes to both Associated Press and United Press International but uses only about 5 percent of their copy. "We use them like a tip service," Stern says. (In contrast, smaller newspapers use a much higher percentage of wire copy because it is cheaper than hiring reporters to write local stories.) All the press releases sent to the newspaper are sorted by employees elsewhere in the newsroom and sent to Stern, who scans them for possible ideas for stories. Other employees cut clippings out of both the *Star* and the *Post,* and Stern puts the clippings in the file, as reminders of events to be covered in the future. People also call in to the newspaper office with tips of possible stories.

One way the newspaper keeps track of police news is by paying several private citizens to call in to report possible stories; Stern says that these "police-radio nuts" call in the information about fires and major traffic accidents. The *Star* also has its own police radio for similar monitoring. Its main resource is the regular police reporters, who routinely call sixty different police agencies in the area every two hours to ask what is going on; these agencies range from state police barracks to fire boards.

For much of the day he keeps track of what each of his reporters is doing, as part of his supervision of the paper's progress toward its four daily deadlines: 8 A.M. for the first edition (if he is working the early shift), 9:45 A.M. for the second, 11:45 A.M. for the third, and 1:15 P.M. for the fourth.

After the deadlines have been met and he has eaten lunch, Stern edits the longer articles, or projects, which appear seven days a week as a hedge against the *Star*'s being scooped by its rival. The better reporters regularly give him lists of projects they want to work on when they aren't covering their beats. "Not all reporters are project-oriented," he says. "Some reporters like to observe an event and write about it."

During what remains of the day, Stern usually answers mail and tends to the needs of his large band of reporters. "You're an amateur shrink, a social worker, a marriage counselor," he says. He also recognizes the need for tact and understanding in his day-to-day relations with his reporters. "You're dealing with thirty-three different people who you've got to treat as individuals. You've got to recognize that people like different stories. They fight if pushed. The best thing is to keep them busy. . . .

"You've got to build up trust, give them feedback. You've got to tell them you've read their story and why it is good or bad. Most reporters want to know the desk is happy. If the story is good, you should tell them right away. If the story is poor or mediocre, don't say that. Always try to give a reason. Don't just say, 'The story didn't do anything for me.' If it's a big deal, when somebody really screws up, call the reporter into the office and talk about what went wrong."

Characteristics of a Good Editor

A sense of news, assertiveness, objectivity

What makes a good editor? Conclusions can be drawn from the typical days just described, and supplemented by the opinions of several editors.

"You have to have a good sense of news, good news judgment, which is acquired in part by experience, academic training, and professional training," says Tom Jenks, *Gazette-Times* editor. But an editor's sense of news must be supported by assertiveness and objectivity: "News judgment comes first of all in the ability and authority to exercise that judgment without any kind of pressure or interference from others on the newspaper."

Rod Deckert, Jenks's city editor, continues: "I have no idea what people at corporate headquarters think about anything. I don't feel much pressure from government. Often, it's pressure from interest groups. It is important that a city editor at a daily not get caught up with political parties, clubs, and organizations . . . [or] with any special interest group. Beyond joining a church, you shouldn't join anything if you're the one relied on to make sure stories are not biased or slanted. That way, when you edit, you can make sure the decisions you make are visible and active."

Willingness to work constantly under pressure

From beginning to end, an editor spends the day under the control of a series of deadlines. Whereas a reporter has one deadline to meet daily, an editor has eight or ten or twenty or thirty—one for every reporter under his or her direction. In Stern's case, this problem is compounded by four editions. Until an editor has edited the stories for the day's newspaper, those stories aren't ready to be set into type. All this takes time, and all the while, the hands of the clock keep moving.

Ability to edit stories and manage people

"Editors have to have an excellent command of the language," says Dennis Stern, "and be good at spelling and grammar and know there is nothing wrong with consulting a dictionary. A lot of people do not have that kind of command. If the desk can't spell after reporters can't spell, misspelled words will get into the paper. You've got to appreciate the written word and encourage good writing; you need to decide, 'Yes this does the job,' or, 'I don't think this story should be written that way.' You encourage your staff to take a different approach—for the sanity of reporter and reader. You look at the story and try to preserve it. If it doesn't work, you go back to the reporter and try to get him or her to do a new approach."

Rod Deckert emphasizes the ability to bring clarity to a reporter's writing. "Some days, a reporter who has been writing clearly and succinctly will turn in a story that misses the point or leaves out basic information or doesn't make much sense. For example, he'll use the phrase 'septic approval.' The city engineer knows what that means, but I don't. So I put the story aside today and rewrite it or have the reporter rewrite it, but it doesn't get in until tomorrow. What I try to look for are things that make sense and are clear. Is someone other than the planner, the architect, the police sergeant, and the city manager going to understand this? It's a constant battle. We start using words our sources use, and jails become 'facilities,' permits for septic tanks become 'septic approvals,' and police cars become 'units.' If words don't mean something, if they don't make basic sense, it's an automatic turn-off for the reader, and the reader doesn't bother. If no one reads your story, it means all of us who put in time on the story are grossly overpaid."

But there is more to good editing than simply good writing. "At least half the job is managerial," says Tom Jenks. "You have to be able to be objective with all of your staffers in doing job evaluations and pay determinations, not letting personal fondness influence you. You have to know about motivating people, especially news people who aren't necessarily motivated by the things other people are."

The management of people regularly involves knowing the strengths and weaknesses of the reporters under one's direction. In Deckert's words: "Some reporters are better at reporting, researching, digging up something; some are better writers. A few newshounds report, dig, and then sit down at a typewriter and put words down in such a way that makes you want to read on and on and on. . . . A city editor has to be sensitive to the talents, interests, and skills of each reporter, so he matches up reporters with the right story."

Editors must also edit reporters' stories without destroying the style of the reporter. "If you're any good at doing your job of editing," says Deckert, "you'll have trouble with reporters. You have to know a lot about writing and reporting. If reporters don't have a lot of confidence in you, you're dead in the water. I've said to reporters, 'You write it, I'll edit it.' That doesn't mean a reporter will not camp in front of my desk so as to wear a hole in the carpet and say, 'What are you doing to my story?' "

Deckert is very much aware of his reporters' sensitivity to editorial changes: "Too many reporters assume all the stories they write are going to be read; some think what they write is etched in stone. Editors shouldn't kid themselves. No good reporter will shrug his shoulders when you've edited a story heavily and say, 'So what? It's just another story.' The good ones always worry about what you're doing and don't like to have questions asked about their reporting."

Stern, too, is concerned for his reporters' self-esteem and does a good bit of what he calls "ego massaging." "They're worried about what it all means. Their story is just not another story to them. One of the things that is certainly true of daily journalism is the ego boost everyone gets from seeing their name in the paper. There are people on the staff who don't feel good if they don't have a story in today's paper. That's why some people can't go to a magazine; they wouldn't get the instant gratification later in the day, or the next morning, there in front of them. People are very proud of their work. When you make a dramatic change without consulting them, people who have come up with a twist of phrase they are wedded to are really stunned."

Good sense of layout and design

"The layout of page 1 is dictated by the photos," says Deckert. "I'm not afraid to run solid local photos big. I want the reader to stop and consider the front page before going to to Ann Landers or sports. After that photo has been selected, we can plan the page. If you get into layout, you need a flare for graphics. To write heads you have to be fast and accurate."

It is usually an editor who decides what goes on what page and whether it will be one column wide or four columns wide. Those decisions determine readability in many cases and need to be made with care and attention, as is merited by the time and effort that went into the reporting, writing, and editing.

Training and experience

No editor can properly gain the abilities already mentioned without time on the job. With time will come the background and experience needed to excel in a demanding position. Only with experience does an editor really know news. Only with experience does an editor become a good idea-person who can spark the interests of reporters, who are sometimes buried in the confines of their narrow beats. Only with experience can an editor deal with reporters, handle copy, write headlines, and lay out the pages of the day's editions.

How is this background and experience acquired?

"An editor should have gone through being a reporter," says Dick King, assistant managing editor of the *Topeka Capital-Journal* newspapers. King has never wanted to be anything else: "I was five or six when I told my mom and dad I wanted to be a newspaperman. I don't know why; I never changed." King came to the *Capital-Journal* newspapers years ago, after working on two smaller dailies. In his time there, he has been a police reporter, general-assignment reporter, state-desk editor, Sunday-supplement editor, and city editor, a post he occupied for nine years.

Dennis Stern had a similar long-standing interest. "I've known I wanted to go into journalism since I was twelve years old," he says, "preferably on daily newspapers. I was editor of the newspaper at Haverford College, but I majored in history. I was an intern on the Milwaukee *Journal* the summer between my junior and senior years. I took a summer job the next year on the Atlantic City *Press*.

"I went to law school at New York University because I wanted to have a specialty. After receiving my law degree, I went to work for the AP. I passed the bar, and the best offer I got was from the Miami *News* as assistant news editor. They trained me to be an editor, and I skipped a few hurdles. After twenty months there I went back to the AP, and after five months the *Star* called, and I was hired to lay out the "Metro" section.

"After thirteen months there was a minor coup, and I was named assistant managing editor, and then metropolitan editor in December, 1975.

"I find editing to be that much more challenging. The responsibility of a whole staff rather than a beat is that much more appealing. It all goes back to my eighth-grade newspaper. Journalism is a thing I tried and liked. Nothing has ever discouraged me."

Tom Jenks of the *Gazette-Times* says that he didn't "have the right reasons for going into journalism." After two years of study at a teachers' college, followed by service in the army, he enrolled at the University of Wisconsin because he felt that a university degree would carry weight. A counselor there suggested journalism, and he liked it immediately. "I thought, 'Man, this is duck soup.' I graduated at a time when there were five jobs for every graduate, nothing like today. I joined a medium-sized daily as a reporter and thought it was great. I saw the best way to get ahead was to get on the desk.

"My first ambition was to do well and advance in the daily-newspaper editorial department. After more and more exposure and finding fault with editors, I decided to become an editor myself. I told myself, 'If you're so damned good, do it yourself, so you won't complain.' "

He started working toward that end, and now, ten years later, he has reached his present position.

His city editor, Rod Deckert, entered journalism by a more roundabout route.

His degree from the University of Northern Colorado is in liberal arts, although he did cover sports for the college newspaper. "I tried a variety of majors in college, and it took me the longest time to decide to get involved in the peace movement," he says. "I got involved in social causes, teach-ins, and debates. When I got out, I decided if I couldn't save the world, I could at least alter it. On and off, I had had the urge to write. I knew in my mind I was headed for that."

He became a county social worker and joined the war on poverty by serving at an Indian reservation in Minnesota. He became a reporter at the Fargo (North Dakota) *Forum* before joining the *Gazette-Times* as a reporter. After two and a half years as a reporter, he became city editor.

The careers of King, Stern, Jenks, and Deckert show the diverse backgrounds of the editors of the three newspapers of this survey. On the experience that contributes to the making of a good editor, Jenks offers the following remarks: "You need to have a variety of jobs. You can't be successful unless you're experienced. Copydesk work is important. You have to know and understand how a desk works so you can make a judgment on how well people are doing their jobs. No editor can get all the necessary experience, or he'd be seventy-five years old. Before getting on-the-job experience you need solid academic training. I'm inclined to favor journalism schools. There are some things a good journalism school should be teaching you: ethics, news judgment, libel, and fairness. These aren't so easily picked up on the job. Small dailies don't have time to help on things like putting leads up high and writing short sentences."

The Different Kinds of Editors

Editors are the next step up in the newspaper hierarchy from reporters. Their duties and responsibilities and power vary with the size of the newspaper. Their titles vary, too: Deckert is a city editor; Stern, who performs the same job but has the wider responsibilities of big-city coverage, is a metropolitan editor.

What are the different kinds of editors?

The *editor* or *editor-in-chief* or *executive editor* is in charge of the entire news department of most newspapers. Although these editors set the policy of coverage, they are seldom involved in the day-to-day running of things. They hire and fire staff members and establish the budget for the news side of the newspaper.

The *managing editor,* as the title indicates, manages the newspaper. If the newspaper is a large one, a number of other editors report to the managing editor. On many smaller newspapers there is no managing editor, and day-to-day management is the responsibility of the city editor, in addition to his or her other responsibilities.

The *city editor,* called a *metropolitan editor* on big-city dailies, is in charge of the beat and general-assignment reporters and assigns the stories they are to cover. These reporters turn in their stories to the city editor for criticism, comment, and changes. After a "first read," the city editor may return the story to a reporter for rewriting. Otherwise the city editor may send it to the copy editor, either directly or (if the newspaper has them) via a VDT and computer system.

As the title implies, a *copy editor* edits copy to improve the writing, to see that style is observed, and to correct spelling errors. This editor also writes headlines. On larger newspapers a copy editor presides over a *copydesk,* which was once a half-moon-shaped piece of furniture, in which the copy editor or copy chief sat in the "slot" and doled out copy to copyreaders at the "rim." The copydesk is now usually several desks pushed together, but the copy editor still performs a similar activity there. On newspapers with VDTs and computer systems, copy editors may be seated anywhere in the newsroom, and the stories are electronically routed to them.

Most newspapers employ a *sports editor* to cover and write about sports; a *women's editor* to discuss such topics as living, fashion, family, children, society, and news of local organizations; and a *business editor* to handle news of business and commerce in the area.

The employment of specialty editors is sometimes determined by the newspaper's locality and its readers' special interests. An *agricultural editor* would be out of place on most big-city dailies, as would an *urban-affairs editor* on a small daily in a rural area. A *foreign editor* is necessary if the newspaper maintains its own corps of correspondents abroad, but not if it uses only wire-service stories.

Beyond this the number and titles of the editors vary, depending on the financial resources of the newspaper and the policy of its management in allotting them. The newspaper may have specialty editors (and reporters) for everything from food and religion to medicine and energy, but the larger, big-city newspapers will have a greater number and variety of them than do their smaller, regional counterparts.

Summary

Editors are crucial to the success of any newspaper. They are on the next level up in the newspaper structure from reporters. Although there are many kinds of editors, the city editor, often called the metropolitan editor on large dailies, is the most important to reporters in the newsroom and to the readers of the newspaper. City editors edit reporters' stories and are responsible for all local stories that go into the newspaper. Editors must be willing to work long hours, able to manage people and edit stories, have a good sense of layout and design, and possess the proper training and experience. Editors deal with many specialty areas in addition to city news. Their number and subject area depends on the financial resources of the newspaper and the policy of its management in allotting them.

Suggested Exercises

1. Interview an editor at the local newspaper, asking him or her to provide an example of how and why a story was edited. Report your findings to the class.

2. Interview various editors on the local newspaper and ask them to describe what they do in their jobs, to trace a story through its progress around the newsroom, and to reveal what they did to put that story into print. Report your findings to the class.

3. Research the various editing jobs on a newspaper and present reports on what each one involves.

4. Research some great editors of the past and try to determine why they were great. Include in your research details of some of the stories they edited.

"*In a news story, say what you've got to say as quickly as possible—the five Ws and H—and get the hell off the stage. The newspaper is a medium competing with radio, TV, and magazines. The reader is deluged. The reader has got to figure out what to accept. You've got to figure out what will attract readers for the most period of time.*"

George Wisner, Reporter,
Corvallis Gazette-Times

8

Writing News Stories and Leads

Inverted-Pyramid Style
Leads
How to Approach a News Story
How Reporters Write News Stories
Attribution
Transitional Sentences
Editorializing

Ask ten reporters, How do reporters write news stories? and the result might be ten different answers to the same question.

"With a great deal of blood," says Bill Monroe, *Gazette-Times* reporter. "The writing takes little time. I pretty much pyramid things; that is, I aim for the most important thing first and miss it more than 20 percent of the time. The only time I don't use this approach is in a feature for a short, humorous item where I'm trying for another effect.

"There are certain types of police stories where, in the interests of time, I write the same way all the time. A blank-year-old man, identification by name and address, was injured seriously (or not) in a car accident, when and where. I can't remember stopping to ask myself if I'd answered the five Ws [*who, what, when, where,* and *why*]. It comes automatically now that I have experience. I can do it fairly easily. No matter how long it takes, no matter how late, you've got to double-check certain things before you go on, like names and addresses. Every time you hurry, you take a chance with a weapon: one of the words you are using. If someone is misquoted, it really affects that person. It is a wrong that happens once. Essentially, you take your time with things."

John Marshall, another *Gazette-Times* reporter, thinks "feature writing needs to be done more carefully. But with news," he says, "I look at my notes and have at it after thinking of a lead in the shower. With twenty to thirty pages of notes, I'll underline things, write down things, pick and choose, then cross out after I've used material. I've never started a story without thinking of a lead. Quite often I'll fiddle with the lead. It's a lot easier with these machines [VDTs] than with paper and pencil; they are a lot easier to type on and a lot faster."

"A hard-news story starts with the five Ws," says Mike Hall of the Topeka *Capital-Journal,* "the most important action taken. We might have had other stories on other issues. The new thing is the action taken and you refresh people's memories on the background."

When reporters learn how to write news stories, they have earned the right to be called reporters. Because its raw material, news, is the essence of journalism, the news story is the most important thing a reporter does. At its best, a news story is simple and straightforward; at its worst, it gives the facts in a way that confuses readers and obscures important details.

A typical news story has two parts: a lead (or first) paragraph and a body (the remainder of the story). These parts are essential, regardless of story length or approach.

Inverted-Pyramid Style

When Bill Monroe talks about "pyramiding things" earlier in this chapter, he is talking about the most common kind of news story construction, the inverted pyramid. Reporters in newsrooms all around the United States take this approach every day.

The *inverted-pyramid* style arranges facts in the descending order of their importance. The most important facts are first, the least important last. This form opens with a summary lead, which summarizes the most important facts.

The inverted pyramid has been a journalistic form since the Civil War, when correspondents filed their stories from the field over the newly developed telegraph. They soon discovered that they needed to write concisely to save telegraph toll charges. They also feared that their complete dispatches might not reach their destinations because of mechanical failure or the enemy's cutting the lines. So, reporters learned to change the structure of the stories they were submitting.

The first war dispatches had been written in a dramatic, opinionated, first-person style that made the reader feel a part of the action but might also leave them wondering, until the end of the story, what had actually happened.

For example, Henry Villard's account of the Battle of Bull Run in the *New York Herald* of July 20, 1861:

> Centerville, Six and a Half Miles from Manassas Junction, Thursday, July 18, 5 p.m.—I have just returned from the thickets of an action of considerable moment, between a portion of the rebel forces and the Fourth Brigade of General Tyler's division, composed of the Second and Third Michigan, the First Massachusetts, and the Twelfth New York Volunteer regiments, under the command of Colonel Richardson; and as the aide of General McDowell, who will carry the official report of the affair to General Scott, and who offers the only means of communication with Washington this evening, is about starting, I have only time to send you the following brief particular of today's operation. [Louis L. Snyder and Richard B. Morris, eds., *A Treasury of Great Reporting* (New York: Simon & Schuster, 1949), p. 134]

Villard then went on to give details of the battle, almost shot-by-shot. His next dispatch followed a similar style and contained much personal opinion:

> Headquarters of The Grand Army, Centerville, July 19, 8 a.m.—Much of the haste and confusion of the retreat was due to the inefficiency and cowardice of some of the officers. I can personally testify to the more than ordinary coolness and gallantry shown by Colonel Richardson during the action. A shower of rifle balls was constantly aimed at him, but they did not for a moment deter him from doing his whole duty. General Tyler also showed great courage on the occasion. He was exposed to the enemy's fire for nearly four hours.
>
> The representatives of the press stood their ground as well as any, in spite of the shot, shell, and rifle balls that kept whizzing past them for hours. [Snyder and Morris, p. 135]

By 1865, however, the new form had been accepted by reporters for writing many news stories. The following account of Abraham Lincoln's assassination appeared in the *New York Tribune* of April 15, 1865. The writer is Lawrence A. Gobright, an Associated Press correspondent.

> Washington, Friday, April 14, 1865—The President attended Ford's Theater tonight and about ten o'clock an assassin entered his private box and shot him in the back of the head. The ball lodged in his head, and he is now lying insensible in a house opposite the theater. No hopes are entertained of his recovery. Laura Keene claims to have recognized the assassin as the actor, J. Wilkes Booth. A feeling of gloom like a pall has settled on the city. [Snyder and Morris, p. 151]

This was the seventh of the eleven dispatches Gobright filed that night. Each one contained new information as the president gradually slipped into death and the army closed in on his assassin. Although it contained some personal opinion and took time to reach the essential details of the story, the above dispatch was a great improvement over dispatches written in the older style. Readers were receiving the real news at the start of the story. It was no longer buried underneath layers of impression and opinion.

The accounts of major battles and the assassination of a president may seem far removed from police-beat news and city-council decisions, but they are not. Reports of all newsworthy events begin as nothing more than a jumble of facts scrawled hurriedly in a reporter's notebook. Reporters must then gather these facts and arrange them so that they will be comprehensible by the readers.

This last requirement—that readers understand what they are reading—dictates everything a reporter does. And because it fills this need so well, the inverted-pyramid style, with its summary lead and account of the facts in order of their importance, has remained the newswriting technique most commonly used in newspaper journalism. Although thought by some to be old-fashioned, the technique has the advantage that it is fast, it is easy, and it works.

Leads

The lead is the most important part of any story because it focuses the attention of readers and establishes a kind of dialogue with them. If the readers are not captured by the lead, they may never finish the story.

Summary lead

The *summary lead* is used most often with stories written in the inverted-pyramid form. As its name implies, this lead summarizes the facts of the story. The long-established formula of the five Ws and H, though thought old-fashioned by some journalists and educators, serves well in writing the summary lead. If a reporter tells readers the *who, what, when, where, why,* and *how* of the story, there is little more to give them. It is usually very easy to include *who, what, when,* and *where* because they are either obvious or easy to discover; the *why* and *how* are often more difficult to determine but very important and worth digging for.

Not every lead can or should contain all of these elements. There are times when such a lead might make the writing awkward, confusing, or strained. A better way is to determine which of these aspects are needed to tell the most informative story. The story will then tell itself.

A summary lead, then, summarizes quickly the facts of the story using as many of the elements of the five Ws and H as are necessary and appropriate to tell readers what they want and need to know.

> A $190,000 windfall to Corvallis in state liquor tax revenue will be used to reduce the city's proposed tax rate, members of the city council decided Tuesday. [*Corvallis Gazette-Times*]
>
> Corvallis Police are looking for the owner of a small dog that bit a girl in the face on a downtown Corvallis sidewalk Thursday. [*Corvallis Gazette-Times*]
>
> Demolition teams descended today on the vacant cannery building that was the home of the Corvallis division of Agripac, Inc. for 56 years. [*Corvallis Gazette-Times*]

These leads are direct and easy to understand. They meet the requirement urged by reporter George Wisner, enabling the reporter to say what they have to say "as quickly as possible . . . and get the hell off the stage."

But writing summary leads for every story can be monotonous—for both reporter and reader. Because of this, a number of other leads have evolved which, if carefully handled, can add interest and enjoyment to a story.

Anecdotal lead

Sometimes, the summary lead may not serve the purposes of the newspaper. Dennis Stern, metropolitan editor of the *Washington Star,* an afternoon paper, encourages his reporters to use other approaches. He always assumes that his morning competitor, the *Washington Post,* will use a five-W lead and that his readers will see the *Star* after reading the *Post*'s account of the same event. "Our reporters have to get a different angle," he says. "They will have to use a different lead than the straight news approach."

The *anecdotal lead* is Stern's first choice. This approach uses an anecdote to interest readers in the story. "I consider this kind of lead most effective," he says. "I'm talking about an example lead in which two or three are used—you might call it a 'scene setter' that paints the scene for the reader."

> Muriel Hodan survived five years of living in the jungles of Africa as a missionary. She thrived on it, in fact, riding her motorscooter from one uncivilized village to another helping the people set up schools and then teaching them how to read and write.

Two paragraphs follow before the one that explains the subject to readers:

> On Friday afternoon, Muriel Hodan was shot once in the head as she sat in the Parkway Beauty Salon in the Hunting Towers shopping center. [*Washington Star*]

Again:

> When Sen. Clarence M. Mitchell Jr., a Baltimore realtor, recently voted to confirm a member of the state board that regulates realtors, few senators considered it a conflict of interest.
>
> When Delegate Torrey C. Brown, D-Baltimore, a physician, introduces legislation affecting doctors, most of his colleagues are pleased he is sharing his expertise in medicine with the legislature.

Four paragraphs follow before the one explaining the subject fully to readers:

> Although the rules of the House and Senate define a conflict of interest as something which tends to impair a legislator's ability to make an independent decision, the working definition of most legislators is much narrower: If it doesn't benefit my personal finances, it's not a conflict. [*Washington Star*]

Delayed lead

The *delayed lead,* as its name implies, delays mentioning exactly what is going on in the story. It attempts to entice the reader to go on by hinting at what is to come. Reporters using this or any other nonsummary lead must be sure to "pay off" or explain it in the second or third paragraphs by using a good transition; otherwise, readers may be so delayed and confused that they refuse to go on. In that case the reporter has failed to accomplish the primary goal, to make the reader pause long enough to read the story.

"Even if you are backing into the story," says Dennis Stern, "by the third or fourth graf—the operative graf—you've got to tell what the story is about. Too many reporters wait until the eighth or ninth graf."

The following examples of delayed leads are from the *Corvallis Gazette-Times:*

What's good for college students may not necessarily be good for their grandparents.

The Corvallis Planning Commission Wednesday night denied a proposal to build a 36-unit "efficiency" apartment complex for the elderly on the west side of NW Kings Boulevard, between NW Arthur and NW Garfield Avenues. [*Corvallis Gazette-Times*]

After a journey of several thousand miles, the year old dream of a Corvallis couple, John and Gloria McManus, made it to within eight miles of their front door Sunday.

Then it was crushed.

The McManuses, who live at 690 NW Oak Ave., bought a white 1973 Mercedes-Benz diesel from a Santa Barbara, Calif. car dealer last week after unsuccessfully scouring Oregon for nearly a year. [*Corvallis Gazette-Times*]

David K. Long, a northwest Corvallis apartment manager, told Corvallis Police Monday afternoon that the weekend burglary of his own apartment was by open invitation.

Long, who lives at 148 A NW Conifer Ave., said he returned home from a weekend absence to find a rear window broken open and about $760 worth of items . . . missing from his home. [*Corvallis Gazette-Times*]

None of these leads makes sense at first glance. One has to read further into the story to find out what is being discussed. The second example is not explained until the eighth paragraph, and the third example is not clarified until the last sentence of the story. But all of them seize the readers' interest.

Question lead

The *question lead* asks a question of its readers. The answer should come quickly, however, and be complete enough to understand.

Does a man who is cooking dinner for six at a price of $1,300 worry a lot?

"Not too much," said O. H. Heintzelman, at work in the kitchen in the home of Dee Andros, Oregon State University athletic director. "I just hope it turns out."

Heintzelman, a retired OSU professor who has gained a reputation in Corvallis as a gourmet cook, prepared the most expensive meal of his culinary career Wednesday night. [*Corvallis Gazette-Times*]

What is Linn-Benton Community College going to do with Washington School in central Corvallis now that it has agreed to buy the building from the City of Corvallis?

Consumer education courses, electronics assembly courses, parent education programs and business training programs are but a few of the uses planned for the building, according to college officials. [*Corvallis Gazette-Times*]

Personal lead

The *personal lead* addresses readers directly by using "you" or implying it in an effort to draw them into the story. As always, the pay-off, or operative, paragraph is very important for understanding and comprehension.

Don't all you burglars, bank robbers and vandals rush down to the city-county law building and switch off the power, thinking that you'll leave speechless cops flailing in the dark.

Members of the Benton Government Committee were told Thursday that, if a power outage occurred in the building, officers in the field possibly could lose radio contact with the dispatch center, creating temporary confusion. [*Corvallis Gazette-Times*]

Beware of bones or scraps of meat that might be found in city parks in Corvallis.

They could contain poison.

That's the message Diane Hall . . . wants to convey to the public after her small dog died of what appeared to be strychnine poisoning. [*Corvallis Gazette-Times*]

Quotation lead

The *quotation lead* begins with a quotation. If the quote is good, this lead will be good. As with the other leads, the transition must quickly pay off the reader and make the story understandable.

> "We're not going to squabble today," said City Councilman Alan Berg as he waited for today's meeting of the Benton Government Committee to begin. And Berg was right. The committee agreed to . . . [*Corvallis Gazette-Times*]

> "If they put one in there, it would make a million bucks."
> Arthur Van Artsdalen watches every day as traffic passes by the service station where he works, across the street from the vacant southwest corner of Highways 34 and 99E.
> He has the same opinion as the businessmen who would anticipate making a lot of money by turning the farmland into a regional shopping center. [*Corvallis Gazette-Times*]

How to Approach a News Story

When faced with writing a news story, reporters should—

1. Begin to think about how to organize the story while they are still gathering the material

2. Cultivate the habit of ranking facts as they write them in their notebooks, important or not important

3. Write down any ideas for a lead whenever they occur to them

4. Go on to another part of the story by starting to arrange material if the lead doesn't come right away

5. Make sure they understand everything they include in a story, because if they don't understand, neither will their readers

6. Try to remember to include all sides of a subject, controversial or not, in a story and gather the quotes and facts while reporting the story; if not, telephone additional sources before beginning to write

7. Look up all additional facts from sources at the newspaper like the library or the morgue and have the material ready as they begin to write

8. Glance through their notes before they begin to write and group material likely to be emphasized by heading; this will make it easy to spot later as the writing is going on

9. Cross out or check off material after they use it, to make sure it is not used again by mistake

10. Double-check the proper spelling of all names and the correctness of street addresses in telephone books, city directories, or other sources, because mistakes in this area can lead to lawsuits and a loss of credibility

11. Keep their eyes on the clock to meet the deadline, but not let this pressure lead to haste and avoidable mistakes

How Reporters Write News Stories

Bill Monroe of the *Corvallis Gazette-Times,* Mike Hall of the *Topeka Capital-Journal,* and Diane Brockett of the *Washington Star* have differing styles but similar reasons for writing their stories as they do. Consider first a story by Monroe, "Youth Beaten by Robber of Gas Station."

The first paragraph presents the most important facts of the story as reported by Monroe, the *who,* the *when,* the *what,* and the *where.* Readers now have all the major details and can go on if they desire. If they go on, they will find that facts touched upon in the lead are related in detail. (See the first and second paragraphs shown on page 152.) In fact, the story leaves unanswered only one important question suggested by the lead, namely, How much money was taken? That information was not on the police report used by Monroe as his source, nor had it been determined by the police at the time Monroe made his inquiries. Because the story was not important enough to follow up, the amount stolen is a detail that readers will probably never know.

The last paragraph attempts to help police by giving a description of the man who allegedly robbed the gas station. This alerts any reader who might know something about the man.

The story is based on a standard format Monroe uses for robbery and police news. "I always put a kind of general lead," he says. "If someone is involved, I publish their name, address, and age in the second graf. Following that, I back up the lead with the nature of what happened. Then I give their description of the event."

A more complicated story requires that the reporter handle details adroitly. There are more details to contend with and the bare-bones approach used in police-beat news does not suffice. Also, the details of the longer story will probably have more significance for readers and need to be ex-

Youth Beaten by Robber of Gas Station

Who:	A 17-year-old gas station employe told Corvallis Police
When:	early Sunday
What:	that he was beaten and robbed
Where:	at the station where he works,
When:	minutes before a police patrol car drove by.
Who:	Ronald L. Foley of 1875 NW Arthur Ave. told an officer
What:	that while working his routine shift
Where:	at Rich Lindsey's Arco, 240 NW 4th St.,
What:	he was closing out the day's credit card receipts
When:	shortly before 2 a.m.
Who:	when a man
What:	came into the station
What:	and asked for a special type of motor oil.
What:	Foley said he went into a back room to look for some and was
How:	followed by the customer, who hit the youth in the face several times and made him sit on the floor.

The remainder of the story expands on *What.*

A 17-year-old gas station employe told Corvallis Police early Sunday that he was beaten and robbed at the station where he works, minutes before a police patrol car drove by.

Ronald L. Foley of 1875 NW Arthur Ave. told an officer that while working his routine shift at Rich Lindsey's Arco, 240 NW 4th St., he was closing out the day's credit card receipts shortly before 2 a.m. when a man came into the station and asked for a special type of motor oil.

Foley said he went into a back room to look for some and was followed by the customer, who hit the youth in the face several times and made him sit on the floor.

The man then went into the station's office and opened the cash drawer after warning Foley he would "kill" him if he tried to get out of the storeroom or stand up.

Foley said he waited for about 10 minutes inside the room, then went outside when he heard a customer drive up.

He told the customer he had been robbed and they flagged down a passing policeman. The gas station is less than two blocks from the city-county law building.

Police described the robber as being 6 feet tall, about 155 pounds, with dark, collar length hair, brown sunglasses and a red-checkered shirt.

Source: Corvallis Gazette-Times.

---

panded upon and often explained. Whereas readers tend to skim a short police-beat item to see if they know anyone involved, they will usually read a longer story in detail.

A good example of this kind of story is Bill Monroe's piece on the reconversion of a cannery into a shopping center. It is written in the inverted-pyramid style of the police-beat item but is more complicated.

"I found out on the day I wrote the story that that was the day the building was going to be torn down," Monroe says. "I realized people would be driving by and see and wonder what was going on. If we had a story, immediacy would be achieved. So the lead states what was happening. The second paragraph tells why it was being done and what will happen. The third gives the name of the industrialist involved." There, in four paragraphs, is the whole story. Readers do not have to go on to learn the essential details: The old cannery is being torn down to make way for a new shopping center to be built by an out-of-town industrialist.

Monroe has already discussed the background of the story. One fact worth noting here is that he protected one of his sources by camouflaging what the source told him with the phrase "the Gazette-Times has learned." In this way he could use the information and still not get his source in trouble. Monroe also thinks that that phrase heightens reader interest. "I used the phrase 'The *Gazette-Times* has learned' because that gives the feeling of intrigue and leads you into what I call 'no comment' comments. It's a lot more exciting if done this way. Readers will want to find out what the *Gazette-Times* has learned, and they'll read."

From this point on in the story, Monroe begins to amplify, bringing in details beyond the tearing down of one building and the construction of a new one on the same site; the additional details maintain the readers' interest and enhance their understanding. "At the end of the story I lifted paragraphs out of the files for background: when the cannery was closed, how many people it employed. I got into a history of the cannery, what happened to it, and who is making it happen."

Old Cannery to Become Specialty Shopping Center

By William Monroe
of the Gazette-Times

What:	Demolition teams descended
When:	today
Where:	on the vacant cannery building that was the home of the Corvallis division of Agripac, Inc., for 56 years.
What:	The building,
Where:	at 637 NW 9th St.,
How:	is being demolished
Why:	to make way for a new shopping center.
What:	The center, which likely will be called "The Cannery," is being built by
Who:	a Portland industrialist, Ira Keller,
What:	who bought the property from Agripac
When:	last December.
What:	The Gazette-Times has learned that the new shopping center will be in a two-story building and will consist of specialty stores in an inside walk-around mall on four staggered levels. The total space for the shopping area will be about 30,000 square feet.

    Following a paragraph on parking facilities, five paragraphs answer various other aspects of *what* and *how*. Monroe knew of a zoning change in that area and that the new building would be in violation of it. He also knew that the city

    Demolition teams descended today on the vacant cannery building that was the home of the Corvallis division of Agripac, Inc., for 56 years.

    The building, at 637 NW 9th St., is being demolished to make way for a new shopping center.

    The center, which likely will be called "The Cannery," is being built by a Portland industrialist, Ira Keller, who bought the property from Agripac last December

    The Gazette-Times has learned that the new shopping center will be in a two-story building and will consist of specialty stores in an inside walk-around mall on four staggered levels. The total space for the shopping area will be about 30,000 square feet.

    Parking will be provided outside. In addition to the building, Keller bought three acres of land from Agripac, but did not purchase an adjoining concrete warehouse, which is still for sale by Agripac.

Writing News Stories and Leads   155

council had not yet acted on the revised plan. He presents this information, adding that a building permit had not been applied for, although one for the demolition had been granted.

Under the proposed revision of the Corvallis land-use plan, a commercial center would not be allowed on the property, planned to be zoned for industrial use. Another part of the revised plan says that new commercial centers outside of downtown Corvallis will be discouraged.

But the revised plan has not been adopted by the Corvallis City Council and present zoning laws allow for construction of the center without approval of the Corvallis Planning Commission.

No building permit applications have been submitted yet to the Corvallis Building Department, but representatives of Keller have discussed the plan with the Corvallis Planning Department.

A demolition permit for the Agripac building has been issued by the city to a Salem demolition firm.

Sources told the Gazette-Times tnat the building will be torn down to its foundation and the new building will be rebuilt on the existing foundation.

The bridging sentence "Nobody connected with . . ." begins seven paragraphs of what Monroe calls "no comment" comments. Basically here he shares with readers the frustrations of reporting. Normally, readers couldn't care less about how much trouble it has been to do the story. That is the reporter's job, they probably reason, let's get on with the story. In this instance, however, such an approach is justified. Monroe wants readers to know that he tried to get more information but could not do so. This increases his credibility with the reader and improves that of the newspaper as well.

Nobody connected with the project would discuss the plans for the new center.

Keller, his Corvallis representative, Lola Dickerson, and a representative of the apparent contractor for the project, Bingham Brothers Construction Co. of Portland, had scheduled a noon meeting today to solidify plans for the tenants of the center. He is reportedly interested in "getting just the right mixture" of specialty shops.

Keller, chairman of the board of directors of Western Sales Co. and a founder of Western Kraft, Inc., is building the center on his own.

He would not discuss the project with the Gazette-Times by telephone today; he was in his office, he couldn't be reached through his secretary, Marian Crayne, who said that in about two weeks a scale model

(continued)

Monroe ends the story with background about the old cannery. Its closing has been a blow to some residents of the community, and its deserted building, now something of an eyesore, a visible wound to the local economy. The newspaper and Monroe did the community a service by reporting all they could find out.

Source: Corvallis Gazette-Times.

of the center and the plans for it will be made public.

"It's still too early," she said about providing information.

There has been no indication when construction might start or when the center will be completed.

The architect for the project is the Salem firm of Payne, Settecase, Smith and partners, but Phillip Settecase, who is apparently designing the building, would not comment, referring questions to Keller's office.

The cannery closed its doors in late 1975 after Agripac officials said that the firm was unable to continue making a profit on it and still meet tough environmental standards with its waste materials.

At peak times during the summer harvest, the cannery employed more than 600 persons.

Keller, when he bought the property, promised that he would develop a "really interesting" use for it.

Stories on council meetings present another kind of challenge for Monroe or any reporter faced with a similar task. As explained in Chapter 6, he had to sit through a long meeting and keep track of what was going on, noting who said what and what decisions were made. Even with an agenda and background packet to help him, Monroe did not find it easy to report on the meeting. In his coverage, he could rely on his background of several years as city beat reporter, bringing into the story things he remembered, even though they did not happen to come up during the noon and evening meetings he covered.

In Monroe's story "Council Rejects Plan for Use of $190,000 Windfall" there were two *what*'s, what the council did do (decide to use the liquor-tax revenue to reduce the tax rate) and what they didn't do (vote to balance the budget and cancel the upcoming election). Both of these *what*'s are stated in the two lead paragraphs. As shown in the gloss, the brief descriptive guide that accompanies this story, the inverted pyramid is completed as successive paragraphs elaborate upon the two *what*'s in the order of their importance, the order in which they were originally presented.

Council Rejects Plan for Use of $190,000 Windfall

*By William Monroe
of the Gazette-Times*

What:	A $190,000 windfall to Corvallis in state liquor-tax revenue will be used to reduce the city's proposed tax rate,
Who:	members of the city council decided
When:	Tuesday.
What:	In earmarking the money for the general budget, the council rejected a plan to cancel next Tuesday's levy election by balancing the budget. However, that would force the city to ask voters for a special levy to finish the second floor of the new city-county law enforcement building, which is already in the budget.

The next two paragraphs expand upon the first *what*, the use of the liquor-tax revenue to reduce the tax rate.

What:	The Oregon Legislature, before adjourning Tuesday, passed a bill to increase liquor revenue allocations. Corvallis will get about $190,000 more than it had anticipated if Gov. Bob Straub signs the bill, which he is expected to do.
What:	The Corvallis City Council, meeting Tuesday night, unanimously decided to use the money to offset the property tax bill of city residents if they approve a special $356,843 property tax levy to balance the city's $7 million operating budget next Tuesday.

A $190,000 windfall to Corvallis in state liquor-tax revenue will be used to reduce the city's proposed tax rate, members of the city council decided Tuesday.

In earmarking the money for the general budget, the council rejected a plan to cancel next Tuesday's levy election by balancing the budget. However, that would force the city to ask voters for a special levy to finish the second floor of the new city-county law enforcement building, which is already in the budget.

The Oregon Legislature, before adjourning Tuesday, passed a bill to increase liquor revenue allocations. Corvallis will get about $190,000 more than it had anticipated if Gov. Bob Straub signs the bill, which he is expected to do.

The Corvallis City Council, meeting Tuesday night, unanimously decided to use the money to offset the property tax bill of city residents if they approve a special $356,843 property tax levy to balance the city's $7 million operating budget next Tuesday.

(continued)

The next three paragraphs expand upon the preceding.

Then the story turns to an explanation of the second *what*, the vote to balance the budget and cancel the election.

What: **Councilmen Richard Evers and Louis Bradley brought to the council floor a motion to cancel Tuesday's election by cutting the budget $186,000—the city's share of finishing the second story of the city-county law enforcement building—and using the liquor revenue to balance the difference.**

The next three paragraphs expand upon this point.

Although the ballots, which have already been printed, say that the tax rate for the levy will be $4.94 for each $1,000 of assessed property value, rough figures given the council by Jerry Hortsch, finance director, indicate that if the $190,000 is added into the budget, the city would have to levy only $145,731 (figuring in an additional amount of uncollectable taxes), for a tax rate of $4.47, one cent less than last year's tax rate.

Voters, in essence, will be voting on a levy greater (more than twice) than that which will actually be levied.

However, the assessed value of most property in Corvallis rose approximately 25 per cent last year, according to C. Lloyd Anderson, Benton County assessor, and the total tax bill will increase accordingly, in spite of the decrease in the tax rate.

Councilmen Richard Evers and Louis Bradley brought to the council floor a motion to cancel Tuesday's election by cutting the budget $186,000—the city's share of finishing the second story of the city-county law enforcement building—and using the liquor revenue to balance the difference.

The $186,000 would then be sought from voters as a separate levy proposal, to be repaid with a lower tax rate over a period of several years instead of a large one all at once.

But Evers and Bradley were the only two who voted for the motion. Council members Robert Wilson, Inge McNeese, Terry Barker, Frank Triska and Lavern Ratzlaff voted against it. Arthur J. "Bud" Schmidt was late to the evening session and didn't vote. Alan Berg was acting mayor, filling in for vacationing Donald Walker.

The story ends with a rather one-sided view of the issue. Monroe quotes two of the council members as to why they voted as they did against the motion to balance the budget. He did not get quotes from the council members who proposed the motion about why they did so.

The council then voted unanimously to put the windfall into the city's budget.

Triska said that the city is committed to finishing the building and should leave the money for the second floor in the budget.

The council's action eliminates the risk of voters turning down a levy to finish the law enforcement building.

McNeese said that if the budget is balanced without a vote this year, it might be more difficult to meet increased costs next year without a seemingly dramatic increase in the budget.

Source: Corvallis Gazette-Times.

"This was the main story I got from the meeting because it had more direct effect on people," Monroe explains. "I used the inverted-pyramid approach, in which I said what the decision was, the amount of money involved, and what it would be used for. Then I went through what they did, using numbers. I use a calculator a lot, particularly in budget stories. I stick to one subject. I try to do this so readers won't get bored and not read the story."

For this reason, Monroe wrote three stories about what took place at this meeting of the city council. The other two dealt with the use of federal money for road construction and the setting up of new planning goals.

Mike Hall uses a summary lead in his account of the Topeka City Commission meeting. "I started with a hard-news lead, 'Two city officials were designated by the Topeka City Commission . . . ,' then went into a reorganization of the department and the mayor's response. Then I used quotes from the audience."

Probe of SCCAA Phaseout

By Mike Hall
City Hall Writer

Who:	Two city officials
What:	were designated by
Who:	the Topeka City Commission
When:	this morning
What:	to examine costs of phasing out a contract with Shawnee County Community Assistance and Action for work for the community development department.

Two city officials were designated by the Topeka City Commission this morning to examine the costs of phasing out a contract with Shawnee County Community Assistance and Action for work for the community development department.

Hall pauses here to back up his lead with a quote from a commissioner about the phaseout plan.

"I think the phaseout is expensive; I think it contains some costs that are not necessary," Finance Comm. Kenneth L. Elder told the other commissioners this morning.

He then tells readers both the cost of the plan and its effect.

Larry Wilson, executive director of SCCAA has proposed costs totaling $93,000 for phasing out the program, following last week's cancellation of his contract by the city commission.

Part of the cost is for termination of 25 employes, including such costs as salary and annual leave. His plan would phase them out in stages on March 31, April 15 and April 30.

One of Elder's objections is to the salaries to be paid during that period. He suggested the entire program could be phased out by April 15.

He quotes the commissioner again.

Elder blasted the plan as having "a lot of bologna in it" and said a community impact statement included in the plan is "political noise."

In the seventh paragraph, perhaps too far into the story, he includes the names of the officials referred to in the lead.

In the end the commission designated Charles Holt, the city auditor, and Craig McLaughlin, the acting community development director, to examine the closeout

More background comes next as Hall reminds readers of the mayor's reorganization plan.

The remainder of the story deals with objections from members of the audience and the response by various commission members.

costs and report back to the city commission.

Wilson said he needed to know what decisions the commission would make concerning the closeout as soon as possible and would request that he be on the city commission agenda for next Tuesday to discuss it again.

Mayor Bill McCormick's proposed reorganization of the community development plan also was on the agenda for this morning's special commission meeting, but McCormick said he had decided that it did not require commission action. He said the only part of it that required commission action is a change of an office manager position to a clerk IV position and that he was withdrawing that temporarily. He said he wanted to discuss it with Ron Todd, the city's new personnel manager.

Glenda Wilson, one of the CD employes to be laid off by the mayor's reorganization plan, interrupted the commission meeting several times to charge that the mayor was apathetic about the plight of the poor people who are supposed to be helped by the program.

She said she was going to sue McCormick, saying: "You and I will fight this out in court."

She contended that she and the other six employes scheduled for layoff were the only personnel in the department with the experience and knowledge to run the program and that they cared more for the welfare of the poor people than the commissioners do.

McCormick denied her charge that he didn't care about the poor people and said that he, too, had seen their substandard living conditions.

Elder defended himself from a similar attack and said it was because of his concern for the poor people that he was advocating eliminating the whole community development department and starting over.

(continued)

Source: Topeka Capital-Journal.

Hall's last paragraph deals with the actual motion and the vote on it. This information should have been placed earlier in the story as part of the news.

"The administrative costs have been exceedingly high. The poor people aren't getting anything. They weren't getting anything before the investigation."

He referred to an investigation that has been under way since Everett Tomlin, the director of the community development department, was fired by the commission in January. The investigation now involves police department detectives, a private auditing firm, the city attorney's office, the U.S. attorney's office and the Federal Bureau of Investigation.

Water Comm. Jack Alexander made a motion later to turn the issue over to Holt and McLaughlin and that motion was adopted 4-0-1, with Park Comm. Harry Felker abstaining.

The next story, by Diane Brockett of the *Washington Star*, is about the appointment of the former superintendent of the District of Columbia schools to a new job in Michigan. The reporter had written a series of stories several years before that had been instrumental in the superintendent's removal from office. Things had become so uncomfortable for Brockett during the earlier coverage that she frequently took another reporter with her to meetings involving the superintendent for protection from the superintendent's supporters. The police also watched her during the meetings because of threats from the group favoring the school head. In short, the group blamed her for the official's eventual ouster and never hesitated to show it.

The present story opens with a summary lead, giving the *who* ("Barbara A. Sizemore . . .") and *what* ("has been selected . . .") of the story.

Diane Brockett continues the description: "The real news here is that she will not be here for the city council position; it had been thought she would be a candidate. I had originally written the lead about the new job, then moved the city-council thing to the second paragraph. The first three paragraphs covered her selection, voted on the night before, and that she was out of council politics.

"I got up high—in the fourth paragraph—that she would not comment because she hadn't heard from the board. [The story resulted from a tip to the reporter, which she then investigated.] Also, something that was not quite so obvious, most of the city did not know she was not working here. Since she was fired in July, 1975, she had been a consultant and teacher.

Because she figured prominently in all discussions of city-council politics, that was of interest. I let her comment; she wants to get back to running a school system.

"I then gave background on her earlier run for the council and also why she had been thinking of running and also applying for another job. Then I wrote a background paragraph on her firing to show the difference in what she was doing versus what she had done. I described where she was going and the parallels between the two cities [Washington, D.C., and Benton Harbor, Michigan].

"I talked to board members about why they hired her. Finally, I put things about the District [of Columbia] up front because District readers are more interested in that than where she is going."

Sizemore Named Head of a School System in Mich.

By Diane Brockett
Washington Star Staff Writer

Barbara A. Sizemore, the District's controversial former school superintendent, has been selected to head a small, troubled school system in Michigan.

Sizemore's appointment as superintendent of the 10,000-pupil school system in Benton Harbor, Mich. dispelled reports here that she would be a candidate this fall for the D.C. City Council.

The Benton Harbor board of education last night voted 4-3 to hire Sizemore, one of 80 candidates for the $38,500-a-year educator's post. She was to be asked this morning to begin negotiations on the particulars of a contract.

Reached last night by telephone at her home near the University of Pittsburgh, where she has been a visiting professor of black studies since September, Sizemore declined to comment on the job because she had not heard from the Michigan board.

However, Sizemore did admit a desire to return to running a school system. "That's my life work, that's what I've been educated to do," she explained.

"I've been gone from there since September" Sizemore added in denying she had ever stated an intention to make a second race for the D.C. City Council.

The former superintendent first ran for a council seat last summer, when she sought to fill the at-large council vacancy created by the death of Julius W. Hobson Sr. She was narrowly defeated by Hilda M. Mason.

Persons close to Sizemore have said in recent weeks that her first desire had been to obtain a superintendent's job, and that the council was an option she was exploring in case the top school post wasn't offered. Sizemore also recently had applied to have her visiting associate professorship at the University of Pittsburgh extended for another year.

City Councilman Douglas Moore,

(continued)

Source: Washington Star.

who supported Sizemore in her bid for the vacant council seat last summer, said late yesterday that she has been actively considering becoming a council candidate but had not yet made a decision.

Sizemore had changed her legal residence from Ward 1 to Ward 5 several months ago causing much talk among politicians about whether she would run at-large or seek the ward seat held by William Spaulding.

Sizemore was fired as D.C. school superintendent in the summer of 1975 after 20 months of running the 130,000-student system.

Her tenure as superintendent was marked by fervent support from several groups of local citizens and constant disputes with members of the board of education, who criticized her administration of the schools.

Her previous administrative experience had been heading the Woodlawn Experimental Schools project for 3,200 in Southside Chicago.

The site of her new job, Benton Harbor, is directly on the shore of Lake Michigan, two hours from Chicago, in the heart of Michigan's farming region.

Although the Michigan community is much smaller in size than Washington, there are many parallels between the two school systems.

A community with a population of about 40,000, Benton Harbor's school system has switched from 75 percent white to 75 percent black in the past 10 years. Many white residents send their children to private schools or pay tuition to send them across the river to the mostly white town of St. Joseph.

A federal judge has recently found the system guilty of running a segregated system and is expected to hand down a desegregation plan shortly.

Implementing that plan will be one of the major tasks facing the new superintendent, explained James Caudill, director of public relations for the Benton Harbor school system.

The schools are also faced with very poor student achievement test results, pointing up the need to concentrate on improving students' basic reading and math skills, Caudill said.

Sizemore was hired in Michigan after capturing the imagination of the community and a majority of the board in a public interview required by Michigan law, Caudill said. She was selected to head D.C. schools following a similar public interview here.

"She really put on a good show," Caudill said. "She really reached the people."

Sizemore dealt directly with her troubles in D.C. during the Michigan session, Caudill said.

She told the audience that part of the trouble had been she didn't know whether she was "working for the board or for Congress," the spokesman added. She also noted that she had had to work for two completely different boards during her less than two years in D.C.

Several of the Michigan board members came to Washington about two weeks ago to investigate her tenure here.

Freddie L. Moore, board treasurer and Sizemore's major supporter on the Michigan board, said last night that the panel believed "D.C. was a real good training experience" in preparation for a community like Benton Harbor.

Attribution

Attribution is the presenting of the source, or sources, of a story. Who told the reporter? What secondary sources were used? This factor is especially important in these days when the credibility of reporters is often questioned. Mention of the source's name or title adds authenticity to the story and gives readers information to use in evaluating its worth. It should be placed high in the story, in the lead if possible. Reporters should cite their sources by name, but if they can get the story only by withholding that information, they may substitute titles or more vague identification. When information derives from a police blotter, of course, only a general form of attribution is necessary; for example, "Police said."

The cannery story did not need attribution in the same sense the other stories did because the demolition of the building had been observed by a reporter. Various other details of the story are supported by attributions. "The Gazette-Times has learned" is attribution in the sense that a source is being protected. "Sources told the Gazette-Times" serves the same purpose.

The same thing applies to the council stories. The reporter attended and observed the council meetings, and the only attribution needed was for quotations ("Triska said" or "McNeese said") or reports or other documents prepared outside the meeting but quoted in the story.

Examples of attribution

Attribution: **Rena Woods, manager of the hotel said**

Attribution: **Mrs. Wood said**

Source: Corvallis Gazette-Times

Fire and water damage from a fire in a room on the sixth floor of the Benton Hotel Tuesday morning totaled only $441, Rena Woods, manager of the hotel, said today.

Firemen contained the blaze in a single room on the northeast corner of the hotel's top floor. It was started by a window curtain blowing into a burning candle on a table. The occupant, Merle Kerby, was not in his room at the time the fire started.

Mrs. Wood said that the hotel's residents were in their own quarters and didn't have to evacuate, except while the firemen were on the scene.

Attribution: Police said

Attribution: A report said

Attribution: Police said

Source: Corvallis Gazette-Times.

Corvallis Police are looking for the owner of a small dog that bit a girl in the face on a downtown Corvallis sidewalk Thursday.

Police said they want to know whether the dog has been vaccinated for rabies.

A report said that the dog was a small pekinese mixed breed, black and white, on a sidewalk outside Olga's Homemade Ice Cream, 310 SW 3rd St., at 5 p.m. Thursday.

A small girl, whose parents were inside the store, began playing with it, but cried out when the dog apparently bit her.

The girl's parents comforted her but didn't notice the small wound until they got home, police said.

Transitional Sentences

A *transitional sentence* guides readers from one paragraph to the next. It is especially important in directing them from the lead to the body of the story. If a reporter confuses or stops readers at this point, they are unlikely to go on to the remainder of the story, and the reporter will have failed. A good way to make this process easy for readers is to pick out a word or phrase from the lead and use it again at the start of the next paragraph.

Fish Disease Expert to Head Microbiology

John L. Fryer, 48, winner of two outstanding teaching awards at Oregon State University and known for his fish disease research, has been named head of the Department of Microbiology at OSU.

Fryer has been acting head of the department since July 1, 1976, when Paul Elliker retired. Fryer's new appointment, which carries a 12-month salary of $34,512, was effective July 1.

Born in Texas, Fryer grew up in Texas and Washington. He earned the doctor's degree in 1964 at OSU after getting two other degrees at OSU. He has been a member of the Department of Microbiology since 1964.

Earlier he had been a state fisheries pathologist for the Oregon Fish Commission and taught in the OSU Departments of Fisheries and Wildlife and Food Science and Technology.

His research has been on infectious diseases of fish, virology, tissue culture and pathogenic microbiology. Fryer was first president of the Fish Health Section, American Fisheries Society, and has been invited to speak on fish diseases in The Netherlands, London, Turin, Italy, and Zagreb, Yugoslavia. He has written many publications about his research.

Fryer and his wife, Mary, have four daughters.

Source: Corvallis Gazette-Times.

In the story, "Fish Disease Expert to Head Microbiology," the repeat of the name *Fryer* makes the transition. Secondary transitional words are the pronoun *he* and the pronominal adjective *his,* both referring to Fryer.

In the next story, "Bullet Pierces House Barely Missing Woman," a repeat of the word *bullet* makes the transition. Secondary transitional words are *Ruth Schrock, she,* and *Mrs. Schrock,* referring back to *woman* in the lead, and *the rifle bullet,* again referring back to the lead.

Bullet Pierces House Barely Missing Woman

A high-powered rifle bullet smashed into a central Benton County home Wednesday evening, narrowly missing a 65-year-old woman.

The bullet was apparently fired from a car passing the house on Highway 99W, 100 feet from the house, according to Benton County sheriff's deputies.

According to the report, Ruth Schrock, who with her husband, Dave, 82, lives in an aluminum house along Highway 99W, several miles south of Corvallis, rose from her reclining chair at 8:05 p.m. Wednesday to adjust her television set.

Seconds after she walked the three feet to the set, the rifle bullet smashed through the living room window above her chair, crossed the room, went through a picture frame, penetrated a wall into the kitchen above a refrigerator and dropped into a plastic dish.

Had she been standing near her chair, her husband said, she would have been shot in the head.

Dave Schrock, a retired farmer, is the father of Benton County Commissioner Dale Schrock, Linn County Commissioner Vernon Schrock and Earl Schrock, a Benton County farmer.

He said he and his wife had finished watching "The Price Is Right" and he went into the bathroom to get ready for bed.

Mrs. Schrock rose to change the channel on the television set and as she was turning it heard a "loud boom." She turned and saw lint floating in the room, apparently from a hole in a curtain hanging in front of the window.

Deputies said the bullet appeared to have been fired from a .30 caliber rifle and said the gunman was probably inside a car.

Schrock said that other relatives who were at a grange hall south of his house, reported hearing a fast car and either a backfiring engine or a gunshot near the grange hall about the same time as the shooting at Schrock's house.

Source: Corvallis Gazette-Times.

Sometimes the reference need not be direct; there need only be a reference to something in the lead, as in the following extract. In the second paragraph the action taken in the lead is summed up in one word, *appointment*.

> Daniel Bartlett, Benton County's assistant director of finance for more than three years, has been appointed director of a new county department of central services. Bartlett will be assisted by Ethan

> Van Eck, controversial director of a county youth employment program.
>
> The appointment was made by the Benton County Board of Commissioners Friday but a decision hasn't been made. [*Corvallis Gazette-Times*]

Consider the next extract. What did Berg do in the lead? He made a *comment* and that is the transition.

> "We're not going to squabble today," said City Councilman Alan Berg as he waited for today's meeting of the Benton Government Committee to begin. And Berg was right. The committee agreed to direct Herb Hammond, law building coordinator, to ask the architects to draw new diagrams for the vacant top floor of the city-county law building.
>
> Berg's comment before the meeting was in reference to a headline on a Gazette-Times article which described . . . [*Corvallis Gazette-Times*]

Farther down in a story, changes in subject can be made with other kinds of transitional sentences: "In an unrelated construction matter the council . . . ," "In other action Tuesday, the council . . ." Words like *however* and *but* can also be used to make a smooth transition.

Editorializing

When reporters express their own opinions in a story not clearly labeled "Opinion" or "Analysis," they are *editorializing*. This is one of the worst sins in newspaper journalism because it causes readers to mistrust the reporter and the newspaper. Readers don't care what a reporter thinks about a subject covered in a story; they want to make up their own minds on the basis of the facts given in the story. Opinion should be reserved for editorials, where there is no doubt that it is the newspaper's opinion, and for signed columns or essays, on the editorial page or elsewhere, as long as the words *analysis* or *opinion* are included too; these last designations are made by the editors.

It is the mark of inexperience and naïveté for reporters to introduce their own opinions into their stories. Their main purpose in covering an event is to represent readers at that event, and this representation must be carried out in a disinterested and objective way. The reporter must find a place with an unobstructed view of the event to be recorded and observe and take notes from that place without actually getting involved. Objective reporting comes with experience in covering both simple and complicated news events; and whatever the difficulty in achieving it—especially when the event being covered is controversial or emotional—this objectivity is absolutely necessary. It avoids even the slightest hint of editorializing and resultant loss of credibility.

At times, the intrusion of a reporter's personality and a reporter's observations into a story is casual and inadvertent. A phrase like "told this reporter" creeps in accidentally. Although seemingly harmless, this kind of approach can lead to the expression of opinion that is editorializing. It also signifies poor writing because it is wordy and interferes with the telling of the story.

A more blatant kind of editorializing occurs when reporters say directly what they think: "It seems to me that the audience was hostile to the speaker," "The mayor stepped way out of line in badgering the witness appearing before the city council," or, worse yet, "I think."

In the foregoing instances, the reporter has expressed an opinion about the events and people involved in the story. It would be far better simply to tell readers the facts of each story, so that they themselves conclude, "That audience was really hostile to that speaker," or, "I think the mayor was out of order in questioning that witness."

Editorializing can also take place because of the words chosen to tell the story. If someone is said to "shout" at an audience, for example, or to "imply" something, it could be editorializing.

Despite the best intentions of reporters and editors, editorializing does appear in news stories. The mere selection of what to cover, what sources to put in or leave out, what or whom to emphasize in the lead and body of the story—all of these choices are subtle editorializing.

Two examples of this subtle, but unavoidable editorializing appear in Bill Monroe's story on the new shopping center presented earlier in this chapter.

> Nobody connected with the project would discuss the plans for the new center.

The sentence might imply that the backers of the project have something to hide. Why wouldn't they talk to the reporter? Later in the story, Monroe said that the owner of the new development would not discuss the project with the *Gazette-Times* by telephone today; he was in his office, he couldn't be reached through his secretary. [*Corvallis Gazette-Times*]

This statement conveys another negative impression, although it is a simple statement of the reporter's difficulties in getting all the facts for the story. He had every right to include both items to explain why he could not give the readers all he thought they should know.

Diane Brockett's use of the word *controversial* in the lead of her story about the former superintendent of the District of Columbia schools is another example. That is clearly an opinion word. "I used *controversial*," she says, "because anybody involved in front-page controversy for two years is controversial."

Some critics of the press object even to the choices noted earlier, of what goes in the lead and of what is covered. But choices have to be made to get the news to the reader. The reporter has to act as a filter in this regard, using experience and accepted journalistic practice as a guide. The alternative is chaos and a situation in which the news is not reported in a form understandable by readers.

Readers, for their part, must learn that a few choices have to be made in the emphasis given to facts and the people interviewed: recognizing that, they would do well to read more than one newspaper's version of a story, look into a magazine's coverage, and watch a television news program's treatment of it before reaching any firm conclusions about the story. If they receive their news from different elements of the press, they will soon develop the ability to distinguish fact from opinion. Admittedly, this approach is an imperfect one, but it is the only one available.

Reporters, meanwhile, need to take pains to avoid even inadvertently expressing their own views.

Summary

A news story consists of a lead (first) paragraph and a body (the rest of the facts). The most common style of writing a news story is the inverted pyramid, which begins with a summary of the most important elements of the story (as many of the five Ws and H as are necessary and appropriate in the lead) and presents the other facts of the story in descending order of importance. A summary lead is used most often, because it summarizes what happened. Its overuse is boring, however, and reporters sometimes turn to creative leads: anecdotal, delayed, question, personal, and quotation. Both the lead and second paragraph and the subsequent paragraphs must be bridged with a transitional sentence whenever the subject is changed. All quotations from sources and other facts in the story should be attributed to the people involved whenever possible. Reporters must never editorialize, that is, put forward their own opinions in a news story.

Suggested Exercises

1. Bring to class five examples of an inverted-pyramid news story. Mount them on pieces of paper and analyze them, noting which of the five Ws and H are included in the lead, where the attribution is, what kinds of transitional sentences are used, where the stories begin to amplify the facts mentioned in the lead. Be prepared to discuss in class.

2. Bring to class examples of poor attribution and rewrite the leads so as to correct the confusion. Why are they bad?

3. Bring to class examples of poor transitions and rewrite the stories so as to correct the confusion. Why are they bad?

4. Bring to class examples of each kind of lead, noting which is which. How good is the transition?

5. Write a story using each kind of lead, being sure to identify it and to use the proper transition.

6. Clip out examples of editorializing in news stories. Bring them to class and be prepared to discuss them.

7. Bring to class examples of leads that do not work; be prepared to explain your evaluation of the leads.

8. Walk across campus, or across town, and find one newsworthy topic or event; gather the material and write a simple story.

"Hello sweetheart. Get me rewrite."

Anonymous Thirties-Style Reporter
to Newspaper Telephone Operator

9

Writing and Rewriting

General Rules of Writing
Rewriting
Rewriting Public-Relations Press Releases
Updating

If ten of the best reporters in the country could be gathered in a room and given the same news story to write, they would probably turn in ten different, but equally acceptable, stories.

There is no "best" way to write a news story. Sometimes the facts dictate the approach taken by the reporter. In one story, the *who* or *what* will need to be told above all else; in another, the when, where, why, or how.

At other times the reporter's background, experience, and even personality or mood influence what appears in print. A trained reporter emphasizes things and adds details to a story that someone new to the job cannot know. In other instances, a reporter bored with the summary lead may choose a delayed lead that will alter the reader's perception of the story.

General Rules of Writing

There are so many ways to write a news story that it is difficult to develop any but the most general rules. Even these rules may be broken at times for special effect.

1. Reporters should use simple, straightforward sentences, each with a subject and verb and not cluttered with unnecessary adjectives, adverbs, or subordinate clauses.

> A 17-year old gas station employe told Corvallis Police early Sunday that he was beaten and robbed at the station where he works. [*Corvallis Gazette-Times*]

> Barbara A. Sizemore, the District's controversial former school superintendent, has been selected to head a small, troubled school system in Michigan. [*Washington Star*]

2. When possible, reporters should keep one or, at the most, two important ideas to a sentence.

> Demolition teams descended today on the vacant cannery building that was the home of the Corvallis division of Agripac, Inc. for 56 years. [*Corvallis Gazette-Times*]

> A $190,000 windfall to Corvallis in state liquor tax revenue will be used to reduce the city's proposed tax rate, members of the city council decided Tuesday. [*Corvallis Gazette-Times*]

> Two city officials were designated by the Topeka City Commission this morning to examine the costs of phasing out a contract with Shawnee County Community Assistance and Action for work for the community development department. [*Topeka Capital-Journal*]
>
> McCormick denied her charge that he didn't care about the poor people and said that he, too, had seen their substandard living conditions. [*Topeka Capital-Journal*]

3. Reporters should use the past tense in news stories because they are describing past events. (The headline, however, not written by the reporter, will often use present tense to create the feeling of immediacy.)

   > A 17-year-old gas station employe *told* Corvallis Police early Sunday that he *was beaten* and *robbed* . . .
   >
   > Demolition teams *descended* . . .
   >
   > Two city officials *were designated* . . .

4. Reporters should group like subjects into the same paragraph, unless that arrangement makes the paragraph too long. In that case, the paragraph can be divided arbitrarily into two paragraphs to diminish the possibility of a gray, dull-looking story on the printed page.

5. Reporters should use the active voice whenever possible, avoiding the passive voice because of the sluggish quality it gives a sentence.

   Active voice: *The mayor told the city council last night . . .*

   Passive voice: *The council was told by the mayor last night . . .*

6. Whenever possible, reporters should let the story tell itself. That is, they should let their sources speak to their readers through direct quotes or at least a paraphrase of those quotes.

7. Reporters can smooth the way they tell their story by using several simple devices. The colon can introduce a topic in a somewhat dramatic and fast-moving manner.

   > The mayor had one topic on his mind: money.

It can also introduce a series of items, if handled properly.

Wrong: *The mayor had several points he said he wanted to bring to the attention of the council. These were: streets, budgets, schools.*

Right: *The mayor said he wanted to bring several matters to the attention of the council: streets, budgets, and schools.*

In this use, however, reporters should not confuse a colon (:), which means go on, with a semicolon (;), which can substitute for a period and means stop.

Another way to lighten the way of readers through a story is to avoid burdening them with a restatement of their original question to the source.

Wrong: *When asked what he wanted to bring to the attention of the council, the mayor said . . .*

Right: *What did he hope to bring up with the council? The mayor said . . .*

8. Reporters should use precise words that quickly tell the story and do not send readers rushing to their dictionaries to determine meaning. The average newspaper reader has not gone beyond high school. More important, however, simple language tells the story better. If reporters use a difficult word, they need to define it for readers—in parentheses, for example, immediately after the first use of the word.

9. Reporters should get into the habit of looking up the correct spelling of any word they have the least doubt about. An attitude of "letting the editors on the desk get it" will result in spelling errors that threaten the credibility of the reporter and the newspaper. Also, in these days of wide use of video-display terminals, the chance of the desk catching such errors is less likely because it is difficult for individuals to catch their own mistakes. Reporters might just as well get into the habit of looking up all words of which they have the slightest doubt. If they are using a VDT, they should look up the words as they go along. If they are still composing their stories on a typewriter, they may underline them lightly and go to the dictionary for proper spelling when they edit the story later.

10. Reporters should also get into the habit of consulting the newspaper stylebook as they write. It is a bad habit to leave the nuances of style to the desk. Preferably, reporters will have memorized the stylebook dur-

ing the first week on the job, so that frequent consultation will not be necessary.

11. Whenever possible, it is a good idea for reporters to leave their stories for a few minutes after they finish writing them and do something else, even if it means going on to another story. This allows them a fresh look at the material and often results in better writing and fewer errors. On a longer story, a reporter might have the luxury of letting it sit until the next day, although this is rare on a newspaper.

12. Reporters must reach a point where they let go of their stories and turn them in. It is a good idea to write them and then revise them at least once, but stories must be turned in to the desk and not held for further, and often excessive, tinkering that does not really improve the writing and may cause a reporter to miss the deadline.

13. Reporters should keep themselves out of the story except in rare instances where they cannot tell what happened any other way.

Rewriting

One of the best ways to improve any kind of writing is to rewrite. Few reporters can achieve a finished, polished piece the first time around. As suggested in the preceding section, reporters should get in the habit of putting the story aside for a few minutes, or until the next day if possible. This time lag will create the necessary detachment for them to view their writing more objectively.

But rewriting on newspapers goes much further than that done by reporters before they submit their stories. Most of it goes on at the copydesk. Editors there check copy for spelling errors and style mistakes. They also make sure the stories read well. Are the leads well written? Do the leads emphasize the right facts, or are these facts buried in the fourth paragraph? Editors must ask such questions as they read the stories submitted to them.

They read the stories carefully, noting portions that are unclear or incorrect. If the lead contains the wrong emphasis, they rewrite it by transposing the appropriate facts. If necessary, they rewrite the story or ask the reporter to do so; if the reporter has missed the point entirely, they return the story for more work, even if this sometimes means holding it back for another day. Although rewriting is usually done by experienced editors, reporters sometimes have the opportunity to do so while serving brief periods on the copydesk or its electronic equivalent.

On large newspapers whose wide coverage may make it difficult for reporters to get to the office, reporters often use the telephone to transmit the facts of a story to a rewrite person (or a dictationist, as at the *Washing-*

Partial Rewrite of "Probe of SCCAA Phaseout"

Two city officials were designated by the Topeka City Commission this morning to examine the costs of phasing out a contract with Shawnee County Community Assistance and Action for work for the community development department.

Charles Holt, city auditor, and Craig McLaughlin, acting community development director, were chosen to make the study, so that the commission can act on closing out the program, which it voted to cancel last week.

Two city officials were designated by the Topeka City Commission this morning to examine the costs of phasing out a contract with Shawnee County Community Assistance and Action for work for the community development department.

"I think the phaseout is expensive; I think it contains some costs that are not necessary," Finance Comm. Kenneth L. Elder told the other commissioners this morning.

Larry Wilson, executive director of SCCAA has proposed costs totaling $93,000 for phasing out the program, following last week's cancelation of his contract by the city commission.

Part of the cost is for termination of 25 employes, including such costs as salary and annual leave. His plan would phase them out in stages on March 31, April 15 and April 30.

One of Elder's objections is to the salaries to be paid during that period. He suggested the entire program could be phased out by April 15.

Elder blasted the plan as having "a lot of bologna in it" and said a community impact statement included in the plan is "political noise."

In the end the commission designated Charles Holt, the city auditor, and Craig McLaughlin, the acting community development director, to examine the closeout costs and report back to the city commission.

Source: Topeka Capital-Journal.

---

ton *Star*). This person will then write the story to appear in the newspaper, using the reporter's general outline and facts.

As an example of the rewrite process, reconsider Mike Hall's story about the Topeka City Commission, "Probe of SCCAA Phaseout." It was not rewritten as extensively as it might have been before it appeared in print. The beginning of the story is reproduced along with a possible rewrite. The rewritten portion appears in italics.

The immediate question in the minds of readers after reading Hall's lead is who the officials are. He buried the answer in the seventh paragraph, using a quote in the second paragraph that reads off the lead but does not really illuminate it. Another variation would be to use the names of the two officials in the lead. That they had been selected and what they were selected to do was the news, however, and their names would have made the lead more complicated for readers.

The necessity of including a name in the lead is more certain in the next example. The story "Bullet Pierces House Barely Missing Woman" was a good one, but the suggested rewrite has the advantage that it moves the woman's name, Ruth Schrock, to the lead and compresses the action slightly; it creates more drama and reader interest.

Partial Rewrite of "Bullet Pierces House Barely Missing Woman"

A high-powered rifle bullet smashed into a central Benton County home Wednesday evening, narrowly missing 65-year-old Ruth Schrock.

The bullet, apparently fired from a car passing the house on Highway 99W, went through the living room window, seconds after Mrs. Schrock got up to adjust her television set.

A high-powered rifle bullet smashed into a central Benton County home Wednesday evening, narrowly missing a 65-year-old woman.

The bullet was apparently fired from a car passing the house on Highway 99W, 100 feet from the house, according to Benton County sheriff's deputies.

According to the report, Ruth Schrock, who with her husband, Dave, 82, lives in an aluminum house along Highway 99W, several miles south of Corvallis, rose from her reclining chair at 8:05 p.m. Wednesday to adjust her television set.

Seconds after she walked the three feet to the set, the rifle bullet smashed through the living room window above her chair, crossed the room, went through a picture frame, penetrated a wall into the kitchen above a refrigerator and dropped into a plastic dish.

Source: Corvallis Gazette-Times

**Rewriting
Public-Relations
Press Releases**

Newspapers are deluged daily with stories issued by, and written from the point of view of, such organizations as churches, clubs, companies, and government agencies. These are called *press releases* or *news releases*.

Such releases may need to be treated with circumspection because they sometimes contain exaggerated claims or are "puff pieces" written without substance for no good reason. The danger here, however, is that reporters and editors may disregard even those press releases that have something important to say, because their time has already been wasted on too many occasions by bogus releases from the organization in question.

The case of organizations that issue releases only when they have something significant to say is more straightforward; newspaper people respect their approach and treat their releases as they were originally intended to be treated, as serious items of information that need to be printed in the newspaper.

When properly used, press releases can be a source of valuable information. They provide tips on new developments in an organization. They detail upcoming events the newspaper may want to cover. They bring word of managerial and political appointments, and financial gains and losses.

A typical release on an appointment might read something like this:

Sam J. Randolph, senior vice-president and chief operating officer of Aurora Oil Company, has been named president and chief operating officer of Ludlow Industries, effective January 1.

Mr. Randolph, 38 years old, also was elected a director of the company by its executive committee. He is a graduate of the Harvard Business School and served in the U.S. Navy.

Mr. Randolph succeeds George Hotchkiss who resigned in October.

Ludlow Industries manufactures agricultural equipment, office equipment, and containers.

A typical release dealing with finances might read like this:

Hatcher-Tompkins Company expects a 20 percent to 30 percent increase in second-half earnings from a year earlier, which would bring 1978 earnings to $4.60 to $4.80 a share, according to James D. Mitchell, chairman and chief executive officer.

In 1977, the producer of construction and building materials earned $20.8 million, or $3.22 a share, on sales of $587.4 million. In the first half of this year, the company's earnings more than doubled to $13.7 million, or $2.03 a share, from $6.7 million, or

$1.07 a share a year earlier. First-half sales gained 25 percent to $322.8 million from $256.3 million a year earlier.

Other company-originated releases might deal with plant expansions, mergers, and annual meetings of stockholders.

Nonprofit organizations issue releases that deal with subjects of more general interest. A typical one from Oregon State University (Figure 9.1) reports on a rise in beef prices.

Another staple of an educational institution is the "hometowner," a release that details the activities of students. (See Figure 9.2.) The release goes out only to newspapers in the hometowns of the students. Reporters there must then rewrite it, emphasizing the local person.

Once the newsworthiness of a press release has been determined, the rewriting begins. In general the rewriting techniques are those used for regular stories, but two aspects of press releases require special attention.

Some releases contain "hype," exaggerated claims and superlatives that render a story unbelievable: "first," "only," "best." These and similar words need to be toned down before the release can be used in the newspaper.

Furthermore, few releases contain the whole story. Although good public relations people do not lie, they often submerge the truth if it is distasteful or harmful to the image of their company, omitting unfavorable details from the release. Reporters and editors, on the other hand, should do some research and attempt to get the whole story.

Even when editors and reporters receive good, objective releases, they should try to add more information to them before using them in the newspaper. What information did the writer of the press release forget to include? Is there a local angle to explore?

The releases presented earlier could easily be expanded into complete stories.

The one on the company appointment could deal with what happened to the old president. Did he resign voluntarily? The newspaper could also call the new president and ask about his plans for the company after he takes over his new job.

The release on the company's second-half earnings could be expanded by asking the president about any plans he has for expansion and about his general views on the company's financial position and on the economy as a whole.

The release on rising beef prices could be the springboard to a broader study on the local situation. Have prices gone up? Why? What do butchers, cattlemen, and consumers think about the subject?

Figure 9.1. Press release: Rising beef prices. (Courtesy of the Department of Information, Oregon State University.)

```
From Oregon State University              RISING BEEF PRICES
Department of Information    6/6/78       BLAMED ON HIGHER
Telephone 754-4611                        COSTS, LOWER SUPPLY
```

After two and a half years of relatively low prices, retail beef prices have reached a new record high, gaining 23 percent over the prices enjoyed by consumers in 1977.

The price turnaround comes at a time when the supply of beef is significantly less than it has been in the past two to three years, reports Stephen Marks, Oregon State University Extension agricultural economist.

This decrease in beef supply stems from the forced liquidation of U.S. beef herds from 1974-77 when farmers and ranchers had to cope with drought as well as depressed cattle prices, he explained. "U.S. cattle numbers are at their lowest point in seven years, so fewer cattle are going to slaughter," said Marks.

"Now that the drought is over and grass is plentiful, ranchers are starting to hold back cattle from market in order to take advantage of the available forage and to rebuild their depleted herds," he observed.

Although consumers are feeling the effects in their pocketbooks, beef prices are not much higher than they were in

(more)

BEEF PRICES RISING 2-2-2-2

June, 1975 when consumers boycotted supermarkets, commented Marks.

Choice beef cuts, including all the cuts from a steer carcass, average around $1.70 a pound now compared with $1.61 in June, 1975, the previous record high. During 1977, however, average beef prices dropped to a low of about $1.38.

Ground beef with 30 percent fat costs $1.19 a pound now, and leaner hamburger can cost up to about $1.59 a pound, estimates Mark.

One reason for the high prices is that, with fewer cattle going to packers, the competitive demand has doubled the cost of slaughter cows for packers relative to the prices that prevailed in 1975 when herds were being liquidated. While ranchers are reaping the benefits of such a market now, Marks points out that they have been operating at a loss for the last four years.

In addition, these price rises are not due solely to the decreased supply of beef, said Marks. Increased marketing costs for such things as transportation, labor, packaging, taxes and utilities, have also boosted retail meat prices.

# # # #

Figure 9.2. Press release: Students' achievements. (Courtesy of the Department of Information, Oregon State University.)

```
From Oregon State University                    LOCAL STUDENTS
Oregon State University     5/18/78             WIN SCHOLASTIC
Telephone 754-4611                              HONORS    AT OSU
```

A total of 264 Oregon State University juniors, seniors and graduate students have qualified for memberships in Phi Kappa Phi, national scholastic honor society.

Membership represents highest scholastic achievement at the university.

To qualify, juniors must rank in the upper 5 per cent of their class scholastically. Seniors and graduate students must rank in the upper 10 per cent.

Those who have qualified for membership this year include:

<u>Albany</u>: Richard E. Thomas, junior in engineering; Steven Alan Dupee, senior in agriculture; Richard Charles Wininger, senior in forestry; Neil Kenneth Poulsen, Eric K. Birks, graduate students.

<u>Aloha</u>: Janet Lee Pettey, senior in business.

<u>Baker</u>: Kevin Michael Fleming, senior in business.

<u>Banks</u>: Dennis Randolph Bays, senior in engineering.

<u>Beaverton</u>: John Palen Pontier, junior in engineering; Steven Charles Troseth, graduate student.

These are examples of the ways releases may be rewritten to put the newspaper's stamp on the story. It is pure laziness to put a release into the newspaper in the exact form in which it was received.

Updating

Updating is usually required for wire-service stories. Because reporters for wire services file their news almost as it happens, the wire machines are running constantly, and stories appear on the continuous rolls of paper or perforated tape every minute of every hour of the day.

At some point, most often several hours before deadline, the wire editor or someone in a similar position will assemble the various stories on the same subject. This editor must now combine the stories so that the most complete and most recent information is what appears in the paper.

Why can't the latest story be used and the other ones discarded? Earlier stories often contain information not included in later accounts. The different accounts must therefore be skillfully blended. This is updating.

Updating might also be necessary on a complicated local story that developed over a long period of time. For example, the holding of hostages and a subsequent shoot-out with police would not be over immediately and would have to be followed closely and updated as the events took place. The same would be true of a local disaster whose details, such as the number of dead and injured and the extent of the damage, might not be available all at once but would become known over an extended period of time.

Here are parts of two wire-service-type stories on the same subject, presented as they might come in at different times of the day before deadline. They show how wire stories sometimes arrive at a newspaper piecemeal, first an advance story, then the one that tells what happened.

> *Detroit—The National Association for the Advancement of Colored People (NAACP) is expected to announce today its policy on affirmative-action programs.*
>
> *Attending a three-day meeting of lawyers and affirmative-action officers from government agencies and private companies, Benjamin L. Hooks, NAACP executive director, said the organization plans a major effort to halt what he called "an erosion in civil-rights accomplishments" . . .*
>
> *Detroit—The National Association for the Advancement of Colored People (NAACP) announced today that it would lead a major lobbying effort to impress upon every member of Congress and the Cabinet the importance of continuing affirmative-action programs.*

> *Officials of that organization also said that they would request a meeting with President Carter to ask that he convene a White House conference on affirmative action.*
>
> *The two efforts were part of a "Manifest for Action" presented by the association at the closing of a three-day symposium on the implications of the Supreme Court's Bakke decision.*

The executive director's comments from his earlier press conference were not included in this second dispatch. The first two stories would therefore have to be combined to arrive at the one finally appearing in the newspaper. The later of the two dispatches might be repeated word for word, followed by an additional paragraph derived from the first dispatch:

> *At a press conference earlier in the day, Benjamin L. Hooks, NAACP executive director, said civil-rights accomplishments had eroded in recent years.*

At other times a new development takes place that partially invalidates the original wire story.

> *Cairo—President Anwar el-Sadat is expected to announce today his willingness to continue negotiations with Israel. Sources close to the Egyptian president said he was prepared to go to Jerusalem, if necessary, to advance the cause of peace as he did in a similar dramatic journey last December.*
>
> *President Sadat will speak at a political gathering on the eve of the anniversary of the 1952 officers' revolution that deposed King Farouk, in which Sadat played a leading role under the late Gamal Abdel Nasser.*

After Sadat's appearance at the meeting, however, quite another story emerged:

> *Cairo—President Anwar el-Sadat declared today that Prime Minister Menachem Begin of Israel was the "only obstacle" to peace in the Middle East.*
>
> *Pointing to what he called Begin's "greediness for land," Sadat said his government was ready to give Israel peace, recognition, and security guarantees, but not Arab land or sovereignty over Arab land.*
>
> *President Sadat spoke to a political gathering on the eve . . .*

Although it was superseded, the earlier dispatch contained information that was important to the story. In the story appearing in the newspaper, the second dispatch might be presented unchanged, continuing like this:

The announcement followed rumors that the Egyptian president was going to announce his willingness to make another trip to Jerusalem . . .

Sometimes, the rush of an on-going news event causes wire-service stories to be outdated as soon as they are filed, as in this instance:

Pontiac, Ill.—Rioting prisoners have taken several hostages and set fire to a cellhouse at the Pontiac State Penitentiary. The rioters blocked a second cellhouse, keeping 200 guards and policemen at bay. They were armed with knives and guns.

Then, a dramatic new development took place as described in a later dispatch:

Pontiac, Ill.—Three guards have been killed by about 600 prisoners rioting at the Pontiac State Penitentiary. A spokesman for the Illinois Department of Law Enforcement said the guards had been killed and a number of inmates injured in the disturbance which began earlier today.

The final story, as updated using information from the earlier dispatches, might read like this:

Pontiac, Ill.—About 600 rioting prisoners, armed with knives and guns, killed three guards, set fire to a cellhouse, and took several hostages today at the Pontiac State Penitentiary. The rioters took control of a second cellhouse and kept 200 guards and policemen from entering it.

Summary   Although there is no best way to write a news story, a few general rules of writing help reporters. These involve such matters as simplicity in writing, clarity of presentation, and attention to spelling and style. Rewriting is an important part of the newspaper process. It is done by individual reporters on their own stories and by editors who seek to catch errors in spelling, grammar, and style and improve overall readability and structure. Press releases received from organizations outside the newspaper can be useful if they are evaluated carefully and rewritten. Both wire-service copy and, at times, local stories need to be updated if facts about them come into the newsroom at different times of the day before deadline.

Suggested Exercises

1. Obtain a press release from a local organization and develop a series of questions to augment the information in the release. Ask the questions of the officials of the organization and write a story using the facts gleaned from your interview and from the release.

2. Compare and contrast the original release noted in exercise 1 with the story you wrote after getting more facts. How do they differ? How does the reader benefit?

3. Take a story written earlier in the term and rewrite it to improve it, keeping in mind the general rules of writing noted in this chapter.

4. Select several stories in a newspaper and rewrite them to improve them, using the general rules of writing noted in this chapter. Present them to the class with reasons for your changes.

5. Exchange your story with another person in the class and edit their story. Compare the two versions and tell the class why you made the changes you made.

6. Interview a newspaper editor and a public-relations person about the press release and its value or lack of value. Write a research paper about the results.

"We look for reasons to run . . . things. We run just about every legitimate thing that comes in: meeting notices, club news, weddings, and obituaries."

Dick King, Assistant Managing Editor,
Topeka Capital-Journal

10

Writing Obituaries and Other Service Stories

Obituaries
Weddings and Engagements
Meetings
Births, Birthdays, and Anniversaries

Every day, just off the main news stage, events are taking place that do not necessarily fulfill the definitions of news discussed in Chapter 2. Governments do not fall because of these events, nor does war break out or the stock market go down.

Yet collectively these events affect more people than do those legitimately defined as news.

Every day, just off the main news stage, people die, are born, have birthdays, are married or become engaged; go to meetings, charity bazaars, picnics, and fiftieth-anniversary celebrations. All the people involved in these events are interested in them. The friends and relatives of the people involved want to read about what went on and, perhaps, see themselves referred to by name as having poured punch or having been elected secretary-treasurer. They may also want to cut out the story and paste it into a scrapbook.

Because these kinds of stories affect such large numbers of readers, newspapers run them as a service. The majority of readers will pass them by, at least until their own fathers die, daughters marry, or clubs sponsor a bake sale.

Most newspapers recognize the need to serve readers by including these stories within their pages. Indeed, many weeklies contain little else. Because the stories are short, often dull and without much significance, however, it is difficult to gather material about them and to write them. Reporters and editors alike dread the thought of spending time on them. Yet they must be included.

On a big-city newspaper, the question of running this type of story is seldom discussed. New reporters prepare the material that does appear and look forward to the day when seniority will release them from such a task. On smaller-sized and medium-sized dailies, however, these kinds of stories must be printed, or editors risk alienating large segments of the readership. Few editors resist, and most find a way to make this kind of story palatable and interesting, even if not very newsworthy.

"We look for reasons to run such things," says Dick King, assistant managing editor of the *Topeka Capital-Journal* newspapers. "We run just about every legitimate thing that comes in: meeting notices, club news, weddings, and obituaries."

Tom Jenks, editor of the *Corvallis Gazette-Times,* finds it a problem "to get along with and satisfy sources who can, at times, appear to be excessive in their demands and annoyances. This used to be more of a problem. We're taking better care of things more quickly like requests from clubs and organizations to get things in the paper and give them a photo when they request one. The women's page area was where the problems were. There are few stories we don't use. When we don't use them, it's not a policy action, we might have just lost them."

Obituaries

The obituary is a report of a person's death. It is the easiest community-service story to write, yet probably the type of story reporters dread most. For years on big-city newspapers, the assignment to write "obits" was a journalistic Siberia; staff members were assigned to write them when the news was slow, and they avoided the process whenever possible. This is still the case.

A level above this kind of obituary is that of prominent people. These miniature biographies are written in advance by both wire services and large newspapers, ready to publish when the person in question dies. Sometimes considered ghoulish by novices in journalism, this practice is the only way that national news organizations can be ready with information in time to serve their customers and readers. When they have the time, reporters for these organizations update the obituaries from existing reference material.

The *New York Times* raised the writing of obituaries to a fine art in 1964 when it assigned Alden Whitman as its chief obituary writer. Until his retirement, he interviewed several hundred famous people to gather material for what would later be in their obituaries. The *Times* has continued this practice.

The obituaries that other newspapers publish are seldom so elaborate. They usually take the form of a small news story that goes beyond the scant facts of a death notice from the funeral home. The information for them often comes from morticians. In Topeka and Corvallis, morticians call in with the facts of the dead person's life, and a reporter puts the information into a standard format.

Information supplied by the mortician may be unreliable, however; it needs to be verified by consulting public records and telephone directories or by contacting the dead person's relatives. In Tom Jenks's view: "Morticians can't spell, or the people with whom they deal don't spell. They don't bother to verify names and names of towns. They do things that don't add up—like five brothers with only four names given. We have a formula written in a formula style. You really don't need a special form. A form wouldn't do you any good. We try to do them all like this: 'Thomas S. Jenks, longtime Linn County farmer, et cetera.' I would not trust the undertaker to pick the most important thing. If you have a form, you still have to rewrite it."

Reporters write obituaries in the most straightforward manner possible. Name of person, age, address, place and day of death come in the lead sentence. If funeral arrangements have been set or have already taken place,

Obituaries

Douglas

Ida Douglas, 74, a long-time Corvallis resident, died early this morning in Good Samaritan Hospital. Services will be at 2 p.m. Wednesday in St. Mary's Catholic Church. Burial will be at 2 p.m. Thursday in the Mt. Shasta Cemetery, Mt. Shasta, Calif. McHenry Funeral Home has charge of arrangements.

Bittes

ALBANY—Jane Adeline Bittes, 55, of 7803 Independence Highway, died Sunday in the Albany General Hospital following a long illness.

She was born Feb. 21, 1922, in Worden, Ill. On Feb. 1, 1947, she was married to Henry Bittes, who survives. The couple moved to Corvallis in 1959 and the next year to their home on Independence Highway. For seven years, Mrs. Bittes worked in the business office at Good Samaritan Hospital in Corvallis.

Mrs. Bittes was a member of the Shepherd of the Valley Lutheran Church in Corvallis.

Besides her widower, Henry, she is survived by her children, Charles of St. Louis, Mo., and Sue Brandon of Bakersville, Calif.; brothers, James Welch of Mt. Vernon, Ill., and Dale Welch of Winnemucca, Nev.; sisters, Shirley McGinley of Scottsdale, Ariz., and Doris Eilerts of Mt. Vernon, Ill.; and two grandchildren.

Viewing hours will be until 9 p.m. tonight and from 9 a.m. until noon on Wednesday in the AAsum Funeral Home, Albany.

Services will be at 2 p.m. Wednesday in the Shepherd of the Valley Lutheran Church, Corvallis, with burial to follow in the Zion Lutheran Cemetery.

The family suggests remembrances to the Shepherd of the Valley memorial fund.

Grace

Graveside services for Otha M. (Sam) Grace, 73, were to be this afternoon in Mt. Union Cemetery.

Mr. Grace died Saturday in Corvallis Manor.

He was born Oct. 6, 1903, in Martinville, Mo. On June 29, 1930, he was married and his widow, Edna, survives. The family moved to Benton County in 1940 and Mr. Grace was employed in the lumber industry.

Besides his widow, Mr. Grace is survived by one daughter, Mrs. Pattey Isaacson of Olympia, Wash.; a sister, Mrs. Oma Leigh of Corvallis; and two grandchildren.

McHenry Funeral Home had charge of arrangements.

Source: Corvallis Gazette-Times.

---

that information should come in another sentence of the lead, including time, place, and minister officiating at the funeral. If services are pending, that fact can go in the final paragraph.

Next should come details of the person's life, beginning with the month, day, and year of birth and including names of parents, date of wedding and name of spouse, and then a brief account of the dead person's education, occupational history, and places lived.

The names of surviving family members should be included next. If the spouse has died, the year of death should be noted in a sentence before this paragraph. Only the names of spouses, children, parents, and brothers and sisters should be used.

A final paragraph can be added if the family has requested that no flowers be sent and has asked for charitable contributions instead. Reporters can use more varied approaches, of course, but this one accomplishes the purpose quickly and easily.

Weddings and Engagements

Newspapers have been so flooded with announcements of weddings and engagements in recent years that many have had to set limits to the amount of space allotted such material. The easiest way to handle this torrent is the most impersonal way; brides and their mothers are asked to fill out a form like the one reproduced from the *Gazette-Times* (Figure 10.1), which asks only for standard information. Thus, the bride-to-be may go to the newspaper office expecting to be interviewed about the most important day in her and her fiancé's life, only to be handed a form by a bored receptionist who does not rate her story very high on the newsworthiness scale.

A few large newspapers have attempted to go beyond this bare-bones approach by writing engagement and wedding stories in the style of a feature story, including details of the couple's romance and the wedding ceremony itself. Most, however, use only the information supplied on the engagement or wedding form, writing it up in a standard format, accompanied by a picture if space permits.

The *Gazette-Times* runs its wedding and engagement stories on Saturdays, all in about half of a page. Weeklies tend to allot more space; big-city dailies allot less, usually limiting the choice of young couples to those from socially prominent families.

The stories written from the standardized information form follow a similar arrangement. The lead includes information on the bride: her name, address, and parents; the name of the groom; and the date and place of the wedding. A variation of this approach uses other information in the lead to relieve the repetitiveness of this type of story.

The next paragraph describes the bride's dress and the flowers she carried. The names of her maid of honor and bridesmaids come next, together with details of their dresses and flowers. If the wedding party included other attendants—such as ring bearers or flower girls—their names appear next. Any unusual aspects—if it was a military wedding, if it had unique flower displays, elaborate decorations—are also detailed.

The names of the best man and ushers appear next, as does a brief account of the reception, including details of the dresses of the mothers of

Figure 10.1. Wedding form. (Courtesy of the Corvallis Gazette-Times.)

Corvallis Gazette-Times
Wedding Form

CORVALLIS GAZETTE-TIMES
PHONE 753-2641

IMPORTANT DEADLINE INFORMATION:

A complete wedding information form and photograph of the bride and groom must be received by the Gazette-Times within 12 days after the ceremony. Because most weddings are on Saturdays, this means that the form and the photograph must be returned to the paper by 5 p.m. the second Thursday following the Saturday ceremony. **INFORMATION PROVIDED AFTER THAT TIME WILL NOT BE PUBLISHED.** If for any reason the couple is unable to select a wedding photograph to meet that deadline, arrangements should be made for a friend or relative to make the selection. If a photo cannot be selected to meet the deadline, the paper will run just the wedding story provided it is submitted on time. **IN NO CASE WILL A WEDDING STORY BE RUN THAT DOES NOT MEET THE DEADLINE.** To avoid dissappointment, please observe the deadline.

The Gazette-Times extends its best wishes for your wedding and requests your cooperation in preparing the story of your wedding. Please complete this form by typing or by printing neatly in ink.

IMPORTANT: Please read the following guidelines before filling out this form:

1. When listing name of a person, include relationship to bride or bridegroom and address.
2. Refer to a married woman as Mrs. Mary Jones or Mrs. John Jones.
3. Do include the name of a deceased parent in the parents' names; i.e., the late John Jones.
4. Make sure that all names are spelled correctly.

BRIDE'S NAME _____

ADDRESS _____

PARENTS' NAMES _____

ADDRESS _____

BRIDEGROOM'S NAME _____

ADDRESS _____

PARENTS' NAMES _____

ADDRESS _____

Usinger-Jackimiec

Mr. and Mrs. Scott D. Usinger are at home in Portland following their wedding April 1 in the St. Elizabeth Church. The Rev. Joseph Huffman performed the afternoon double-ring ceremony.

The former Christine Ann Jackimiec wore a white Qiana gown with a full-length train and a fingertip veil held by a Camelot headpiece.

Mrs. Steve Peters was matron of honor. Mrs. Brian Kelly, the bridegroom's sister, Jody Fast, Susan Wright and Janine McLeod were bridesmaids.

Steve Peters was best man. Ushers were Dr. Brian Kelly, brother-in-law of the bridegroom, Greg Geelan, Floyd Freck and Randy McLeod.

Robbie Jackimiec, brother of the bride, provided organ music. Randy Westfall, guitarist, sang "The Wedding Song." A reception was held at Hillvilla Restaurant. The couple honeymooned in Hawaii.

The bride, daughter of Mr. and Mrs. John Jackimiec, Philomath, was graduated from the University of Oregon School of Dentistry. She is employed by dentists in Oswego, Milwaukie and Portland.

Usinger, son of Mr. and Mrs. Alexander Usinger, The Dalles, was graduated from Oregon State University and is employed by Contractors Construction Supply, Tigard.

Source: Corvallis Gazette-Times.

---

the bride and groom. Occasionally, even the names of those who served punch and cake are added here.

This information is followed by details of the bride's and groom's lives, their educational backgrounds and current jobs. The wedding story ends with the location of the honeymoon and the address of the couple upon their return. If the names of the groom's parents have not been given before this point, they can be added.

The engagement story is shorter and usually does not include a picture. It gives details of the bride-to-be, her parents, and the groom, in much the same way as the wedding story, but mentions only the date, time, and place of the wedding and any plans for bridal showers.

Meetings

Notices of the activities of local clubs and organizations can inundate a newspaper. An editor recognizes that although their activities are not really news in the classic sense, such organizations do constitute a segment of the paper's readership and should be served in the best possible way.

These readers can also become the most vocal of a newspaper's critics if they think their needs are not being taken care of. "Where I do feel pressure," says Rod Deckert, *Gazette-Times* city editor, "and where people work on me and suggest that a story be done and not be done is invariably with local people." His editor, Jenks, adds that "some of those folks wouldn't be satisfied if we gave them the whole newspaper."

Jenks has eased some of this kind of criticism by instituting a new policy of handling what he calls "chicken dinner" news, the accounts of local clubs and organizations that are of narrow interest. People who want to have the newspaper run such information fill out an information blank giving the name of the organization; the time, date, and place of the meeting or event; the program, and whether the meeting is open to the public. (See Figure 10.2.)

Reporters compile these items into a calendar of events that is printed as a full page on Saturday (Figure 10.3) and in a smaller amount of space during the week. Separated into categories ranging from organizations and government to sports and entertainment, the items include the name of the organization, the time and place of the meeting, and general details of what

Figure 10.2 Information blank for newspaper's "calendar" page. (*Courtesy of the* Corvallis Gazette-Times.)

CORVALLIS GAZETTE-TIMES

CALENDAR

Name of Club or organization _____

Time, date and place of meeting or event _____

Program _____

Members only ☐   Open to the public ☐

Whom may we call for additional information?

Name _____   Phone _____

Return to Calendar, Corvallis Gazette-Times, 600 S.W. Jefferson, Corvallis, Ore. 97330

Corvallis Gazette-Times

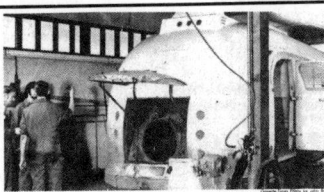

Figure 10.3 Public-service page: *Calendar of the week's local events.* (*Courtesy of the* Corvallis Gazette-Times.)

> ## Wednesday
>
> *Organizations*
>
> Demoforum, noon, Big O Restaurant, Cliff Trow and Robert Marx, Democratic candidates for the State Senate District No. 18, will speak. Buffet lunch $2.75 or $1 cover charge for coffee. Call Karen Nibler, 2750 S.W. DeArmond Drive, or Barbara Boucot, 2850 S.W. Fairmont Drive, for reservations.
>
> Kiwanis Club of Corvallis, noon, The Towne House Restaurant. Members and their guests only.
>
> Women Studies—OSU, 2:30 p.m., Center for Women Studies, Dr. Solly Dreman, "Israeli and American Sex Stereotypes."

Source: Corvallis Gazette-Times.

is to take place. (A typical format is shown for a Wednesday schedule of events.) Information about whether the meeting is open to the public or for members only is put in as well. If a speaker will appear, that information is noted, along with the price of admission if applicable. Items about government agencies are longer because they list the agenda to be considered.

After the meeting has taken place, a follow-up story might appear if anything newsworthy happened, such as the appearance of an interesting speaker. If the speaker was notable enough, a reporter from the newspaper might have been assigned to cover the appearance as a news event.

"In our calendar, we run everything open to the public," says Jenks. "If we did otherwise, we'd be serving as a newsletter. We will run a photo for any fund-raising event to help drum up a crowd and run an advance story to draw a crowd."

This approach serves readers but also avoids having to run hundreds of separate stories that are difficult to lay out and easily overlooked by readers.

Births, Birthdays, and Anniversaries

Unless an "important" baby is involved—the child of a president or a king, perhaps—announcements of births seldom rate more than a brief notice. Such accounts include the names of parents, their address, the weight and sex of the baby, the name of the baby, and the time and date of birth. They are compiled from official records.

Birthdays are most newsworthy when the person has reached a milestone in life, 100 being the age that usually draws special attention. The story that results is really a feature story because it includes an interview with the person about what it is like to reach such an advanced age.

"Pioneers' Daughter to Be 100," from the *Corvallis Gazette-Times,* is a good example. Because the woman was a longtime resident of the area, the "pioneer" theme works well. Her comments were interesting, and quotations are interwoven with the account of her life.

In anniversary stories, fifty is the magic number to merit coverage. In such items, the details of the couple's life together and the day, time, and place for the celebration are included. These stories, too, can sometimes make good feature stories.

Pioneers' Daughter to Be 100

*By John Atkins and Janine O'Neill
of the Gazette-Times*

On Jan. 30, 1932, Cecil Maud Taylor Rennie pasted a "Recipe for Old Age" into a yearbook full of recipes for more mundane dishes.

Mrs. Rennie, who no longer remembers why she cut it out, must have followed it, anyway, because Friday will be her 100th birthday. Friends and relatives will observe the occasion with a party at her residence in the Corvallis Care Center.

"I think I'm the only one of the Callaway-Taylor family that has lived to be anywhere near that age, and I've had every disease going," says Mrs. Rennie from her bed, where she spends much of her day reading the Gazette-Times front to back—no particular favorite part—with the aid of a magnifying glass. Among other things, she had pneumonia when she was one year old, was in a wheelchair while she recovered from typhoid fever and was "in bed sometimes for six months," not to mention the time she fell off a ladder while hanging curtains and ended her piano-playing days forever.

Mrs. Rennie's ancestors may not have been long-lived, but they were illustrious.

Her maternal great-grandfather, Samuel Cecil, for whom she was named, was descended from Lord Cecil of England and was himself a native of England.

Mrs. Rennie's parents were James C. Taylor and Lillian Callaway Taylor. Mrs. Taylor crossed the plains by wagon train in 1864.

When she was growing up, Mrs. Rennie says, Corvallis' population wasn't over 1,500.

"The Averys were the oldest people in town," she says, referring to the founders of Corvallis. "I knew them personally. I knew everybody personally.

"The people were close, too, just like one family."

It was, although it's difficult to believe so much has changed in one person's lifetime, an era before home electricity, telephones or telegraph service, an era of daily steam boat runs to Portland and a ferry across the Willamette River where the Van Buren Street bridge now crosses.

Mrs. Rennie, whose family home was across from where the Whiteside Theater stands, remembers standing on Sixth and Jefferson in 1881 and watching the golden spike driving ceremony for the coming of

(continued)

Source: Corvallis Gazette-Times.

the railroad. She was four years old at the time.

Later, as she grew up, she remembers riding horses and going to Portland to shop and dine at the Portland Hotel. "It was nice," she says of the hotel. "It would be nice today but it was torn down."

When she was 16, after two years of study at "the college on the hill," Mrs. Rennie married Alexander "Alex" Rennie, who was to serve in the Oregon House of Representatives five sessions with his wife as his secretary.

The elopement was written up in the newspaper in the language of the day: "It was not a conventional affair, in that the parents of the bride were not aware that the expected event was to happen so soon; but for all that they extended the popular couple a warm welcome on the latter's arrival in town early Saturday morning. Both bride and groom have plenty of friends who hope that they may be spared a superabundance of the storms and squalls sometimes incident to wedded life."

Apparently they were: The marriage lasted 48 years until Rennie's death.

His widow, who says she eloped because she "didn't like algebra and that kind of thing," says she thinks women today need to be educated equally with men. Still, she remains a strong supporter of marriage and says the best thing she knows is to "find somebody you love and make a home."

Despite the old age recipe in her yearbook, Mrs. Rennie says emphatically that she never expected to be 100, herself.

"And I'm well, you know," she says. "There's nothing the matter wrong with me, except old age. I still can think and read, which is good. Lots of old people sit and do nothing."

And, despite her feeling that people were closer when she was a girl, she says she thinks the world has improved since then.

Even young people?

"All the ones I know are doing nicely," she says.

Summary

Every day events are taking place that do not necessarily fulfill the standard definitions of news—births, deaths, marriages, engagements, meetings, anniversaries, and many other, often very personal events. Such events can be mundane to the readership as a whole, and frustrating for the reporter to cover. But because every reader is at some time affected by such events, they are reported as a public service. They reach the printed page as small news stories and are written in the manner of news stories, with the most important element first. They generally have their own fairly rigid format, especially obituaries and reports of engagements, weddings, meetings, and births; this is the easiest way to handle such stories, but it can also be the most impersonal. Birthdays and anniversaries become newsworthy when a milestone in life has been reached (such as a 100th birthday) and can make interesting feature stories.

Suggested Exercises

1. Clip several obituaries from the local newspaper and analyze them. Do they contain all the information noted in this chapter? Rewrite them to make them more readable, explaining why you made the changes you did.

2. Read and analyze a famous person's obituary in the *New York Times* or in a wire-service story. Analyze it for class, noting the writing style used and the kinds of information included.

3. Clip several wedding stories from the local newspaper and analyze them. Do they contain all the information noted in this chapter? Rewrite them, explaining why you made the changes you did.

4. Interview the presidents of several clubs on campus. Obtain the material needed to write several meeting announcements; then attend the meetings themselves and write brief stories on them.

"The deadliest way to write a speech story is to say, 'Cows are giving less milk this week because of the drought, says so and so.' Speeches are one of those exceptions to the hard-news rules of not backing into a lead. The news most often is what the speaker said, not who he is, or where, or when. The best way is to back into the where, how, what, who, when. *For example, on the example above, I'd write, 'The Oregon dairy industry is worried about the cost of milk this summer. Consumers may feel the pinch.' I put the attribution at the point where it fits."*

John Atkins, Reporter,
Corvallis Gazette-Times

11

Beyond News: Writing Speech Stories

Speech Stories: Routine and Frequent
Covering the Speech Story
Writing the Story

Speeches are given every day in all kinds of settings—at schools, universities, at club meetings, before government bodies. Although most of them are of less than oratorical quality, speeches are important in any consideration of beginning journalism because there are so many of them. New reporters, both those on campus newspapers and those entering full-time reporting for the first time, are often assigned to cover speeches.

They are natural news stories—planned, predictable, and readily available to the assignment editor. If the newspaper serves a college town, the people giving the speeches may be well known and what they say interesting.

Even if the speakers are not notable, another reason for the new reporter to cover speeches is the opportunity they offer to witness an event without having to interview anyone, though the reporter may find it helpful to ask a few questions, too, before or after the speech. Listening to a speech also offers good experience in rapid note-taking, a skill that will help later in personal interviews and in dealing with many subjects in a single story.

Speech Stories: Routine and Frequent

Because speech stories are so common, this chapter will detail the proper reporting and writing of them in some detail: first by presenting several good speech stories along with comments by the reporters who wrote them; secondly, by including specific rules for writing speech stories.

"I try to cover a variety of different things in a speech story," says George Wisner, a reporter for the *Corvallis Gazette-Times*. "I go in for two principal elements: the speaker and the people who listen. I keep my eyes open and get the reaction of both parties. At times I've recorded what the speaker says, then leaned over to others sitting near me and asked what was being said. Sometimes you get a startling reaction."

Wisner followed this approach in an assignment he had to do a story on the appearance of Alex Haley on the Oregon State University campus. Because of the author's tight schedule, Wisner guessed he would not be able to interview him personally. So, he did the next best thing: he covered an informal talk Haley made at the campus Black Cultural Center before giving his main speech later the same night.

As soon as the reporter arrived at the center, an old house on the edge of campus, he knew his hunch had been right. There would be no time for a one-to-one interview. He sat back and heard what Haley had to say.

"I listened to the people as they were reacting to him," recalls Wisner. "I decided that was my role here. When you go in, you make that decision." The reporter therefore began to react like a member of the audience; that is, as an anonymous member of the audience he could ask more pointed questions than might be asked by a reporter in an interview. "I had to ask

Black Achievement Is Overlooked, Says Haley

By George Wisner
of the Gazette-Times

The story begins with a summary of Haley's main theme, and an identification of where he spoke, when he spoke, and to whom he spoke.

The civil rights movement in America today is not dead, Alex Haley, author of the bestseller "Roots," told a standing-room-only crowd at Oregon State University's Black Cultural Center Wednesday afternoon. It has just changed its shape in the last 15 years.

The next paragraph continues the summary of his theme.

Early black leaders in the civil rights movement opened the educational doors for blacks and the most important thing the black youth of today can do to support their efforts, and the movement, is to choose their careers early and strive for excellence so that they may become future leaders.

The third paragraph outlines the range of topics discussed by Haley.

Haley talked with the crowd for about an hour at the center on topics ranging from civil rights to his status as a folk hero before speaking at OSU's Gill Coliseum later in the evening. Earlier in the day the 55-year-old Pulitzer Prize winner spoke at Eastern Washington State College.

The fourth paragraph begins to use description like that normally used in a feature story: the chair Haley sat on and the place at which he was speaking. The story also brought in his answers to questions. This paragraph also uses a direct quote for the first time, unusually late; quotations are regularly in or near the lead.

Seated on a metal folding chair in the informal living room setting of the cultural center at 2320 NW Monroe, Haley responded to a question about the vitality of the civil rights movement and said that 15 years ago "there were two major civil rights leaders—Malcolm X (whose life story Haley wrote) and Martin Luther King." The big push at that time was to open college and university doors to blacks, get them educated and into influential positions. The movement succeeded.

(continued)

By the sixth paragraph, the reporter is describing the way Haley talks ("a slow, deep voice").

The reporter continues by alternately quoting and paraphrasing the talk.

Midway through the story, the reporter stops the flow of the speech to note the reaction of the audience, that of two members in particular.

The reporter continues: what Haley said about the lawsuit involving his book.

Now there are black mayors in many of America's large and small cities and there is an increasing number of black doctors and other professionals coming from prestigious universities, Haley told the predominantly black audience that crowded around him.

Speaking in a slow, deep voice he said "Instead of two leaders, we have leaders throughout the country . . . and the most important thing that they (the young people) need to do now is decide as early as possible what they want to get into (for careers) and strive for excellence in it."

More attention should be given (by the media) to the positive work being done by blacks, Haley said.

There are about 10 or 12 outstanding black students at Harvard, Haley said, "and I'm so happy that I could split." But they are drawing far less publicity for their academic accomplishments than they might if they got into trouble with the law.

Those listening seemed pleased with what they heard.

"I'm mesmerized by the man," said Sam Pierce, a pre-med student at OSU. "I believe it is important for us to use what we have."

Mevelyn O'Ray, an accounting student from Portland, said "I'm impressed with him." She, too, believed that more publicity should be given to the positive rather than the negative.

During his talk, Haley denied that he copied any portions of his novel from a 1966 novel called "Jubilee" as alleged by that author, Margaret Walker, in a lawsuit. Restating a comment he gave to the media in April, Haley said: "It took me 12 years to finish this book and if I were copying I'd type faster than that."

He added, however, that he met the book's author several years ago and that he considers her a hard worker. "I respected her then and I respect her now . . . I am a reluctant adversary," he said. "The only thing I will stand on is that her accusation is not true."

It is not uncommon, Haley said, for such charges to surface when a novel such as his becomes a big seller. It happened with "Gone With the Wind" and to a more limited extent with "Jaws."

Then: what Haley said about his status as a folk hero.

Answering a question about how he copes with his status as a folk hero, Haley said that it is a role he accepts reluctantly.

"I'm really not so much a folk hero as I am a writer," said Haley, "and it has become difficult to find time to work . . . I haven't written a sentence" since "Roots" was finished.

"I travel too much and sleep too little," said Haley. "But I'm not complaining."

The story ends with more Haley quotes, about the difficulty of being a famous writer.

Between now and Christmas he has 802 requests to appear in places throughout the country.

But he plans to return to his typewriter soon. Possibly in July he will begin work on a story about his search for "Roots."

Source: Corvallis Gazette-Times.

---

questions of him because there wasn't time to have a personal interview. I generally don't do this, unless it's a type of thing I can't get at. But I needed to ask him about the lawsuit he's involved in."

Haley answered the questions and Wisner got the feeling of the audience for his story, which read more like a feature than the record of a talk. Later that night another reporter covered the speech itself.

With his approach to writing "Black Achievement Is Overlooked, Says Haley" Wisner gives readers a behind-the-scenes look at Haley not talking about things he talks about in his big speech. Also, the reporter has perhaps captured a more relaxed Haley because he has been speaking before a largely black audience.

The story of the major speech, "Ancestors Watching, Says 'Roots' Author," is written with a more conventional approach. The reporter backed into the lead with a quote from a Haley ancestor. He saves the identification until the fourth paragraph. His use of direct quotes also begins in the next paragraph.

From here on, the reporter follows the speech chronologically using both direct quote and paraphrase. The reporter sticks to the theme of "remembering your roots" introduced in the lead and used as a main approach by Haley. He also includes details of the author's life and how he got into writing.

Ancestors Watching, Says 'Roots' Author

*By Robert Goldstein
for the Gazette-Times*

"They sittin' up there watchin' you to see what you gonna do," Cousin Georgia once remarked to Alex Haley about his ancestors.

What he did was write a best-selling novel about them called "Roots," and he hopes they're pleased.

He certainly is. The book has now sold more than 1½ million copies and been translated in 22 languages. It was the basis of an acclaimed and highly popular television mini-series.

Haley's nine years of genealogical research and three years of writing produced more than merely a recounting of one family's heritage, he told about 2,500 listeners in OSU's Gill Coliseum Wednesday night.

"Roots is symbolically the saga of a whole people. If you tell the story of one family, you tell the story of all (black) families," he said.

Haley said he first learned of his family's past from stories he heard in his early childhood from his grandmother and older sisters.

"I remember them talking," he recalled. "I wasn't quite sure what a slave was then."

Like biblical parables he learned in Sunday school, Haley had memorized most of the stories by the time he reached grade school.

But the idea of committing those stories to writing did not enter Haley's mind until he visited the National Archives in Washington D.C. to look up the names of deceased relatives in old census reports.

Haley said he noticed that people at the archives were intent in their studies.

"These people are here to try and find out who they are," he remembers saying to himself.

He began poring over microfilm documents. After about an hour's search he located the name of a long-lost relative—Tom Murray.

"I didn't really know it at the time, but I had just had my first bite from the genealogy bug, from which there is no cure."

Haley pursued his search, but soon ran into a dead end. Through a relative he managed finally to locate "Cousin Georgia," the last surviving storyteller of Haley's youth.

She was living in Kansas City, Kan., so that's where Haley went.

"She told me the whole story, lock, stock and barrel," he said.

"Cousin Georgia" died when Haley was in Gambia, Africa, where her stories had led him. Haley said he later discovered that Georgia died within an hour of his setting foot in the African village where he uncovered the final link of his family's past.

"She was the last survivor of the line," Haley said. "It was as if it was Cousin Georgia's job to be with me . . . to help me find the way to that village."

Haley said the writing of "Roots" has drawn attention to the rich "heritage resource" families possess in their eldest members.

He said it's too bad today's children are "growing up removed from their grandparents."

"Parents," he said, "are guilty of allowing their children to grow up rootless."

Families that take pride in their heritage are families that care for themselves, he said. And "that can literally change the face of a society."

In addition to "Roots," Haley is the author of "The Autobiography of Malcolm X," a book he created from tape-recorded interviews with the black nationalist leader who was murdered in New York City in 1965. The book has sold 5½ million copies.

Haley's writing career began while he was serving a stint in the Coast Guard during World War II.

He said the long intervals at sea were boring so he would take out his typewriter and compose letters.

"I just got in the habit of taking out my typewriter and writing letters to old friends, schoolmates . . . anyone. Things really got rolling" after awhile, he remembered.

Haley's friends began noticing his talents, and soon enlisted his help in writing letters to girls they met on liberty.

"For the rest of the war I wrote love letters," he said.

Haley stayed in the service until 1959.

One day he tried copying from a book just to get the feel of what professional writing was like. He wrote seven days a week for eight years before his first freelance article was published, he said.

"It isn't talent," said Haley about his craft, "one must develop an extraordinary amount of self-discipline and one must do more work than any parent or teacher."

He urged students in the audience to become family historians to stem what he called the increasing "rootslessness," in the United States.

"We don't want to lose our heritage and the ties that bind generations together," he said. College-age people should take the lead in organizing family reunions, interviewing elderly family members for valuable information and searching old trunks that serve as family archives.

"Grandparents sprinkle stardust in the lives of children," he said. "They can do some things for boys and girls that others can't."

Source: Corvallis Gazette-Times.

Two stories by reporter John Marshall are further examples of speech stories. For the story on a speech by former evangelist Marjoe Gortner, Marshall opens with a description of the film shown during the presentation.

This goes on for three paragraphs before the reporter makes a transition to the present—"Marjoe is a minister no longer. Now 31, he is an aspiring actor . . ."

For the rest of the speech, Marshall uses a combination of direct quote and paraphrase and personal description. The only reference to the story's reporting speech comes in the fourth, transition paragraph.

Evangelists Con Men Too, Says Former Minister

*By John Marshall
of the Gazette-Times*

The image flickered onto the screen—a curly haired moppet, in a white suit with red carnation, standing in between two adults as he performs their marriage ceremony. His squeaky child's voice intones the familiar words with plodding, memorized delivery.

But what's most noticeable about this shot from the 1972 documentary about evangelist Marjoe Gortner is not little Marjoe. The eye soon focuses on the young couple being married.

They stare stiffly ahead and not even a hint of a smile crosses their faces. It's obvious they see nothing the least bit peculiar about being married by a 4-year-old. Afterall, the child is a minister.

Marjoe is a minister no longer. Now 31, he is an aspiring actor in disaster movies and TV dramas. But ministry and evangelism was his topic last night when Marjoe spoke at Oregon State University as part of the Big CONference being held this week.

Although his message at OSU still was delivered with an evangelist's zeal—full of waving hand motions and frenzied verbal sprints—what he said was far different from what he used to say in packed tents with dirt floors.

"From the beginning, I never really believed what I was saying," Marjoe said. "The only vision I ever had was my mother saying, 'You will learn that sermon tomorrow!'"

A slim, Hollywood handsome figure in jeans and plaid shirt, Marjoe had an overflow crowd of 800 in Milam Auditorium eating his words like candy. He was glib, funny, cynical and sometimes raunchy—and all his disdain was focused on the "con" of evangelism as he and others practice it.

"At a revival, what those people in the audience want is a show, an entertainment," he said. "I was just giving them what they wanted to hear. And I'd work the audience just like an actor does."

In the documentary which was shown before Marjoe began his talk, his preaching style showed a distinct debt to the mad prancing of Mick Jagger, the lead singer of the Rolling Stones. And Marjoe emphasized in his talk that, yes, he used to copy stage techniques of rock performers like Jagger.

But although he admitted that he was performing for profit as an evangelist, Marjoe was less than harsh on the people in the audience who used to take his words as gospel.

"Everybody's got to get off on something—that's the rule of life," he said. "Those women you saw rolling in the aisles in the film were in a state of ecstasy. If Bob Dylan were up there, they'd boo. But in a religious meeting, they can get up and have an orgasm right in front of all the people."

Running his hands casually through his curly hair, Marjoe continued, "Those women may work all week in a Delco factory. But when they're on that stage, they're the star. I was doing them a service."

That some people would seemed to be "cured" by his preaching was only evidence that many people's ailments are mainly in their minds, Marjoe added. He cited the example of a time when a boy who'd been blinded in an auto accident was brought to him.

"I said to my mother who was behind me, 'What do I do now?' She said, 'Pray.' So I put my hands on the boy and he could see. I was shocked. It turned out that his eyes had not actually been injured in the accident; he was suffering from traumatic blindness.

"That he could see again was a very legitimate miracle. But I didn't do it. It was his believing that did it."

In a question and answer session, Marjoe was asked if other famous evangelists are con men.

His response was instantaneous: "Yes—famous evangelists are con men. Billy Graham may be very sincere and he believes in what he says—but so did Hitler, man.

"A lot of people believe what they do is right."

Source: Corvallis Gazette-Times.

Marshall's lead for the story on a speech by novelist John Barth could almost be used in a feature ("His eyes light up, his face turns ruddy and out of his mouth come marvelous and unexpected words at quick pace"). The reporter saves the transition and the identification of the speech as a speech until the third paragraph.

From here until the end, the story uses many direct quotes and observations. Marshall has let the story tell itself and the speaker speak for himself.

Novelist John Barth Describes the Con Men of Literature, Myth

By John Marshall
of the Gazette-Times

His eyes light up, his face turns ruddy and out of his mouth come marvelous and unexpected words at quick pace.

And John Barth, the novelist, is such a charming conversationalist that it doesn't really matter all that much if the words make little sense, as they sometimes do. For he is a bonafide wordsmith crafting the beauties and subtleties of language.

Barth gave evidence of this during a noon talk Wednesday at the Corvallis Public Library—part of the Big CONference being held this week at Oregon State University.

A measure of Barth's verbal magic was that he captivated the crowd of over 200 with what, in less witty presentation, would have given a class of college students an instant trip to napland.

Barth's topic was the Shape Shifter in fiction—an illusive figure who serves first as a foil, then as an aide to the wandering hero in mythology. The Shape Shifter is, in effect, a changeable con man and Barth said he first became aware of the figure after some critics had pointed out just such a figure in "The Sot Weed Factor," one of his own works.

"Since this was something I wasn't even aware of, I thought this was clear proof that I was a genius," Barth laughed. "I thought it showed that the muse was speaking directly through me."

Barth—a thin, jovial man in a tan suit—then turned to a blackboard behind him, drew a circle and then took his listeners on this life journey of a mythological wandering hero:

"He's born to a virgin and is reportedly the son of a god. Early on, an attempt is made on his life—usually by a paternal grandfather or an uncle (a word of warning to you here)—but he escapes.

"At puberty, he is summoned to adventure and sets out—usually westward, as the sun goes down in the evening—toward the threshold of adventure. He meets a magic man and goes out of the daylight realm into a shadowy realm filled with fluid forms. As he continues his descent, he undergoes one of a series of ordeals.

"Among his adversaries is the Shape Shifter—usually appearing as an adversary, but potentially helpful (as was Proteus). The hero tries to get ahold of the Shape Shifter until the hero undergoes a transformation and goes to the Bottom of the World, where he has a sacred marriage and starts his ascension.

"He goes through a metamorphosis and may have to elude pursuers. He is much changed by his adventures.

"He enters his period of reign—armed by his experiences, he usually gives laws or builds cities. But it usually doesn't work—the city is built but doesn't last, for example. He is exiled, goes lonely again and his death is as mysterious as his birth. Afterwards, apostles misinterpret his message."

The point of his long ramble, Barth said, was that the mythological wandering hero's journey "actually corresponds to the biological rite of passage we all go through."

And Barth also said that the Shape Shifter—the elusive adversary, turned guide—had particular appeal to him because he is "a projection of what the writer himself does for his readers."

Barth paused at the thought for the briefest of seconds, then added, "This is probably the longest telegraphed punch of this conference. But the Shape Shifter is also a metaphor which says that we are not one person in our own lives—that we too go through changes as we race to the grave."

He continued, "That's one of the reasons writers are drawn to this figure. Among my motives in writing is the wish to deal with the horrifying fact that I am but one person.

"If I couldn't project myself into characters' lives, I'd go bananas."

Source: Corvallis Gazette-Times.

Covering the Speech Story

Research

Secondary source material can be useful in advance of a speech. Before going to cover a speech, reporters should try to find out information about the speaker (title, job, background, recent accomplishments, controversial aspects) and read pertinent books, articles, or other material that will enable them to evaluate the speech intelligently. This is particularly true if the speech is on a technical subject. Background information is also important when the speaker is controversial and newsworthy; reporters without a thorough understanding of the controversy would miss an important element of the story.

Note-taking

Note-taking is difficult; reporters should try to relax and enjoy it. Covering a speech the first few times is a hard job. A reporter must listen to what the speaker is saying while remembering what they have just said and writing it down. In the meantime, the speaker has gone on to something else. There are always places to catch up, however: pauses to breathe, to drink water, and to enjoy applause. Also, there may be things that can be left out. As reporters take notes, they should try to write down whole sentences to avoid the horror of being compelled to dot their paragraphs with fragmentary quotations, a phrase here, a phrase there.

Reporters should not rely on advanced texts of speeches. Speakers seldom have them, unless they are political figures and government officials. If such a text is available, reporters must follow it closely for places in which the speaker departs from it. When Lyndon Johnson announced that he would not seek reelection as president in 1968, for example, he tacked that announcement onto a speech about Vietnam. Reporters who had gone home after filing a story based on the advanced text would have missed the bigger news.

Tape-recording

Tape recorders can be useful, but they can also be a problem. It is wonderful to have everything down on tape. Then it is no problem to get full quotes and correct quotes for the story. The speaker can't deny having said what he or she is quoted as saying. Speakers seldom object to being taped; most of them accept the idea if they have spoken before large groups for any length of time.

But there are problems associated with the use of tape recorders. Anyone using a machine should be sure that it is in proper working order. Otherwise, there on the rim of the stage at the speaker's feet, the tape recorder will get a strange buzz and will have to be repaired in front of 500 people.

Also, there is a time problem associated with tape recorders. Reporters who work for daily newspapers do not have time to sit and listen again and again to the tape to take the notes needed to write the speech story. Few offices have machines with foot pedals to stop the tape and earphones to make listening easy. A tape recorder can be useful as a backup tool, however, especially if the speaker has a troublesome accent. In this case, a reporter might be wise to take notes *and* use the machine.

"I don't think it's necessary," says reporter George Wisner. "Using a tape recorder slows the process down. You get tied up in words that lose their impact. I would use it only in situations where I couldn't get notes because I've got a lousy memory. It will get quotes right. I will use it if I'm going to cover a strange accent. It's good to capture dialect and get a realistic flavor of what is being said. It's one of a reporter's freedoms to select whether to use one or not."

Writing the Story

Going over the notes

Notes of a speech should never be allowed to get "cold." Reporters should get in the habit of going over notes when they get home or back to the office, inserting things they did not have time to write down the first time around. This should be done with a darker pencil than, or pen of another color than, that used originally, to write out words abbreviated during the speech itself and those that might not be legible if too much time passes before the speech story is written. In this way, the notes will be more valuable.

Organization: the use of bullets

In a speech on many topics, the main ones can be covered in paragraphs, then bullets can be used to set off the other topics. Bullets are marks like this: •. In typescript they are indicated by marks like this: ., *, or #. Careful organization helps the reader sort out the ideas presented in the speech. The use of bullets does this, too, and avoids the need for a great many transitional sentences. Bullets are especially useful in reporting the sort of speech, usually by a government official or politician, that is followed by a question period; question periods often raise subjects not covered earlier.

The best way to use bullets is to categorize the subject and then use a quote:

> *Jones also discussed:*
> - Science in the Soviet Union. *"Direct quote."*
> - President Carter's science policy. *"Direct quote."*
> - Cancer research. *"Direct quote."*

A further word about question periods: Reporters should not mention them ("A question and answer period took place after the speech") unless something said during the period is newsworthy. But neither should reporters ignore them, because something more notable than the speech itself might be said during a question period.

Editorializing

In writing the speech story, reporting should not be confused with writing editorials. The reporter should not use a particularly provocative word uttered by the speaker without putting it in quotation marks or explaining that it is the speaker and not the reporter who is saying it. Nor should he or she react like a member of the audience and indicate agreement or disagreement with the statements of the speaker. Reporters need to present the material objectively, without comment, and let the reader agree or disagree with the speaker from what the story tells them. At the same time, they should not forget that they are reporters. If a demonstration takes place, a riot breaks out, or half the audience boos the speaker and leaves, that is news and a part of the story. In fact, a demonstration or riot might be big enough to supersede the speech story.

The lead

Like writers of any news story, writers of speech stories are looking for the most important element to grab the reader's interest and attention. In a speech story, what the speaker said is the most important thing, not where he or she said it or the kind of group addressed.

Consider the following lead:

> *John Jones spoke tonight in Milam Auditorium at Oregon State University before an audience attending the annual science symposium. He talked about new advancements in gene engineering.*

This lead says nothing that could not have been said in an advance story, and readers of it would be unlikely to go beyond the first sentence.

A careful reporter will therefore feature what the speaker said in the lead, using either a dramatic direct quote or a paraphrase of a quote that presents the most significant point or points of the speech. This approach tells readers more about the subject, and they will be more likely to read the entire story than they would the kind of lead illustrated above.

With the exception of newspapers of record like the *New York Times,* newspapers rarely reprint a verbatim account of a speech. This means that the lead quote or paraphrase of a quote will very likely be taken from somewhere in the body of the speech. Occasionally, it might even come from the question period that follows a speech. It will seldom be found at the start of a speech; no one would read a lead quote that said, "Thank you, Mr. Smith, for that generous introduction. I am happy to be here tonight."

The two examples that follow illustrate the effective use of quotation and paraphrase, respectively, in a lead.

> *"Gene engineering represents a dangerous new era in science with more risks than benefits connected to its development," said John Jones, assistant director of the National Science Foundation. He spoke to an audience attending the annual science symposium on the Oregon State University campus last night. "More stringent controls need to be placed upon it," he said.*
>
> *Gene engineering contains more risks than benefits, and John Jones hopes to see more stringent controls placed upon its development.*
>
> *Jones, assistant director of the National Science Foundation, told a science symposium audience on Oregon State University campus last night that . . .*

The quotation lead uses a dramatic direct quote found in the speech, followed by identification of the speaker, place, date and audience, and another quote. The main disadvantage of the quotation lead is that its first sentence is somewhat long because of the addition of the attribution material; furthermore, it is often difficult to pick out a good quotation, because a speaker seldom highlights main points in a single sentence. The paraphrase lead solves the problem and probably is interesting enough to entice the reader into pressing on. In it the attribution is given by mentioning Jones's name.

Identifying the speaker

Identification of the speaker should be given as high in the story as possible—not only the speaker's name but, where appropriate, such details as his or her title, profession, qualifications. It helps, too, to specify the kind of group addressed if that is appropriate information. From details like these, readers can better evaluate the worth and authority and context of the speaker's statements. This is what is done in the second and third examples in the preceding discussion of leads. This kind of format is especially important when an unknown name is tossed into the lead (a *John Jones* or a *Mary Smith*); the person must be identified as soon as possible.

Paraphrase and quotation

If paraphrases are used, they should be used with care and quickly backed up by a direct quote. A good format for reporters to follow is one that alternates paragraphs of direct quotation and paraphrase. It is fine for reporters to paraphrase, because obviously there is not time or space to use all the material in the speech. But they should give enough of the speech in direct quotes for readers to get the flavor of it. Reporters should be careful, of course, not to put the paraphrased material in quotation marks.

To paraphrase a quotation is to put it in one's own words. This requires great care, however; the meaning of the original quotation should never be changed. The lead paragraphs discussed earlier illustrate the correct way to paraphrase a direct quotation. The quotation:

> *"Gene engineering represents a dangerous new era in science with more risks than benefits connected to its development. More stringent controls need to be placed upon it."*

The paraphrase:

> *Gene engineering contains more risks than benefits, and John Jones hopes to see more stringent controls placed upon its development.*

First, *represents a dangerous new era in science* has been discarded, and the word *contains* added. A simplified attribution, *John Jones,* comes next, followed by a paraphrase of the second sentence of the quote, using the key words *more stringent controls* and *placed,* as well as *development* from the first sentence. The only words that are wholly new are *hopes to see,* put in as a supposition by the reporter after reading the direct quote.

Only in rare instances should quotes and paraphrasing be combined in the same sentence. The phrase *more risks than benefits* could have been in quotation marks in the paraphrase above, but was not. It is disconcerting and confusing to be "reading along" and have "certain words" placed "in quotation marks" and others not. It is better to include sentences that are all in direct quotes or all in paraphrase. The major exception would be in a lead where a few words were placed in direct quotes to show that it is the speaker and not the reporter who is saying them.

Whether they quote or paraphrase the words of a speaker, reporters should not strain to avoid using *said*. *Said* is a perfectly good word and expresses what happens in a speech very adequately. In a longer speech, a reporter can soon run out of substitutes (*implored, implied, concluded, noted, related*) and the result can be laughable.

Summary

Speeches are a routine and frequent assignment for reporters. Many of them are given, in cities of all sizes, and they are natural news stories—planned, predictable, and readily available to the assignment editor. Although speeches are news stories, they require a special approach in coverage and in writing. Although reporters might use a tape recorder in covering a speech, that machine should be used only as a secondary resource. It is better to learn to take notes rapidly. Background research is necessary before covering the speech. Reporters should not let their notes get "cold" between the time they listen to the speech and write their stories. After writing begins, what the speaker said should be featured in the lead, either by direct quotation or paraphrase of that quotation. Speakers should be identified early in the story. Reporters should keep their own opinions out of the story.

Suggested Exercises

1. Clip a speech story from a newspaper, mount it on a piece of paper, and analyze it. What kind of lead does it have? Where is the attribution? What kind of transition has been used? How does the reporter handle the direct quotes and paraphrases?

2. Listen to a major address or press conference by the president of the United States and write a speech story about it.

3. Practice taking notes by listening to radio and television news interview programs ("Meet the Press" or "Face the Nation") and writing down what is said. Try to develop the ability to take down whole sentences and to devise your own kind of shorthand.

4. Cover a speech on campus and write a story about it.

"You've got to try to control the interview without alienating the interviewee so he'll cut off the interview. At times you have to give up and say in the story, you tried, but your source wouldn't answer the question."

Mike Hall, Reporter,
Topeka Capital-Journal

12

Interviewing

Preparing for the Interview
The Interview Begins
Interviewing
Notes, the Tape Recorder, and the Telephone
After the Interview

John Atkins had been given exactly three and one-half minutes in the seat next to Ronald Reagan, no more, no less. The former governor of California was campaigning by bus through Oregon's Willamette Valley before the 1976 primary election in that state. Atkins, a reporter for the *Corvallis Gazette-Times,* had been assigned to gather material for a background piece on the candidate. Entering the campaign bus, Atkins sat behind the only seat with a table in front of it, which he guessed would be Reagan's.

"[Reagan's] staff was keeping the national press at a distance," Atkins recalls, "but had allowed local reporters to interview [him] as the bus carried him to his speaking engagements. I didn't want an angle story on the campaign or to use up valuable time on parochial questions. I wanted to get the political flavor of the campaign.

"I wound up tossing him a couple of softball questions. The first question was on dams. I also asked him, 'What is your vision of America?' He repeated a speech from the campaign of 1964 and my time was up. He had memorized those speeches."

Luckily for him, after his own lack of success, Atkins was near enough to tape the answers to other reporters' questions when he resumed his seat—by leaning and stretching and perspiring a great deal.

He spent the rest of the trip standing up and awkwardly holding his tape recorder and microphone in the general direction of Reagan as the bus lurched and swayed down the valley. A Reagan aide eventually asked him if he wanted to put the microphone on the table. "The Secret Service men are afraid you'll have a heart attack," he said.

All reporters who have many past interviews to choose from, have a similar "worst" interview.

The interview is the key tool of the reporter for getting the job done. Typing ability apart, it is the one thing a reporter cannot stay in the business without mastering.

The interview is the two-way exchange of information between reporter and news source that keeps newspapers and other parts of the press functioning. There are few events that do not involve interviews; a reporter will have to talk to at least one person for answers to questions in even the most elementary stories, and more in more complicated stories.

In all but a few publications like *Playboy* and *U.S. News and World Report,* which treat the interview as a special department in each issue, there is no such thing as an "interview story" per se. Rather, reporters use the material from interviews to write news and feature stories. Because of this, Chapter 12 will not contain material on writing. Suggestions on writing news stories are given in Chapters 8 and 9; feature writing is the subject of Chapter 13.

Preparing for the Interview

Research and question preparation

Preparation for the interview begins even before the reporter receives the assignment to write an interview story. "You should do your homework," says *Gazette-Times* reporter George Wisner. "You may not get the chance at the time of the assignment, so you should read the daily paper and the news magazines just in case. You never know who you'll have to interview and you've got to be prepared." Wisner uses the background information to prepare questions for the interview in advance. It is a good idea for the beginning reporter to write out the questions to be asked, almost in script form, beginning with a brief statement of what the story is about and how this person fits into the story. People may not automatically know why a reporter has called them for information, but they will usually be satisfied and willing to set up a meeting if the reporter can tell them readily.

"You need to know more than they do before you go and talk to them," says Atkins. "If you are dealing with a public official over a specific issue, it is wise to understand why it is you're asking the questions." Diane Brockett of the *Washington Star* puts it this way: "I write down a list of questions about areas I want to cover. I always try to look through the background material I would have gotten from the newspaper's library, like clippings on the subject. I generally go through a list of questions. I don't go through them in any particular order. I take a lot of notes because I have a very bad memory. I also write notes to myself about things that come up."

Where to meet and with how many

An office is the best place to conduct an interview, especially if the subject has been asked tactfully to cancel phone calls and avoid other interruptions. The person is thus on home ground surrounded by familiar things and feels more at ease and in control of the situation. At times, a reporter might want to conduct the interview over lunch or dinner at the reporter's expense, of course. This is a pleasant gesture, and it relaxes the interviewee; but it also makes things difficult for the reporter, who must now juggle a pen and a fork and avoid spilling salad dressing on the notebook. At other times, a reporter might want to assume greater control of the interview and meet the source on neutral ground or at the newspaper office.

For a feature interview, a reporter might conduct at least part of the interview at the home of the interviewee, to get a feeling of how he or she lives. At times, a reporter might want to protect a source by meeting with the person at a shopping mall or airport waiting room or a more secluded place, where they can meet inconspicuously. Sometimes, another person might be present at the interview, either as a witness to or as a participant in the interview.

Generally, however, it is best for reporters to avoid interviewing two people at the same time. In interviewing two people, it can be difficult to keep track of who said what; there is also a danger of losing control of the conversation. A company official often asks a public-relations person to be present at the interview. This is permissible as long as that person remains unobtrusive; interruptions like "I don't think you should answer that, J.B." give the reporter every reason to end the interview.

Setting up an appointment

Arranging an appointment with the interview subject may not be as easy as it sounds, especially if the reporter is facing a deadline. Persistence is the best way around an obstructive secretary or a reluctant interviewee, even if it means that the reporter arrives unannounced at the office or home of the person to be interviewed. Or it may mean a mild form of "hot pursuit," in which the reporter walks or runs along and talks to the subjects as they enter or leave the building in which they work. In negotiating for an interview, reporters should always identify their publication and the fact that they are reporters.

The Interview Begins

Starting smoothly

Once an appointment has been made, reporters have no excuse for being late. An out-of-breath arrival with the reporter mumbling apologies and explanations gets the interview off to a bad and defensive start; it will undermine the reporter's ability to establish careful control of the interview and get the information needed to write the story.

At the interview itself a reporter needs to break the ice gently and may begin the exchange by making small talk about the person's office or living room. Even after the interview begins, the reporter should build up gradually to any controversial questions, leaving those of the "why-do-you-beat-your-wife" variety until last. Then, if the subject becomes angry, the reporter will have obtained most of the essential information and can leave quickly.

"You should save the hardest or most insulting question until last," says Bill Monroe. "I get along with people, so by the time I get to the question when I have to zap them, the question can usually be asked." John Atkins adds: "There is the 'gonzo' theory of journalism [practiced by Hunter Thompson of *Rolling Stone*] where you call up your subject at 2:30 A.M. and see what they say. It has its place, precisely at the point you are getting no cooperation from a subject. It's important to make an effort to get cooperation first."

At the start of the interview, the reporter begins to size up the interviewee. "You develop a feeling for the people you're dealing with," says George Wisner, "and there's no way to explain it. You develop a sixth sense about it." After conducting many interviews, reporters learn how to tell in advance how someone will react. Hostility and courtesy are both easy to determine when walking into an office or home. Boredom or nervousness are signs of how an interview is going. Such signs will provide useful clues to the most tactful ways to treat the interviewee.

Overall, the best approach for reporters is the open approach; they should ask appropriate questions in a friendly manner, and leave as quickly as possible unless invited to stay on by the interview subject. Above all, they should remember that they are there at the sufferance of the interviewee, and taking up valuable time.

Interviewing

Asking questions

The direct approach is best in asking questions during an interview. "I'm not very calculating," says Diane Brockett. "Something I'm not very comfortable with dealing with, I'll wait a bit. Most of the time, I don't ask sources nice questions; that's a waste of time." Questions should always be phrased in an easily understandable manner and not include the opinions and biases of the reporter. Reporters should also avoid asking leading questions with predetermined answers ("Don't you think this is true?") or that can be answered with a simple yes or no. A particularly laconic and taciturn interviewee will stifle an interview if given these kinds of questions. The reporter will have gone through a whole list of questions in ten minutes and have only a half page of unusable notes to show for it.

Mike Hall of the *Topeka Capital-Journal* describes his own technique as follows: "When I get into the interview itself, it's like a conversation. I start out by saying, 'I don't know much; bear with me.' My style is pretty informal. At first, I tried to interrogate more. I think I used to ask too many leading questions." Hall's style is now quite the reverse: "Not, 'Isn't it true you did so and so,' because they can answer yes or no. Instead, I say, 'What did you do?' Sometimes, the way a person explains the answer makes a better direct quote."

If a person refuses to answer a question or be drawn out on a subject, reporters should leave it for the time being and come back to it later. Some questions may never be answered, but a person will usually not grant an interview unless he or she plans to say at least something about the most likely topics of the interview. "Certain people can be highly evasive, hard to pin down," says Hall. "That happens with politicians and school-board members. You just have to persevere and keep after them. 'I understand what you're saying, but you haven't answered my question.' You've got to try to control the interview without alienating the interviewee so he'll cut off the interview. At times you have to give up and say in the story, you tried, but your source wouldn't answer the question."

Reporters should also try to group their questions by subject, so that the interviewees are not forced to jump back and forth in their thought processes.

At times, they may also need to steer the interviewee back to the subject at hand; by accident or intention, people talk sometimes about things that have nothing to do with what the reporter has come to discuss. If this happens, reporters should simply restate the original question and bring the person back to the subject.

Handling difficult interviews

At times, because of the topic or the person being interviewed, a reporter will know in advance that the exchange is going to be a difficult one. "I wade in and go at it," says Wisner. "I needle, hammer away. There is no sense beating around the bush. If I can't get a straight answer, I trap them, trip them up. There's always 'no comment' and you can try to get it elsewhere. But you just don't hang it up after that."

Diane Brockett had trouble every time she interviewed the former superintendent of schools in the District of Columbia. She knew she would have trouble in advance but there was little she could do about it. "She [the superintendent] credits my work with half the reason she lost her job," says the reporter. "She hates my guts. I was uncomfortable with her and had a hard time asking her difficult questions. I never figured out what was happening in the interview in terms of how I felt. I'm not proud of it. I was an issue. I am identified as her enemy."

At other times, interview subjects turn out to be difficult when the reporter least expects it. Brockett continues: "I did a series on cable TV and had an interview in New York with an influential attorney. He had a plush office in Rockefeller Center, and I was totally flustered; he treated me like a child and I acted like one. He gave me a few pronouncements and ushered me back out. I haven't to this day figured out why he flustered me."

John Atkins thinks an interviewee difficult if the person constantly tries to get away with what he calls freebies, that is, statements the reporter needs to challenge and does not just put into a story only on the interviewee's say-so. "My pet peeve on a feature story where I'm trying to get the reader to meet the person I'm talking to," he says, "is to give them what I call freebies, to let them have their say without challenging them politically or sociologically. I ask them where they got that information just for clarification and definition. If not, you leave the impression that what they say is supported, and it may not be."

Following up on new information

Occasionally, reporters will pick up something during an interview that they will recognize immediately as more important than the original subject. When this happens, they should seize the opportunity to question the source, without appearing so anxious to do so that they overwhelm the person being interviewed. In these instances, it is best if reporters do not let the source know how valuable the new information is, in case they decide they have revealed too much and refuse to talk.

Going "off the record"

Only experienced interview subjects will use the device of placing the interview "off the record," that is, making it unavailable for publication and for use only as background information. Many of the people using the phrase really mean "not for attribution"; they do not want to have their name identified in the story. The best approach on controversial interviews in which the problem may arise is for the reporter to work out ground rules in advance. In this way, information can perhaps be unattributed, and the rest usable as part of the description of the actual interview.

It is not acceptable for a person—frightened about what he or she has said—to put something "off the record" or "not for attribution" during or after the interview. If this should happen, and the interviewee cannot be reasoned with and talked out of such an approach, it is best to find sources on the same subject who will allow their statements to be published.

Notes, the Tape Recorder, and the Telephone

Taking notes, or not

A reporter should never be caught without a pencil or pen and notebook. It really gets an interview off to a bad start if a reporter has to borrow something to write with. Nor should a reporter try to hide the fact that notes are going to be taken. It is strange but true that an interview subject will sometimes wonder why the reporter is writing down everything that is said, even though the topic has been discussed in advance. George Wisner keeps his notebook out of sight if the person he is interviewing seems to be tightening up. "I shoot the breeze and leave my notebook in my pocket until they loosen up," he says. "Then I say, 'Mind if I take a few notes? I've got a lousy memory.' If one question makes them tighten up again, I'll put my notebook away and then run to the bathroom after I leave and write down what they've said."

Other approaches have their merits, too, and the reporter may prefer to keep the notebook and pencil in plain sight right from the start. This eliminates entirely the risk of making a grand gesture in pulling them out after the interviewee has warmed up and has begun to talk; with that approach, the interview subject might become nervous and freeze up to the extent of refusing, or being unable, to continue. Furthermore, quotes are sometimes remembered only imperfectly, and failure to take notes from the beginning will leave the reporter wholly unprotected if a source later denies having said something the reporter included in a story.

Note-taking

Reporters should begin their note-taking by writing at the top of the first page the spelling of the person's name, and the date and location of the interview. This makes for easy reference to the correct spelling of the name and for ready identification of the notes later. They should also number each page in case the binding of the notebook becomes loose. Taking notes is a difficult skill to learn. Reporters need to learn how to write rapidly but legibly and take down what a person has just said while listening to what he or she is saying next. They should never ask the source to slow down, however, because that would destroy the spontaneity of the interview by making the source conscious of the note-taking. There will be ample opportunities to catch up as the source pauses for breath. Reporters should use a form of shorthand: for example, using the ampersand (&) for *and,* substituting "w/o" for *without,* and leaving out the articles *a* and *the.* "I don't try to take things down verbatim," says Diane Brockett. "I write down key phrases and later remember the rest pretty accurately."

Tape-recording

The question of whether to use a tape recorder in interviews is as old as the development of the machine itself. It is comforting for reporters to know that everything said in the interview is being recorded on the machine quietly whirring on the desk between them and the interviewee. With the interview on tape, there is no question about accuracy or whether a statement was made or not made; some reporters do feel more secure for having a taped record of everything said. On the other hand, the use of only a tape recorder and no notes requires that the reporter sit through the interview again and again to transcribe it. A daily newspaper's deadlines make this practicable only in the case of a timeless feature article or a series of articles written over a long period.

"I don't like them," says Bill Monroe. "For a daily, you've got to sift through the tape, start and stop, stop and start. I can't see using it." John Atkins likes them once in a while: "They are useful to have on occasion, like working on stories out of town. In the Reagan interview, I couldn't have done without one."

A good compromise is to take a tape recorder along on important assignments, as a supplement to notes; the notes will be the primary source for the story, the tape will be the reserve source. A tape recording can also be useful in recapturing a personality or a dialect.

Tape recorders are usually disruptive, however; it is a rare source who does not keep glancing nervously at the recorder and is not self-conscious about its presence. At times, it is as though people think of the recorder as someone eavesdropping at the door. If an interview subject objects to the use of a recorder, the reporter should never insist on its use but should quickly turn it off and not touch it again. Nor should the reporter ever try to conceal a tape recorder during an interview; not only is this practice illegal, it is highly unethical.

If the tape recorder must be used, and its use has been agreed to, the reporter should make sure the machine is working properly *before* going to the interview and be careful not to be constantly pushing buttons and intoning "Testing, testing" into the microphone. Such actions will disrupt the smooth start of the interview and call attention to the tape recorder.

The telephone

The telephone is one of the reporter's most useful tools. When a deadline is looming or a person is out of town, the telephone is invaluable. It also serves well in gathering details of shorter news items or in checking facts on longer ones. Diane Brockett adds: "It depends on time and whether I know the source and how much I need to get from them; I guess part of it depends on complexity. If it's getting facts and figures on how a program works, I'll always use the telephone."

Use of the telephone should never become a mere crutch, however. Excessive use of the telephone, for every kind of story from substantial news to feature articles is wrong; it is the approach of the lazy person. A reporter cannot possibly hope to assess people and their answers, or to describe how they look and act, if they are only voices on the telephone. "You need to make face-to-face contact on something that's important," says Monroe. "If you do it on the telephone, the person you are interviewing can have time to think and structure a response."

After the Interview

The notes

It is a good idea for reporters to review their notes as soon as possible after the interview, to see if any questions have not been answered. They should also make sure they understand everything discussed during the interview. If they do not understand it then, still less will they understand it when they try to write the story later. Even if everything seems complete, it is wise for reporters to have left an opening to call the person back in case they discover anything later they do not understand.

There is nothing more difficult for a reporter to use than "cold" notes, a record of an interview that has been allowed to sit around for a long time, so that the reporter cannot read handwriting or remember all the unrecorded details of what went on. It is better for reporters to work on their notes as soon as they have returned from their interviews, even if they are on deadline. They should read them quickly, writing in the spelled-out versions of words abbreviated in haste during the interview. They should also add observations on the physical appearance of the person, or perhaps descriptive details of the room in which they talked. If they remember things that were said during the interview but were not written down, they should note down that information, too. A few minutes taken to do all this now will save time later when the story is being written.

The sources

Reporters should never agree to show the source the finished story before it is published, even if it is controversial or technical. If they do, they run the risk of having the story rewritten by the source, or losing it altogether because the interviewee decides to change or eliminate things said in the interview. It is a rare person who can avoid trying to "improve" upon what he or she said earlier.

Reporters should, if necessary, talk to sources on the telephone, reading them parts of the story that may need clarification; this will ensure accuracy and avoid the unacceptably long delay that would result from sending a copy of the complete story for review and waiting to get it back. Even when he reads parts of the story to sources on the telephone, Bill Monroe does not let them change what they said earlier if it was accurate. "A reporter shouldn't be afraid to ask people for corrected quotes," he says. "But by the same token, when someone lets something slip, when you go back to him, don't give him the opportunity to change."

There is no better tool for the reporter than the interview if it is used well. These suggestions may help the beginning reporter avoid unpleasant or unproductive interviews. There are times, however, when nothing helps; a reporter knows from the minute the interview begins that it is not going to work out. "If the interview is obviously turning out dull, drop a bomb, change the story," says Monroe. "You've got to be able to roll with whatever punch comes. You've got to be able to bluff. The interviews I like best are ones where you can see half way through that they are leading to something else . . . where people you are interviewing know more than you think. You build the questions one on top of the other, you remember what others told you, you protect sources."

Monroe still recalls his worst interview. "It happened shortly after Gerald Ford had lost the election to Carter, and Earl Butz, the former secretary of agriculture, was on campus. I asked him questions about world food production and got back to the office to write the story. When I walked in, the city editor asked me, 'Well, what did he say?' 'About what?' I replied. 'Does he think his remark [a slur against blacks that caused him to be fired] cost Ford the election?' I felt embarrassed and chagrined. I hadn't thought to ask him that question."

Summary

The interview, a two-way exchange of information between reporter and news source, is crucial to the successful completion of any assignment to write news or feature stories. The interview process is complicated and must be handled carefully for best results. It includes careful advance preparation, a good start, and the interview itself, during which a reporter builds up gradually to tough questions and knows how to deal with difficult interviewees. Questions about note-taking, and use of a tape recorder and the telephone have to be considered too. After the interview, a reporter must work on notes so they won't be unintelligible when they have to be used.

Suggested Exercises

1. Interview a fellow student, using five questions planned out in advance. Use the interview material to write a short profile.

2. Study the interview techniques of three well-known mediums—for example, *U.S. News and World Report, Playboy,* and "60 Minutes." Write an analysis of how the questions were developed and arranged and how completely they were answered. How were controversial questions asked? How good were the questions?

3. Write a story using the information gleaned from one of the interviews recommended for analysis in exercise 2.

4. Research and develop the questions for an interview; conduct an interview with one source and write a 500-word news story from the information gained.

5. Repeat the process suggested in exercise 4, interviewing two sources.

"Features are much more descriptive [than news stories]. For example, in a crime follow-up, we use quotes and are much more liberal with attribution. Instead of saying something happened 'according to police,' we'd do this: 'Charley Jones was not having a good day. First, his wife and daughter moved out. Then, his German shepherd was run over. Finally, he was laid off.' Then we would get into the story.

The same story with attribution: 'Charley Jones did such and such, according to police. First, his wife and daughter moved out, according to neighbors. Then, he was laid off, according to a source at work.' The story moves much more quickly without the attribution."

Dennis Stern, Metropolitan Editor,
the *Washington Star*

13

Beyond News: Writing Feature Stories

News Features
Sidebar Features
Short Features
People Features
Investigative Features
Preparing and Writing the Feature

Larry was a natural subject for a feature story from the moment reporter Bill Monroe knew of his existence.

"When I first heard of him, a juvenile who had been thrown out of the house and got in trouble trying to steal food," says Monroe, "I wrote it from the policeman's side. The city editor said to talk to the mother, too, and because there was no room in the paper the first day, the next day I went to her and got a better story."

"Larry" exemplifies the good feature subject: a somewhat dramatic situation that can be treated at length, using good quotes and ample description to evoke sympathy, empathy, or humor from readers.

Monroe picked up the story on his regular police beat rounds. Had he treated it like a routine item from that beat, it would probably have been written like this:

> *A 14-year-old boy has been sent to live with his stepbrother in Texas following the failure of efforts by his foster mother to control his behavior.*
>
> *Corvallis police said the boy, who had no previous record, was arrested Wednesday trying to steal three empty soft-drink bottles from a locked storage area at Waremart, 930 N.W. Kings Blvd.*

That would have been the extent of the news account. Beyond those bare and somewhat dull facts, however, Monroe found a story in which he could really become interested and involved.

The lead immediately attracts attention because of the way Monroe wrote it. Who is Larry, and why should readers say goodbye to him? The reporter answers these questions in the next paragraph with a direct quote from a law official. He answers it again in the next paragraph with the quote from the boy's foster mother.

In the fourth paragraph, Monroe picks up the last sentence of the preceding paragraph ("I wanted him to get caught") with two words ("He was"). Then he begins to fill in the gaps left earlier: that the boy is fourteen, had been in jail, and was now on a bus for Texas. Then he details the boy's subsequent arrest for stealing empty soft-drink bottles from a grocery store.

Using this preliminary information to set the scene, Monroe tells readers why they might want to continue his story: It is typical of the problems of juveniles in the city.

Then, following a transitional sentence to carry the reader along ("Here is the story she tells"), Monroe uses quotations and paraphrases of quotations from the boy's foster mother to tell his story up to the point several days

Larry, 14, Was Told He Had to Leave Home

*By William Monroe
of the Gazette-Times*

Say goodby to Larry.

"He's got every right to be a juvenile delinquent," a law official said.

His foster mother said: "I cared desperately, but it would be to all our benefit to have him picked up for something. I wanted him to get caught."

He was. Larry, 14, was jailed Wednesday, and the next day he was gone—shipped out of town on a bus for Texas following a month of survival in Corvallis streets, friends' houses and Benton County forests.

After, that is, he was put out of his home and told not to return.

He was picked up by Corvallis Police Wednesday after being caught trying to steal three empty pop bottles from a grocery store.

Larry isn't his real name. Authorities said the boy's tale of survival, emotional instability and adversity isn't a typical one in Corvallis.

His foster mother, who has discussed with many other foster mothers the problems she had with her adopted son in the past few years, thinks it may be more typical than anyone cares to admit.

Neither she nor her husband could handle the boy.

Here is the story she tells:

Larry was born one of seven children of a welfare recipient in another Oregon city. The mother didn't want to lose him to the state, so she sought out a friend and asked her if she would adopt the 10-month-old baby.

The child knew from the first that he was adopted. In fact, his foster mother and father (who died nine years ago) even adopted his natural grandfather to keep some family ties.

But the family moved from the city to Corvallis out of concern that people would talk about the adopted son and that might somehow affect him.

Through the years, the boy was a model child.

He rarely caused problems and made it through the trauma of his foster father's death and foster mother's remarriage.

It wasn't until he was 12 that the problems started.

Then, his foster mother said, Larry started smoking marijuana at school (she said she was told that the school could do nothing to stem the tide of marijuana into its playgrounds). He also got marijuana and liquor from a neighbor.

His behavior changed, she said. Larry became combative at home. Told 'no,' he would scream and bang his head against the wall. He yelled obscenities out the door at passing cars.

A Corvallis pediatrician told Larry's foster mother that he was probably not mentally disturbed, but rather that his emotional maturity hadn't caught up with his extremely high IQ. He would be all right when it did, she understood the doctor to say.

(continued)

She blames the marijuana for Larry's failure to adjust.

His emotions never caught up.

"I told him we could either go spend 50 bucks an hour for the doctor to tell him what he was doing to all of us or he could have a new bike he wanted," she said. "That summer was the quietest time we ever had with him, but then when school started, it got worse."

He stole money from his family and grandmother.

The fits and obscenity continued. He ate and slept at home, usually went to school, but disappeared for days at a time after fights with the family. The foster mother believes that he stayed high on marijuana or liquor when he was away.

She said she was advised by a school counselor to let Larry have his way, including the use of foul language, but after trying the method for a day, she couldn't put up with his swearing and slapped him.

Larry's foster mother tried to get the Oregon Children's Services Division to place him in a foster home.

But she couldn't because the youth didn't want to go and threatened to run away. Finally the division referred her to the Benton County Juvenile Department, which recommended they continue to see a mental health department psychiatrist (whom they had been seeing) before trying to commit the boy to the custody of the court.

In late May, however, things came to a head between Larry and his parents.

Following the death of his foster grandmother and serious illness of his real grandfather, Larry, his foster mother said, threatened to beat her up one evening in the garage, below the room where he slept.

"He blamed us for everything, so how could I help him?" she said. "I told him he had to go."

Go he did, living part of the time in nearby woods, staying sometimes with friends, lurking around the family's house, watching when they left, then sneaking home for something to eat.

"We knew more about him when he was gone than we did when he was just eating and sleeping here," the foster mother said. "People would call all the time.

"I knew it wouldn't be long before he was picked up and something would be done."

Wednesday afternoon, Larry was caught by an employe at Waremart, 930 NW Kings Blvd., trying to steal three empty pop bottles from a locked storage area.

Corvallis police said the boy had been drinking and was out of control when they arrived, so he was handcuffed and taken to the law enforcement building. On the way, he managed to undo his seat belt while handcuffed, pulled the lock of the car door open with his teeth and was starting to open the door when police stopped the patrol car and restrained him.

A check of police files couldn't turn up any police record on Larry—a normal-looking 14-year-old with shoulder-length brown hair, about five feet tall. He was wearing dirty blue jeans and a ragged T-shirt when arrested.

Police called the youth's foster mother. She told them she didn't want him back.

His foster father went to the station but Larry was being questioned about some burglaries (of which he was cleared). Larry's foster parents agreed to leave him in jail.

"I didn't want him home again," his foster mother said. "We just would have been up all night."

Officers had to physically carry

him—kicking and resisting—to the juvenile detention area of the Benton County Jail, where he stayed until the Oregon Children's Services Division found a foster home for the night.

The next day, Larry's foster parents still wouldn't have him back home (although he wanted to return). It was agreed that he would go live with his stepbrother in Texas, an Army man whose wife is expecting their first child.

Neither the Children's Services Division nor the juvenile department had anything to say about the matter since Larry wasn't a ward of the court. The Benton County District Attorney's Office released him from charges on the pop bottle thefts to allow the trip to Texas.

By 2:30 Thursday afternoon, he was on a bus to Texas, where he was expected to arrive by Saturday morning.

Meanwhile, Larry's foster mother, who has four other children at home to care for and who babysits during the day, remains perplexed by what happened to her foster son and to the family.

Partly, she blames the marijuana for changing his mind. Partly, she blames a system that she doesn't think helped her out and one which she thinks is too lenient with youthful offenders.

And although she believes Larry will make it all the way to Texas, she isn't sure what will happen to him when he gets there.

"I cry a little and pray a lot," she said.

The family, which lives in a nice home, well-kept, is apparently religious.

A printed prayer, framed on the kitchen wall, starts, "Lord, slow me down."

Goodby Larry.

Source: Corvallis Gazette-Times.

---

before, when he had been taken to county jail. He tells readers about the decision to send the boy to live with his stepbrother in Texas.

He ends the piece by bringing readers into the foster mother's living room ("Meanwhile, Larry's foster mother . . . remains . . . perplexed by what happened"). Readers learn that she blames both marijuana and the system for his plight. She isn't sure what will happen to him.

Monroe never identifies the people involved in this story. Even *Larry* is a pseudonym. He does this to protect the family, but he really does not need to use identification; their story is interesting on its own, and their names would not heighten its impact.

"I wanted the lead to be kind of a grabber, to elicit empathy from the reader for both the boy and his mother," Monroe says. "I knew I would have to featurize the story. It came at the end of a string of dull government stories, and I was kind of feeling my oats.

"I used a delayed lead to catch the readers and get them in. Then I used the quotes to let the situation bleed a bit before I went back to do the surgery. I got in a narrative account of the weeks before. I had started out writing my original version from the standpoint of the police, but some of the facts were wrong and it made me think I should do it from the other side. I wondered,

'What kind of a woman would turn her son onto society hoping he'd be arrested and taken off her hands?' "

Monroe—and his readers—found out that it wasn't that simple.

Most reporters enjoy writing feature stories. The subject matter is often more interesting than routine beat news. Also, they can abandon some of the constraints of the news story in a feature—the inverted-pyramid structure, for example—to tell the story in a more interesting way.

The characteristics of a feature include an unusual subject, written with greater structural freedom than, and longer than, the news story. Features are usually timeless and can appear whenever the reporter and the editor want to run them, unlike a news story, which must run immediately.

News Features

The most common kind of feature is the *news feature*. This is a story based on the news but treated at greater length and in greater detail than a news story about the same event or issue. "Larry" is a good example of a news feature. It takes readers behind the news to detail the story of one juvenile delinquent.

Another example, by *Washington Star* reporter Diane Brockett, deals with Forest Haven, the District of Columbia institution for the mentally retarded.

"This was a series, but you don't know that until you've got the material in hand," she recalls. "You sit down and figure out what the issue is about and then talk to the metropolitan editor. It was the most logical way to organize it."

The lead describes a scene at Forest Haven. A retarded young man is staring out a window. Immediately, Diane Brockett has captured her readers with the drama of the scene. "The lead attempts to paint a picture and draw the reader in," she explains. "It was a bleak picture show of frustration, hopelessness behind the situation, and [since the newspaper's earlier series on the subject written several years before by another reporter] nothing had changed."

Her next paragraph emphasizes the horror portrayed in the lead by telling readers that the same man had been at the same window two years before when another reporter had visited Forest Haven to gather material for earlier articles. Indirectly, she has made the point that nothing has changed despite the pledges of officials at the institution. The point is made explicit in the next paragraph, where Brockett, now viewing the scene through the eyes of "a visitor," makes the direct observation that "things have not changed." Next, she uses a quote from an employee to reenforce this viewpoint, so that the reader will not have to take her word alone.

Forest Haven: After Two Years, the Forgotten Still Suffer

By Diane Brockett
Washington Star Staff Writer

In the Curley Building at Forest Haven, the District's institution for the mentally retarded, a profoundly retarded young man with gaunt cheeks stares balefully from the same tall, narrow window day in and day out. His view is of a dilapidated, brick administration building across the road.

The man was at the same window two years ago, staring blankly at the world outside, when an investigation by The Star called attention to the miserable plight of Forest Haven's 1,300 residents. Local and national officials professed outrage and vowed that things would change.

But a visitor to Forest Haven still would see the young man at the window, his lonely days still filled with emptiness, a squalid symbol that things at Forest Haven have not changed.

"It tears me up to see him there every day when I come to work and every day when I leave," said a Forest Haven employe who was at the institution when promises of reform were made.

Forest Haven is a bleak, sprawling collection of 17 one- and two-story brick buildings, looking like a decaying college campus from the 1920s. It is set in rural Maryland, 22 miles from Washington, just off the Washington-Baltimore Parkway near Laurel.

The institution's 1,050 residents, a decline of 250 over the last two years, range from the profoundly retarded with an I.Q. level of about 35, to the nearly normal, some of whom are merely illiterate. Like most homes for the retarded, Forest Haven has been used all too often as a repository for unwanted and problem children.

A catalog of Forest Haven's problems, 1976 edition, is almost a reprint of the 1973 version: overcrowded, understaffed, underfunded, and a demoralized staff that knows the institution has been forgotten by the public. But the size of the staff has shrunk even further since 1973, and Forest Haven's budget, in terms of buying power, also has diminished.

A series of inspections of the institution conducted by The Star over the last month found such problems as:

• A cafeteria so unsanitary D.C. Environmental Services officials want to close it down (they only have authority to shut restaurants and private facilities, not the District's own operations).

• A shortage of funds so acute that Forest Haven residents are forced to pay out of their own meager pockets for custodial supplies, soap, disinfectant, mops, to keep the buildings clean. Staff members also buy many of the daily necessities such as aspirin and light bulbs.

Among the myriad supply shortages at Forest Haven is the linen problem. Parents frequently take bedclothes home with them to wash so there will be enough to get through a weekend. When the institution runs out of diapers for residents without toilet control the precious sheets are ripped up to make substitutes.

(continued)

- As a result of staff shortages, parents report that their children have been straight-jacketed as a result of staff shortages, although they have never needed to be restrained in the past.

Employes regularly work 16-hour shifts, an undesirable practice in a situation where patient abuse is a constant danger. Counselors are so overworked they do not have time to make sure residents swallow their medicines. Overtime costs run $46,000 a month.

- Forest Haven's school buses are so old that children who attend special education schools in the District sometimes don't get there because none of the vehicles is operating.

The institution's buildings are in such bad shape that repairs will cost $8.2 million to be added to the institution's budget over the next eight years. Congress appropriated the first $1.2 million for fiscal year 1975.

The new superintendent has set the institution on a course of preparing as many residents as possible to return to their communities—about 400 of the total 1050 residents, Queene estimates. He has made modest gains in improving the lives of those who will remain.

But Queene himself insists that living in an institution such as Forest Haven is "worse than being in jail." He has refused to admit any new residents except under court order. Still, Queene says, there are instances of poor commitments, as in the case of a recently committed delinquent teenager with a relatively low I.Q.

"His problem is delinquency, not mental retardation. What can we do now but give him three meals a day and a place to stay? We have absolutely no programs for him," Queene said.

The Curley Building—a cold, low-slung, cement and brick dormitory opened in 1971 as the institution's show piece—now has become the most troubled cottage at Forest Haven. As the home of 200 profoundly retarded residents, it is the place where the shortages seem especially cruel. . . .

When there are two counselors on duty, one can give individual attention to a single resident while the second watches the remaining 19 residents doing nothing.

Because of a federal court order, 55 residents of the Curley Building are in school six hours a day, learning things such as the names of colors and how to hold eating utensils. But for the remaining 145, everyday life everyday is depressingly like the scene in the day room—monotonous, aimless and lonely.

Those 145, most of them older, did not receive any educational services when they were school age because no federal court order existed. There is virtually no hope now that the years of neglect will be made up to them or to the other several hundred older residents around the institution who have been similarly cheated.

"Everybody has potential," Queene said of the profoundly retarded Curley Building residents, people who repulse many visitors, in part because of the surroundings which make them seem like animals in a zoo.

"If we only had the staff," said Queene. "They can at least be toilet-trained and trained to feed themselves. We don't really know their potential. They can experience pleasure, feel love in their way, know when they've been hurt both mentally and physically."

Original plans for the Curley Building called for a staff of 116 nursing assistants and nine nurses. It currently has 82 nursing assistants and two nurses.

For the more capable residents, who live in cottages with 30 to 70 residents, the world consists of a bed in a vast dormitory without a place to keep personal possessions; a dismal dayroom furnished with dilapidated furniture and a television set blaring at all times. The resident gets three meals a day in a barn-like eating hall. The food is such that staff members eat off the grounds.

No one watches what the residents actually eat, so some probably live on a steady diet of cake, Queene said. A balanced if unappetizing meal is available, however, in unlimited portions.

Staff shortages affect every aspect of life at Forest Haven. In the infirmary, which houses bedridden patients, many of them severely and profoundly retarded, nurses' aides must sometimes bathe, diaper and feed 13 persons. They have been trained to give some stimulation and affectionate care to each patient as they work, but with so many people to care for there is little time for lingering.

In cottages where residents are not bedridden, yet still are not self-sufficient, one counselor may be faced with helping 35 persons brush their teeth, bathe and dress each morning, making it impossible to teach one how to button a blouse properly or which shoe goes on which foot.

Peeling and filthy paint, dirty floors, dim lights, broken steps and barren, windswept fields comprise the Forest Haven environment.

"The only city code we can meet is that of how much smoke we produce burning our garbage," Queene said, referring to lax health and safety conditions throughout the institution. He said the backlog of repair requests is over a year old, the result of too few maintenance men and too little money to stock parts.

There have been plans for over two years to close down the Forest Haven laundry, where residents work in inhumane heat during the summer and comfortable temperatures in winter, but the bureaucracy has never followed through, Queene said. One improvement since The Star wrote about conditions at the laundry in 1973—when residents worked in the heat until they collapsed—is that the toilet facilities in the building have been made usable.

Some improvements are planned and will go forward despite the District government's curtailment of most other construction projects, according to Terry Peal, head of the D.C. capital improvements program.

Some 200 residents work on the grounds, a few more work in D.C. or Laurel. About 60 school-age children go to special education schools in the District and the other 217 children, aged 7 to 16, attend school daily on the grounds. But half of the 1,050 residents still have nothing to do all day, Queene said.

They stare at television sets or into space, shuffle around the grounds. They sit in hallways, some begging for money. One old man repeatedly wanders away from the institution to set small fires in nearby fields.

Judy cries "every time we see her because she just wants something to do besides watch television," said her troubled mother.

Queene offers little hope to the parents of changing Judy's life or that of the man in the window in the foreseeable future. "And it's not that we don't know what needs to be done," he said with some bitterness.

Source: Washington Star.

The next three paragraphs describe very concisely the institution, its residents, and its present problems compared with those of 1973, the year of the earlier series. She tells readers that the staff has shrunk and the budget declined.

Diane Brockett continues: "After doing that, I tell readers what I am talking about by describing the institution. I use a series of bullets to describe, briefly and succinctly, a series of the most horrible things that happened. Then I go on to describe the effect of the first series.

"Then I turn to the most ghastly situation and go into detail. I talk more broadly about the rest of the institution as specifically as possible, using examples wherever possible about the efforts that have failed to improve things. I end up with quotes from the superintendent. If I have something that ends logically, I use it. Otherwise, I just end a story after summing things up in the last graf."

She spent a month on the reporting and writing and plans another visit to see if things have improved, though she thinks the officials will try to keep her out. She plans to talk with sources "off grounds" first, then request formal interviews: "I'll go through these interviews, be limited severely in what I get, then go to the mayor."

Sidebar Features   The *sidebar feature* is a self-contained story set off from the main story to treat one aspect in detail. This allows a reporter or an editor to break up a large topic into several smaller and more manageable stories. Each sidebar covers part of the larger story in a way that heightens reader interest. If all the material were grouped together in one story, readers might be disconcerted by its length and take no interest in it. Sometimes, on a very broad and complicated subject, several reporters can be assigned to do different sidebars on the story.

Figure 13.1 illustrates the use of the sidebar feature. The issue being reported is a proposed new land-use plan for the City of Corvallis. Bill Monroe treated the issue in a number of sidebar features. His "Most Controversial Issue Is Boundary for Growth" is a sidebar feature to the small news story "Schedule of Hearings" (see Figure 13.1); it sets the scene by explaining the background and purpose of the hearings to be held later in the month.

Further sidebar features by Monroe appeared on subsequent pages. For example, one feature gave a background look at various ideas given by experts in preparing the plan and detailed its components. Another detailed the property owned by the people making the decisions on the plan, and the property's location in relation to the proposed boundaries. Another covered the population density assumed by the plan.

Figure 13.1. Sidebar features on a proposed plan for urban growth. *(Courtesy of the* Corvallis Gazette-Times.*)*

One story on this complicated subject would have had readers reaching for stronger eyeglasses—or stopping and giving up before they had read information that was valuable to them as voters and taxpayers. The use of sidebars made the subject easier to read about; it also helped Monroe as he wrote it.

In another instance, George Wisner wrote two local sidebars for the community page, about a national news story appearing the same day on the front page—the controversial Allan Bakke case, on reverse discrimination, which was heard before the Supreme Court. (See Figure 13.2.) "Will Bakke Keep White Males on Top?" outlines a debate on the subject that took place on the Oregon State University campus. "No Quotas in Oregon's Schools" expands upon the subject by bringing to readers' attention the admission policies at the state medical and law schools.

In writing a sidebar, it is important to refer early to the main news story that it accompanies. Readers may then tie the two together and use the information in one story to understand the other.

In the article on the debate, Wisner discusses the Bakke case in the lead as he sums up the conclusions reached: "White males and friends of the boss will get all the job and educational opportunities if Allan Bakke wins a discrimination suit now being reviewed by the U.S. Supreme Court." He interweaves the background of the Bakke case with the substance of the debate as he continues his story.

His article on the lack of quotas in Oregon schools relates the result of his own survey of the medical school and law school. His lead summarizes his findings: "There are no quotas for the admission of minorities or women to medical or law schools operated by the University of Oregon, officials at both schools say." He then uses quotes to back this up.

Short Features

The *short feature* deals with a humorous, sad, or ironic incident that can be treated in an interesting way. In the short feature, timing is everything; the story may fail if its funny, sad, or ironic aspects are revealed too soon—it would be like giving the punch line of a joke prematurely.

The best way for a reporter to write this kind of story is to use a delayed lead, as Bill Monroe does in the short item on the manager's "invitation" to a thief. This kind of lead can thus entice the reader before the subject is explained, or "paid off," at or near the end.

Monroe raises a question in readers' minds at the end of his lead when he says the burglary was "by open invitation." He then details what was taken and does not begin to answer the question raised in the lead until the third paragraph: "Long told police that as manager of the apartment complex he is required by the owner to leave a notice posted on his door every time he

Figure 13.2. Sidebar features on the Bakke case. (Courtesy of the Corvallis Gazette-Times.)

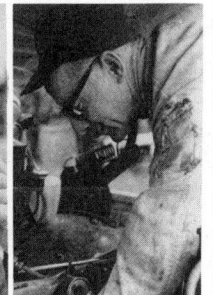

News, News, and More News

Source: Corvallis Gazette-Times.

Manager's Note Was Invitation to Timely Thief

David K. Long, a northwest Corvallis apartment manager, told Corvallis Police Monday afternoon that the weekend burglary of his own apartment was by open invitation.

Long, who lives at 148A NE Conifer Ave., said he returned home from a weekend absence to find a rear window broken open and about $760 worth of items, including a television set, stereo equipment, a watch, a hair dryer, and a calculator missing from his home.

Long told police that as manager of the apartment complex he is required by the owner to leave a notice posted on his door every time he leaves.

The notice, he said, gives the dates and times he will be gone.

---

leaves." The last paragraph fills in the missing details that will leave readers amused: "The notice, he said, gives the dates and times he will be gone."

In the sad story of Terri Stokes, "The Hardest Decision, at 17," Monroe uses the unusual approach of a letter to a dying girl to convey the facts and his own part in them. In this instance, a "short" feature was not all that short.

The Hardest Decision, at 17

Dear Terri,

You remember how I kiddingly told you in June that I write lousy obituaries . . .

It seemed like a light-hearted joke then—a mistake I'll never make again; a cheery crack to a happy young woman who had wiped the cancer from her system after two years of painful treatments that made her hair fall out and left her lean. Remember how we chuckled?

Well, I'm not going to write it. No, I'll let someone else tell the world—probably later this week, your doctor says—the statistics of your life; where you were born, where you lived, who is left.

You're a woman, all right. You're matured way beyond your 17 years.

And you've decided to die.

I'd come to your house in Albany in mid-June to interview you for a follow-up on our story from last September when we told about how you had set aside your own troubles with terminal cancer and pounded the pavement door-to-door to collect

$127.25 for Jerry Lewis' Muscular Dystrophy campaign because, "those kids . . . must be spectacular to be able to live with it."

Things looked pretty good then, didn't they? The doctors couldn't find any of the cancerous growths on your bones of the months past.

Remission. Prayers answered.

Your hair was growing back, you were strong, talking about all kinds of things you were going to do . . . school, another year of campaigning for muscular dystrophy victims . . .

So why did it come back?

Why did my wife, Glenda, have to call me from work at the Albany hospital in tears two weeks ago to tell me you'd been admitted again, getting more treatments, more needles poked into your arms, more blood transfusions?

How come it hadn't appeared as leukemia at first, instead of a bone cancer? Would it have made things different?

And how many times did you ask yourself those questions before making your decision last week to quit the chemotherapy treatments?

Now, you live each day, one at a time, every moment and movement precious. When you and your dad, John, cried together Sunday, he said you couldn't breathe very well and he told you, grinning through his tears, "Don't you cry, honey, I'll cry enough for both of us."

I understand your decision, I think.

It's like your mother, Rose, said to Glenda and me when we came to see you Saturday afternoon.

"She was told that the chemicals could give her another year or year and a half at the most; but it's such an agony, the pain and pressure is just too much. This way she can go without having to endure it any more. She can control it herself."

When we walked in you sure didn't look all that sick, lying there on your side on the divan in your favorite blue shirt and bluejeans, smiling at an occasional joke.

One wouldn't know that inside you was raging the battle being won by the white cells in your blood—200 times more than there should have been and multiplying every day, crowding out the life-sustaining red cells.

No one could tell other than from the slow way you walked and held your stomach that you have a bleeding ulcer and other internal bleeding that won't stop.

And only the faintest quiver of your lower lip, between grins as you listened to your mother's and father's voices, could give away the graveness.

Your best friend from the hospital called while we were there and you talked for a while, then left the room after hanging up. "She only cries after someone she really cares for calls," your mom said.

I hear your grandmother from Washington and brother from Montana got here Sunday. I'll bet you're glad to see the whole family together, mom, dad, grandmother and two brothers and a sister.

At first they weren't going to come until later in the week, but the doctor said they should get here sooner.

I remember your mom telling you about how she called your grandmother and explained the urgency of the situation.

"I hope you didn't scare her," you said.

Your folks say the hardest part is telling everyone what's going on. Your dad asked Glenda to tell everyone at the hospital. Whenever anyone there asks how you're doing now, all he can say is, simply, "not well."

Your mom told us about watching you during the days of the past two years, suffering the agony of the chemical therapy.

(continued)

Then, when your dad came home from work, you'd somehow find more courage and put on a good front.

Those hand-painted ceramic plaques you were making for your parents' anniversary are beautiful, even if, as you told us, "I guess I won't get them finished."

And your leather work—the hand-tooled belt your dad wears and the collar you made for Tippy, your little dog . . . he liked it up there on that divan with you, snuggled against your leg, with a couple of paws hanging over the side.

I won't forget one of your dad's favorite stories of the past few weeks, when there was a memorial service for another terminally ill patient at the hospital. Your mom never met him but she knew his parents from hallway conversations in the hospital.

Your dad kept quiet when your mom put that $5 they could hardly afford into the offering.

Then came the beautiful surprise a few days later when your mom's church took up a collection for you and gave your folks $175.

You laughed Saturday when your dad told that one. A "pretty good investment," I think your mom called it.

Just before you went to the medical center in Portland last week, you told my wife, "Well, I guess Bill wrote that article (about the apparent remission) too soon."

When a mistake is made, we correct it with a story under the heading "We're sorry." It is the hardest kind of story a reporter has to write, a hazard of the trade, I guess.

This is by far the toughest, most sincere, "We're sorry" I've ever written.

Go with God, Terri, and our love,
Bill and Glenda Monroe

Source: Corvallis Gazette-Times.

In "The Passenger Really Got Mad!" John Marshall turns one aspect of police-beat news into an amusing account of a drunk-driving investigation. This short feature relies less on a delayed or punch-line ending than it does on a detailed account of an unusual incident, in which a passenger reacted so violently to his friend's being stopped for speeding that he, not his friend, ended up in jail.

The one-sentence lead sets the scene ("He was only a passenger in the car") and the second paragraph continues it with allusive details designed to interest readers. The third paragraph jumps ahead to tell the outcome, again to sustain reader interest. In the fourth paragraph, Marshall fills in some of the missing details: how fast the car was going, that the driver had been asked to take a sobriety test, the thing that really irked the passenger. The next three paragraphs tell what the man did.

By this time, readers may be asking, What happened to the driver? Marshall tells them by reporting that he was given the sobriety test, found not to be intoxicated, and issued only a speeding ticket. This sets up the final payoff in the last paragraph, the information that the passenger had to spend

The Passenger REALLY Got Mad!

*By John Marshall
of the Gazette-Times*

He was only a passenger in the car.

But he was darn mad when it was stopped early today by a Benton County sheriff's deputy on U.S. Highway 20, near the Midway Drive-In Theater.

The passenger was so mad that by the time his encounter with officers was over he had to be cuffed on both his wrists and his ankles. He was so mad that while he was handcuffed he broke out a rear window in the patrol car—using his head.

According to sheriff's reports, radar had shown that the car was going 83 miles per hour and it was 1:15 a.m. So when an officer stopped the car, he asked the driver to step out and take some sobriety tests.

This really irked the passenger, a 32-year-old Corvallis man. He got out of the car and approached the officer, spouting a series of profanities.

He was asked to get back in the vehicle. He wouldn't. He was told he might be arrested for disorderly conduct, and still he didn't budge. The officer called for assistance on his radio and the man got angrier.

After the assisting officer arrived, he and the deputy who had stopped the car had to throw the passenger to the ground to put cuffs on his wrists. Then they had to carry him to the patrol car. All the time, he continued his string of threats and profanities. His friend tried to quiet him, but was unsuccessful.

Standing next to the patrol car, the man vented his anger on its rear window. He smashed it with his head. That was when officers applied stronger cuffs on his wrists and another set of cuffs on his ankles.

Only then were they able to complete the sobriety tests for the driver. He was found not to be intoxicated and was issued only a speeding ticket.

His passenger, on the other hand, was transported to Benton County Jail, where he spent the night. And this morning he faced charges of disorderly conduct, resisting arrest and criminal mischief.

Source: Corvallis Gazette-Times.

---

the night in jail and faces charges of disorderly conduct, resisting arrest, and criminal mischief.

People Features   The goal of the *people feature* is to make the subject come alive. The people written about in this kind of story must have an interesting reason to be written about—something they have done or said, or their unique personality—and that is what the reporter needs to capture on paper. Physical description helps, and so does an accurate account of what they say in the interview.

Ironically, people features can also be written about animals, things (an old hotel or a locomotive), and places (a ski resort or a ghost town). Their common link is the interest they hold for readers. The task of the reporter is to find out enough about the subject to make it worth reading about.

John Atkins accomplishes this goal readily in "Easing the Pain at the Check-out Stand," a feature about a checker at a local supermarket. By sacking groceries for a few hours, he has the chance to observe a very nice lady as she tries to help customers forget how much their food bills are going up.

Easing the Pain at the Check-out Stand

By John Atkins
of the Gazette-Times

Anybody who's been in a grocery store lately—any grocery store—knows that going through the check-out counter can be a painful experience.

But it stings less in Flo Arbeiter's check-out line at Albertson's.

What Flo's customers appreciate is that she sympathizes with them over the high cost of eating.

And she's outgoing and cheerful, calling out the prices in a melodic voice while she rings them up.

It's no accident that the same shoppers keep showing up in Flo's line week after week. In 15 years as a check-out clerk, she knows most of them by name.

"She's super," remarked a shopper unaccustomed to Flo's disarming style of singing out prices, of making small talk and of dispensing shopping tips. Flo will inquire, for example, as to whether shoppers have remembered to bring coupons for a specially priced item, or whether they've checked the eggs for cracks.

Maybe that's why, two years ago, when the Mayfair Market where Flo worked 13 years went out of business and she switched to Albertson's, many former Mayfair customers did the same.

"My husband calls you 'Smiley,'" a shopper said as Flo handed her a receipt. "You make this almost fun."

"Oh," answered Flo, grinning. "Thank you. That's nice to hear."

The exchange was overheard one afternoon last week as I worked as a bag boy at Flo's counter. Usually she packs the groceries herself.

"Now don't put all the cans in one bag," she told me. "It'll make them too heavy to carry."

She said to be ready for lots of chicken because a special was on that day. Though prewrapped in plastic, each fryer was to be wrapped again in brown paper, Flo said, to protect against drips.

The same went for prewrapped Alaskan crabs.

"Be sure to put them in a separate bag, too," she said when a woman brought two of them to the checkstand. "How can anything that smells so bad taste so good?" said Flo. The customer said she didn't know, and laughed.

To another shopper with a half-dozen fryers, Flo said, "Chickens are a good buy today. Aren't they beautiful?"

At 39 cents a pound, said the customer, they were beautiful indeed.

A woman with a pint of ricotta cheese came up and asked if it could be exchanged.

"It's frozen," the customer said.

"Ooh, they've got that cooler too cold," said Flo. With apologies, she directed the customer to the dairy cooler. "Check to make sure you get one that's good," she said.

When the customer came back, she had a half-dozen other items with her.

"Might as well get these, too," she said.

With an older couple, shoppers whose names she knew, Flo exchanged pleasantries as she rang up their selections. The man was smoking a cigar.

"Is that a White Owl?" asked Flo. "It must be. I can smell the feathers."

The man chuckled.

"Yeah, that's an old joke, isn't it?" Flo admitted.

To a man who asked where the baking powder was, Flo said, "Table 2A," then named the brands available.

"No Clabber Girl?" the man asked.

"No," said Flo in a sympathetic tone. "I haven't seen it for a long time. I don't know whether they're still making it."

As another customer wrote out a check, Flo remarked, "Oh, you're left-handed. Did you ever notice that your left thumbnail is wider than your right?" Flo said the opposite is true with right-handed people.

The customer, a woman, said she hadn't heard that before, and checked her thumbnails.

The clerk at the next check-out stand hadn't heard that before, either.

"Really?" he said, holding up both thumbs and comparing them. "Huh, it's true."

During a lull at the check-out stand, Flo said she hears more complaints than she used to about the price of groceries.

"I don't take it personally," she said. "You can't blame them."

Used to be, she said, that a checker could memorize the prices of items because they didn't change very often.

"Now you have to look all the time," she said.

Her job calls for her to be on her feet two hours at a stretch, with a 10-minute break in the morning and afternoon and an hour off for lunch.

"The breaks are a lifesaver," she said.

Has she thought about looking for a job that doesn't require standing up all the time?

Sure, she said, but other jobs don't pay as well as the one she has, "not for a woman who's 55 with only a high-school education."

As a member of the retail clerks' union, Flo's union-scale pay is higher than that for most secretarial and clerical jobs.

"I never learned how to operate a typewriter, anyhow," she said, and if she were going to learn how to operate anything, it would be a piano.

"That would be wonderful," she said. "But I've never been able to find the time." So far, the only musical instrument she's learned to use is the one she was born with, her voice.

She sings in the St. Mary's Church choir and, though not technically a senior, in the Corvallis Senior Citizens' Recycling Band.

(continued)

Source: Corvallis Gazette-Times.

Flo said many of the numbers she sings in the band are songs she learned as a girl, listening with her nine brothers and sisters to a battery-powered radio on a farm in Iowa.

"There was no other entertainment," she said. "We learned the words together. One of us would take the first line, the other the second, and so on."

Though she doesn't actually sing for Albertson's customers, a touch of melody and rhythm comes through when Flo rings up sales at the cash register.

Having totaled the bill for a woman with a cart full of groceries, Flo sang, "That's fifty-one eighty-one today."

"Oh," said the customer, more to herself than to Flo. "What have I done?"

"I know," said Flo in sympathy, "I know."

He sets the theme of his article in the lead: Going through the grocery store check-out counter can be painful (because of high food prices). He ties this theme to the subject of his profile in the second paragraph ("But it stings less in Flo Arbeiter's check-out line at Albertson's").

Why? readers will ask. Atkins tells them in the next few paragraphs: She is sympathetic, outgoing, and cheerful, and she knows many of her customers by name. He tells readers that she went to work at the market two years before, bringing with her many of her customers from another market, where she had worked for thirteen years.

By the tenth paragraph Atkins has told readers that he worked an afternoon as Flo's bag boy to observe her, slipping into the first person to do so. He relates her instructions to him about not putting all the cans in one bag and being ready for "lots of chicken" because it was on sale that day.

Atkins spends the remainder of the article in giving readers evidence to back up his earlier description of her. Using quotations and descriptions, he takes them with him to the check-out counter as he reports what happened. Along the way he smoothly weaves in information about her education, her ability as a singer, her childhood with nine brothers and sisters on a farm in Iowa. He ends with one last anecdote, which sums up Flo and reenforces the theme of her concern for her customers.

The people feature "He's Paid to Ask too Many Questions" is a profile of city editor Rod Deckert. In it Bill Monroe tries to capture the essence of Deckert's job, discovering in the process that he is too close to his subject.

"We went over to a bench on the courthouse lawn and talked for three hours," recalls Monroe. "He knew this was his chance to tell what kind of an animal was making this newspaper tick. He went into great depth. It was hard to write; I was too close to try to unravel and explain the story in that amount of space. To this day, I think he's disappointed."

He's Paid to Ask Too Many Questions

*By William Monroe
of the Gazette-Times*

Rod Deckert lets his fingernails grow on weekends.

Then he gnaws at them Monday through Friday as deadline pressures build.

He'll likely be munching on one or two of them as he reads this story—and he'll be the first in Corvallis to see it because Deckert is the city editor of the Gazette-Times, the person who makes most of the front-line decisions on local news.

Every day he climbs into the newsroom driver's seat and guides an important part of the paper down a road strewn with soft lead pencils, scraps of notes, story assignments and over-used carbon paper.

At the end of the trip are 13,235 doorsteps on which the newspaper is laid.

The city editor directs the coverage and influences the content of the Gazette-Times' local news coverage and many of its feature stories.

He oversees a staff of seven full-time reporters and two photographers. Family and social news, sports coverage, Oregon news, and national and international news are handled by other editors. All five desk editors are responsible to Thomas S. Jenks, the paper's editor.

A city editor is many things to many people.

To the seven staff reporters, he is a fellow who asks too many questions and demands too many answers. It's one of his jobs to see to it that difficult or murky stories are clear to the reader, to make sure nothing important has been left out.

Deckert does not change the facts of a reporter's story, but he exercises control over how the story is presented. Usually, an unclear point will be discussed with the reporter. Often, entire paragraphs may be rewritten or deleted.

His job is to get the news covered and written so that the reader can understand what happened—and why.

What he does, what he has others do, and where he puts what they do in the newspaper can mean the difference between critical Readertorials, complaining phone calls, or an award for general excellence among Oregon newspapers, which was won by the Gazette-Times in 1975.

Those who know Deckert the least are those most affected by what he does—the readers.

A typical day for the 32-year-old city editor starts between 8 and 8:10 a.m., when he walks in a side door after a five-minute drive in an old Volkswagen camper from his home, three miles south of Corvallis.

He stands in front of a mirror for a moment to comb his hair forward over a receding hairline, then walks into the newsroom.

Reporters and photographers come to his desk individually or in pairs.

Within 10 or 15 minutes, Deckert knows what the staff will produce for the day's paper. He sorts the information in his mind as he pulls a handful of sharpened, soft-lead pencils from a desk drawer.

Reporters return to their desks or leave the building on assignments while photographers begin the day's picture-

(continued)

taking. Deckert thumbs through a stack of publicity releases, saving those of local interest for another look later, and tossing the rest into a wastebasket.

By 8:45, Deckert is ready for the only break he will take until the paper is sent to press. Downstairs in the lunchroom, below the noise of teletypes, typewriters and telephones, he buys a machine-brewed cup of coffee, grimaces with the first sip, and starts scanning the previous day's papers from other cities in the state.

At 9 o'clock he joins Don Alan Hall, copy and state wire editor, and Jeanne Danielson, national and international wire and front-page editor, in Jenks' office for a morning news conference.

Jenks meets every morning with the desk crew to determine the placement of the day's news in the paper. Together the group decides what to put on page 1, how to play certain stories, and what to move to inside pages.

At 9:20, Deckert is back at his desk where he begins to read or edit local copy—which most reporters have been turning in since beginning work at 8.

For the reporters, the news deadline is 11, unless a late-breaking important local story goes past the deadline. Late-breaking "spot" news—fires, crimes and serious accidents—may be written up to 1:30 p.m. and still make the day's paper. The press rolls at 2 p.m.

The Community Page, page 2, is the showcase for local news not appearing on page one. It must be off of the copy editor's desk by 11:30. Stories are first read by Deckert for clarity and approach, then passed to Hall for further editing.

On a hectic day, as many as a dozen pencils may be dulled to round ends by Deckert's and Hall's editing.

11:30 comes and goes. Page 2 is off to the composing room and Deckert picks up a paper clip, unbends it and picks his teeth as he reads a page 1 story. Occasionally the blunt bend in the clip will make a trip into his ear as Deckert looks blankly out the window in front of him, dreaming up a headline.

At 1, the last page "dummy," or mock-up is gone. Deckert is finished with his juggling and can go to lunch. Favorite spots are a nearby lunch counter or a walk-in hotdog stand. He often returns to the G-T building sipping a milkshake.

In the afternoon, there are conferences with reporters, sometimes with critiques of their work. There are assignments to make and feature stories to plan.

Part of the afternoon is spent talking to Jenks. The two evaluate the day's paper and plan some of the content of future issues.

Finally, by 5:30 or 6 p.m., Deckert goes home. Usually his work week will include an hour or two on Saturday, sometimes Sunday.

The city editor has few outside interests beyond OSU's basketball team and his family. He reasons that a city editor should be beholden to no organization, and he averts possible conflicts of interest by being a member of none. It's okay for an editor to be a member of a church, Deckert says, but only if he's nervous.

Deckert is the youngest child of an Ottertail County, Minnesota, dairy farmer. Two of his brothers still farm. Another owns a grocery store.

He became a social worker, first on a Minnesota Indian reservation, then in a welfare office in Fargo, N.D.

In 1967, fed up with red tape and "too much irrelevant paperwork," Deckert went to work for the Fargo Forum, a morning and evening daily serving 60,000 subscribers.

For $90 a week, he wrote obituaries

and chased accidents. Later he became city hall reporter and feature writer.

In 1970, Deckert decided to move west. He came to work for the Gazette-Times after Robert Ingalls, the publisher, convinced him that Corvallis was the place to be.

He covered education and politics for the G-T until 1974, when he was named city editor.

Hall, the copy editor, is most directly associated with the city editor, rereading most everything Deckert does. Their desks touch.

"He'll surprise you," Hall says. "You don't know it, but Rod always has a long-range goal in mind; he knows where he wants this thing (the newspaper) to go.

"I always think he's on top of the cab somewhere looking around, but he's right there. You think he's paying no attention, then he zaps you, wondering about a story or something else you were supposed to be working out."

Deckert was reluctant to become a Monday profile in the newspaper.

"I know that I have a lot to do with what makes the G-T, but I have no grand scheme on the part of either myself, the town or the publication," he explains. "We'll go wherever Corvallis takes us."

The city editor's phone often rings with complaining readers at the other end of the line. Their arguments are prepared, his answers impromptu. Compliments are few.

The most popular criticism—and most incorrect—is that the paper slants its news.

"We are accused of being fiscal conservatives in our coverage of budgets and radicals when we run a feature about an adult bookstore," Deckert says. "I don't see it in those terms."

His news judgment and decisions on feature article choices are influenced by a compelling interest in people.

"Every newspaper can give the wire news. We want to give people something more," he says.

"We've got to get close to the situation. The stories get more sensitive; sometimes they get more emotional, harder to write. Then they have more impact. They're more meaningful."

Deckert listens patiently to nearly every caller, in spite of the newsroom activity. The exception is between 11 and 1, when the action at the desk is at its peak.

"The thing I'm proudest of is that I have survived. I haven't gone bonkers, I haven't been fired and I'm not bitter or disillusioned," he says.

"I'm proud of that. It's the best and hardest job I've ever had."

Source: Corvallis Gazette-Times.

Investigative Features

The *investigative feature* has grown in popularity and usage by newspapers in recent years. This kind of story could be categorized as a news feature, except for its great length and the unusual techniques often needed to get the desired information. Quite often, smaller newspapers do not have the time needed for reporters to research, report, and write this kind of feature. They have left the specialty to big city dailies and the wire services.

The typical investigative feature takes weeks to research and often costs a newspaper money in travel expenses and telephone bills incurred by the reporter or reporters involved.

The investigative feature has been more prevalent since the 1960s as issues in the United States have become more complicated and in need of explanation to readers. The Vietnam War, urban riots, youth rebellion, the drug problem, environmental deterioration, energy crisis, and the Watergate scandal all demanded answers for a public not accustomed to such chaos and trauma. After such events were investigated by reporters on the national level, their local counterparts were investigated by newspapers around the country.

Since the Watergate scandal was uncovered by two reporters for the *Washington Post,* many newspapers have hired their own investigative reporters or assigned staff members to do such work. Dennis Stern, metropolitan editor of the *Washington Star,* thinks all good reporting is investigative by nature. "All good reporters should be doing investigative reporting," he says. "Most reporters cover press conferences and rewrite press releases. That is not reporting, not considered the news we're looking for. Who is making the profits off of the thing announced in the press release? We don't cover an election via a news conference. We go, see the style of the candidate. We never go with that one dimension. It takes more work; one-dimension reporting is easier.

"It is difficult to take a reporter and say, 'OK, you're an investigative reporter; I want you to go out to this county and find scandal.' A better way is to have good reporters on beats who do investigative reporting as they go along."

The *Star* publishes investigative pieces all the time. Typical is the series Diane Brockett and two other reporters did on pornography in the District of Columbia.

"Basically," she says, "we have a fascinating tale to tell, and I take the readers through it. I paint a picture of a scene in figuring how to catch people's attention and describe it. Then I tell people what I'm talking about, that this has been a nine-month investigation by police that we didn't hear about because it failed. I make the point that a successful investigation by the District of Columbia police would get mentioned."

The article "The Perilous Task of Probing Smut" is reproduced here. Consider the techniques. A dramatic, narrative lead catches the attention of readers. "Police Detective David 'Angelo' Penque was wired for sound," but readers don't know why. The next paragraph describes the way he is wired.

Penque is getting nervous by the third paragraph as the narrative goes on, and the sentence that follows it explains why: Penque is accepting a bribe from the owner of a nude club. The owner frisks him and pulls a gun on him before passing him two $100 bills. The high drama continues, and no doubt, the reader is sufficiently interested to go on, inside the newspaper. (The story continued on another page.)

On the inside page, Brockett details more activities of the owner of the nude club. Then, far into the story, the "operative" paragraph: The club owner's arrest, the highlight of a $100,000-investigation that began to fall apart immediately afterward.

The explanation for running the story continues in the remainder of the long article, which tells readers what the Star's reporters found out in their own investigation.

Brockett takes up the analysis: "I go on to tell what the investigation is about. Then I use bullets, one of the best things ever invented because people find it easy to read and it forces reporters to organize things.

"I name several of the interesting things that happened during the investigation—interesting and worth mentioning. Then I go sequence-by-sequence. I wrote it in chapters, chronologically; each step along the way, I tell what is happening and why. I use bullets later as a means of condensing.

"I try to be as specific as possible on everything I use to tell the story. I try to show what the policemen felt. I had to piece this together because none were allowed to talk, others wouldn't talk. I don't say who the sources were.

"It was written because it was a fascinating tale. It appears that the reason the investigation was handled so strangely is that men lost their perception and judgment. I've never gotten a good answer as to why it was stopped.

"The story resulted from a tip that I nursed for three months. We didn't get in the end what we thought we'd get. It was a good lesson. You never know what you'll get in the end."

Reader interest heightens with the account of the murders of two police informants. The last quarter of the story details how and why the pornography investigation fell apart; and at the end one of the men arrested for pornography is acquitted, the other receives only a light sentence. Meanwhile, the detectives involved in the investigation are beginning to fear for their safety. The contrast is an effective one, and Brockett has given sufficient information about the policemen to gain the readers' sympathy for them; indirectly, she is also telling readers of the futility of the whole investigation.

An article of this length must be interesting, both the subject and the writing style, to sustain readers through the long columns of type.

The Perilous Task of Probing Smut

This article was prepared by Washington Star Staff Writers Diane Brockett, Allan Frank and Michael Kiernan.

D.C. Police Detective David "Angelo" Penque was wired for sound.

A tape recorder hung next to his service revolver on his right hip, and a thin wire led from the recorder to a small microphone taped to his chest.

Penque was getting nervous. It was the third time in recent weeks that he had entered the nude club on 14th Street to accept a cash bribe from the club owner, Lothar Kutscher.

In the club's kitchen, Kutscher nervously patted down the detective's jacket looking for a tape recorder, his hand passing right over the wire on Penque's chest.

"Where's your gun?" asked Kutscher, surprised he hadn't even felt Penque's shoulder holster. Kutscher nervously pulled out his own handgun and stuck it into the policeman's ribs.

The detective feigned anger. "Why the treatment?" he asked. "I'm tired of getting frisked all the time. I have more to lose than you."

The money then changed hands smoothly. Kutscher pulled out two $100 bills and handed them to the detective.

Kutscher insisted that all he wanted in return was a promise from Penque that some minor police and liquor board charges pending against his club would be dropped and that he would have no further trouble with police.

Kutscher, after all, had great plans. He wanted to help open a casino in Atlantic City. He didn't want any troubles in the District.

But today Kutscher, 56, still has troubles in Washington. In December he pleaded guilty to attempting to bribe a policeman after being confronted with the evidence collected by Penque, and last week he was sentenced in D.C. Superior Court.

But if Kutscher is unhappy, so are the detectives who snared him.

Indeed, Kutscher represents something special to Penque and a team of six other detectives who carefully planned the steps leading to the arrest of the bar owner.

Kutscher is the highlight—the one shining moment—in a nine-month, $100,000 investigation that began to fall apart almost immediately after Kutscher was arrested last April.

Successful investigations by D.C. police get good publicity. The various Sting operations, for example, made national headlines. But little mention, if any, is given to other investigations—those which fall short of their goals.

This is the story of one of those investigations as pieced together by The Star. The investigation, called CAKE, began in November 1976 and ended abruptly last July.

The probe—designed to pinpoint the ties of organized crime to the city's booming sex industry—remains one of the more secret and controversial D.C. police investigations in recent memory.

Before the CAKE operation ended last

July, according to The Star's investigation, the following events took place:

- A club owner, Kutscher, was arrested for attempted bribery.
- A go-go dancer, who was also a police source, was murdered. For a time Penque was a suspect.
- Two detectives involved in the probe were accused of police brutality during the arrest of an adult book store employee.
- One detective told superiors his car had been run off the road, and several detectives said they received threatening calls.

Here is the full story of the CAKE probe, based on scores of interviews as well as examination of public and confidential documents.

Detective Sal "Sonny" Nasca, from the 1st District, was sitting at the bar of the Butterfly Club when Lothar Kutscher first approached him.

Kutscher had reason to dislike the plainclothes detective. Nasca's beat was primarily narcotics, but in recent weeks he had cited Kutscher's club for several minor violations—like employing an underaged waitress. Nasca was becoming a nuisance. Maybe, Kutscher reasoned, the two could reach an understanding.

"What do you do off duty?" Kutscher asked Nasca at the bar.

"Not much," Nasca replied.

"Why not come in regularly and sit at the bar," Kutscher said. "You'd be taken care of."

Nasca declined the offer.

But the conversation worried Nasca. Word was out on the street that new people were moving into the Washington sex industry—that they were tied to organized crime.

Maybe Kutscher knew something.

Nasca reported his conversation with Kutscher to his superiors.

It was among the first of many reports on the Washington sex industry that began filling up 1st District police commander Herbert Horowitz' in-box in the fall of 1976. Horowitz, too, was getting worried—worried enough to call then-Police Chief Maurice J. Cullinane.

After several conversations with Cullinane, Horowitz was given permission to launch an unusual probe into the Washington smut scene and its possible ties to organized crime.

Unlike most investigations of organized crime, this one would be run by Horowitz out of the 1st District, rather than by headquarters. And rather than using organized-crime detectives, this probe would involve street detectives who knew the area well. It was to be top secret.

The probe, as Horowitz envisioned it, had three goals.

First, he wanted to check all public records to determine who—at least on paper—was in control of the city's expanding sex business.

Second, he wanted details on these sex industry leaders.

Third, Horowitz wanted to catch Kutscher at the Butterfly Club offering a policeman a bribe.

In November 1976 Horowitz hand-picked the leader of the probe—Detective David R. "Angelo" Penque from the 1st District's felony division.

The two then selected the rest of the team: Detective Harry A. "Uncle Tony" Daino, from felony investigation; Detective Larry "Biggie" Leatherberry, from gambling; Reamer "June Bug" Shedrick; Carl "the Occ" Occhipinti; Patrick "Moon Man" Mooney, and Nasca, all from narcotics.

(continued)

The men were chosen for their street contacts and other special talents. Daino and Leatherberry, for example, were skilled in record searches. Occhipinti has an encyclopedic knowledge of the mob.

All were ordered to go undercover. A secret headquarters, rented at $450 a month, was set up at the Skyline Inn in Southwest Washington.

Special precautions were taken. A peephole was built into the apartment door, locks were changed, a secure telephone line was installed and the curtains were drawn shut.

Expenses for the probe, with its $2,200-a-month budget, were paid out of Cullinane's "confidential office" funds, rather than the 1st District's budget.

The investigation's code name was CAKE. The seven detectives were, as one said later, trying to bake a cake for Kutscher.

By January, the CAKE team had a plan to snare Kutscher.

They would give him a cop to bribe.

Word was put out on 14th Street that Detective Angelo Penque, newly assigned to the strip, was the man who controlled the vice officers on the east side of 14th Street.

Penque loudly ordered Nasca and Mooney to stay out of the Butterfly Club, just as Kutscher had wanted, and the detective gave everyone the impression there would be no more liquor board violations for the Butterfly.

Then, on a Friday night, Jan. 14, 1977, Penque was approached by Kutscher in the club's main room. Saying that he wanted the dismissal of the liquor board and misdemeanor charges pending against him, Kutscher told Penque: "I'll bet there is no one who can help me in this mess."

"Things don't look good," the detective agreed.

"I'll bet you $1,000 there isn't anyone," Kutscher said. "And if I win the bet, you win anyway."

Leaving the bar, Penque hurried back to the Skyline Inn and notified his bosses that the bait had been taken.

Kutscher and Penque talked several more times, sometimes with Nasca along, over the next three weeks before any payment was made.

The detectives obtained a sophisticated taping device—described as powerful enough to hear bills coming off Kutscher's money roll. The recorder was concealed on Penque's belt, and the microphone was taped on his chest during the four money transfers as well as at other meetings.

Kutscher instructed Penque to drop by the Butterfly "sporadically," never indicating on which visits he would be paid.

The first payment, two $100 bills, was made in Kutscher's second floor office above the Butterfly just two days after the misdemeanor charges were dropped.

On the tapes made of conversations with Kutscher, he promised that he had "bigger and better things" ahead for Penque and Nasca if they played along.

There was also lots of bragging about his connections. He told the officers that he had already "fixed" one of the charges pending against him and that a city council member had promised to appoint him as head of an important commission. Kutscher even dropped the names of Horowitz and Cullinane.

Kutscher also made serious allegations. He said he personally had made "loans" to other D.C. policemen.

Despite the drama of the Kutscher case, the members of the CAKE team spent most of their time doing mundane and often boring work.

They wanted to gather all they could

about the pornography business in Washington, hoping they would uncover a network to lead them from the clerk behind the counter to the Mafia don on top raking in millions.

Their most arduous task was checking raw, public records on bookstores and other sex-related businesses in a six-block area in downtown Washington.

Leatherberry, the team cameraman, and Shedrick did surveillance work, sitting outside book stores, noting license plates of delivery vans to trace suppliers, recording descriptions of people entering the bookstores.

Under the guise of checking occupancy and business permits, Mooney and Occhipinti talked to store employees. Telephone numbers posted near the cash register often gave hints about who was in charge.

Occhipinti contacted police departments around the country to obtain intelligence on organized crime and pornography, material which could provide pieces to their puzzle.

Sources provided leads the seven planned to explore:
- An apartment on 14th Street, with one room richly paneled in dark wood and mirrors, and two other nearby locations on 14th Street and Vermont Avenue—all said to be studios used to make X-rated movies.
- Chicken films (pornography using children as actors) reportedly could be bought at a store on 14th Street.
- Two D.C. policewomen had close ties with two figures the CAKE team was investigating.
- Several D.C. bookstores, bars and massage parlors were reportedly used for laundering money made from illegal activities.

By mid-April the Seven-Ups—as they had begun to call themselves—were in good spirits. Everything seemed to be going smoothly. They had arrested Kutscher on April 15 after he had paid Penque a total of $800 in alleged bribes. Now they were hopeful of bagging even bigger game.

Then on April 24 Carolyn Hiawatha Valdez Todd, 34, a longtime drug user, was found dead in Northeast Washington. Todd was a paid police informant who only days earlier had been quizzed by Occhipinti about certain figures in the D.C. sex industry.

The CAKE detectives never determined whether her death was linked to their probe. Even now—10 months later—D.C. homicide detectives acknowledge that there is "maybe a 50-50 chance" that Todd was murdered.

At any rate, the Todd death rattled the sex-probe team enough to cause them to take extra precautions. They began taking alternate routes to and from the Skyline Inn, and they made sure their hotel apartment was double-locked at all times—even when they were working inside the suite.

Then, two weeks after Todd's death, a second police source, Mary Frances Reilly, 28, was murdered within an hour after talking to Penque.

The woman, a part-time go-go dancer and secretary, was found shot to death along Indian Head Highway. Penque, it turned out, was the last person known to have seen her alive.

Police had met Reilly several times in the past and had paid her for information about D.C. drug traffic. In the early spring Penque had begun to quiz her about the people who operated along the 800 block of 14th Street where she had worked for several years.

Shortly before 2 a.m. on Friday, May

(continued)

7, Penque talked to Reilly briefly, paid her for information, and then dropped her off near DuPont Circle, according to Prince George's County police sources.

Officially, county police say little except that the murder is still under investigation.

At the end of May, Mooney and Occhipinti wrote a report to Cullinane outlining their findings on "the extent and control of the pornographic traffic" in D.C.

They said that the city had two major pornographic bookstore owners—Donald Epstein on 9th Street and Jack Gresser of Bon Jay Sales Inc. on 14th Street.

In addition, they concluded that three distributors, the District's main sources of smut, all have "organized crime ties outside the D.C.-Baltimore area, specifically in Cleveland and California."

They concluded, "The undersigned investigators are in the process of showing that the pornography traffic, mainly in D.C. and the rest of the United States, are controlled by one main interest and is in fact a monopoly."

Cullinane agreed to continue the investigation for at least three months through August.

June 7 was warm and sunny as Occhipinti and Mooney walked into the Circle Arcade at 1106 14th St. NW.

As they had many times in countless bookstores over the last seven months, one detective looked around the shop while the other showed his badge to the man behind the counter, George Rohanna, and asked to see the licenses for the store.

The two officers then left, returning to their unmarked rental car, with Rohanna coming out after them to record their license plate.

What happened next is still in dispute, but two things are clear: Rohanna was arrested for disorderly conduct and there was a fight.

According to the officers' version, Rohanna, after screaming at them to stop harassing him, slapped Occhipinti in the face. Then, they said, they arrested him. A fight broke out, they said, as they tried to subdue Rohanna.

Rohanna, in a civil suit filed against the two officers, said they assaulted him first "by striking him with their fists and kicking him with their feet." Then, according to his version, they arrested him for disorderly conduct, using "excessive force."

The officers' version did not look good: Rohanna was then 69 years old.

Returning to the hideaway office, they faced five disappointed cohorts. The team speculated about the impact the incident might have on the future of their investigation as well as whether Mooney and Occhipinti had been set up.

Rohanna has an extensive arrest record, both in obscenity and gambling, dating back to 1933.

After the Rohanna incident, the CAKE team kept working, but clearly their special investigation was in trouble. A request to attend an out-of-town conference on pornography was turned down. They were excluded from a police department meeting on local porn problems.

Then, on June 14, Horowitz told them they had 30 days to complete their reports. The CAKE probe, Horowitz said, was over.

There were several explanations. Horowitz told Cullinane that the probe had gone beyond the scope of the 1st District and that it was time for headquarters to take over. He reportedly told the CAKE investigators that, among other things, he feared for their safety.

Clearly, however, the Rohanna incident also played a key role in ending the probe. The investigation had become tainted with allegations of police brutality.

No doubt Horowitz questioned the wisdom of continuing a top-secret investigation when two of his investigators were embroiled in Rohanna's lawsuit.

In July a D.C. police truck pulled up to Skyline Inn. The CAKE team helped load boxes of records to be shipped to the 1st District station.

There the CAKE files were stored in a large two-drawer filing cabinet in the corner of Horowitz's office. A special lock was installed.

By August much of the dust had settled. Six members of the CAKE team were back on their regular assignments. A seventh member, Daino, left the department to become a private investigator.

In December, six months after CAKE was terminated, the gray file cabinet was still sitting in the corner of Horowitz's office.

On Dec. 30 Assistant Police Chief Burtell Jefferson was named to replace the retiring Cullinane.

A week later Horowitz went to Jefferson's office to tell him about the CAKE files.

The next evening, during an interview with The Star, Cullinane said he was surprised to hear that the CAKE materials had not been turned over to the department's organized crime squad. "I don't believe that to be true," Cullinane said.

Asked about the file cabinet, he responded: "You know more about that than I do."

Cullinane said that he had been present when Horowitz had given the organized crime unit a lengthy report on the CAKE investigation.

But the only reports written about the nine-month effort were the 13-page report written by Occhipinti and Mooney in May and a shorter final summary by Penque.

Immediately after the telephone interview with The Star, Cullinane called Deputy Chief Robert L. Rabe, who heads the department's organized crime unit.

Several officers from organized crime went to Horowitz's office the following Monday to start going through the gray file cabinet.

But the night before their visit, a coat locker in Horowitz's office was broken into. Horowitz had previously placed the transcripts of the Kutscher tapes in that locker.

Pages of the transcripts were strewn around the office and 96 pages of copying were unaccounted for on the station's Xerox machine.

Horowitz, in a recent interview, denied that a break-in had occurred and said there was no investigation of a break-in.

Several CAKE investigators continue to worry about their own safety. Within the past few weeks Penque has complained to colleagues that the brake lining on his wife's car was deliberately cut. Occhipinti has said that his car was run off the road and his house burglarized.

The homes of both men, according to sources, are under protective surveillance by Prince George's County police.

Rohanna was acquitted Feb. 1 of charges stemming from the fight with the two CAKE detectives. His civil suit is pending.

Kutscher, meanwhile, who pleaded guilty in D.C. Superior Court Dec. 16 to a single count of bribery after agreeing to cooperate with prosecutors, was fined $500 last week and put on probation.

Source: Washington Star.

Sometimes, a commitment to investigative reporting does not work out, despite the best intentions of the editors and investigative reporters involved. At the *Corvallis Gazette-Times,* reporter John Atkins was named investigative reporter in 1976. After a year in that assignment he has returned to beat reporting at his own request.

"Investigative reporting is where you seek to get information and a story many others want to keep quiet, the publication of which results in people getting into trouble," says editor Tom Jenks. "For over a year John Atkins looked at half a dozen things, and we had very little success. That either means it [the wrongdoing] isn't there or we're not good enough to find it. I accept the former. It makes me conclude that this is not Jersey City."

Jenks says the newspaper approached the problem in the right way, by sending Atkins to a seminar on investigative reporting and rearranging the beat system, so that he would be free to pursue his new work. "But in no case did he catch people with their hands in the till," he continues. "It doesn't mean we won't do this kind of story, but we concluded that rather than assign somebody to turn over rocks and see what crawls out, we would wait for tips and see what looks suspicious. Rather than form a list of investigative topics, we would wait until it flies in the face. In every case a good story that came from a tip has held up; in no case has this kind of story come from something we dug up."

Atkins found the year a frustrating one. "Because we have looked into leads and come up empty-handed, we have concluded that there isn't much going on or we haven't found it. I guess we have a pretty honest local government."

One of Atkins's first stories dealt with a local state-human-resources official who was using staff and state time to get an advanced degree at Oregon State University. The revelation caused the official to be transferred to the state capital.

Another series of investigative articles—his most ambitious while doing this kind of story—covered the Chicano-Indian Study Center of Oregon (CISCO), a federally funded improvement program set up on an abandoned U.S. Air Force base north of Corvallis.

Atkins's stories revealed financial error and general administrative carelessness. "CISCO Owes Feds $26,000, Audit Shows" was one of the early stories. "There is no question," Atkins says, "that these reports led to a federal audit which led to reorganization of CISCO and, after that, its ultimate demise, unfortunately for the Chicanos and Indians of Oregon. On the other side, they were not getting the services they deserve and were being victimized, in a way, by not getting supervision or educational opportunity."

CISCO Owes Feds $26,000, Audit Shows

By John Atkins
of the Gazette-Times

ADAIR—Federal auditors say the Chicano-Indian Study Center of Oregon owes the U.S. government a $26,000 refund because of accounting and bookkeeping errors in the management of tax-supported programs for Indians and Chicanos.

An audit by the Department of Health, Education and Welfare found that some expenditures by CISCO were not documented and that other expenses were not allowable under the terms of federal grants.

The audit covered the period June 7, 1971 to March 31, 1976, and was conducted between April and July of this year. A copy of the audit report, submitted Aug. 16 to the Region 10 HEW office in Seattle, was obtained by the Gazette-Times.

The audit report included point-by-point responses to the auditors' findings and recommendations by John Talley, chairman of CISCO's board of directors, and Noreen K. Saltveit, CISCO lawyer.

Though they generally concurred with the auditors' findings, Talley and Saltveit requested that HEW waive the recommendation that refunds be made.

They said the disallowed and undocumented expenses "represent a very small percentage of the total grants and are due primarily to lack of administrative expertise together with lack of technical assistance including accounting assistance in spite of numerous requests by CISCO staff."

The two said that the auditors' recommendations are being implemented, or soon will be, and that mistakes such as those revealed by the audit "should be avoidable in the future. In terms of effectiveness we would welcome comparison with state, federal and other programs designed to help minorities, particularly those who have been unemployed for the length of time that CISCO clients in general have."

Talley said today in a telephone interview that the reason CISCO has asked that the refund be waived "is very simple: we don't have any money."

If a refund is insisted upon, he said, CISCO will need time to try to raise the money. But he said CISCO is not going to go under.

"It's the first audit CISCO has had in five years," he said. "There should have been an audit earlier, and we could have used some technical assistance."

Talley said CISCO's financial troubles began the day it gained title to 10 abandoned buildings on 14 acres of land at former Adair Air Force Station in 1973. The buildings, many of them dilapidated and vandalized, were to be used to establish a "live-in, learning environment" for disadvantaged Mexican-Americans and Indians. The center was to provide vocational training, general education and other social services to its clients.

Talley said it took until this year to get heat to all the buildings.

"CISCO has been vastly underfunded," he said. "Its programs were launched by people without professional

(continued)

Source: Corvallis Gazette-Times.

experience in accounting and administration. I think it is amazing that we have done as well as we have."

Kenneth E. Sill, HEW regional audit director, said a decision on the auditors' recommendations will be made by Bernard Kelly, HEW regional director, in consultation with George E. Hoops, regional director for federal property assistance.

The audit report said CISCO received $365,158 from six federal agencies between May of 1972 and March of 1976: Office of Education, $180,103; Office of Human Development, $22,500; Rehabilitation Services Administration, $20,555; Office of Child Development, $40,000; Alcohol, Drug Abuse and Mental Health Administration, $95,000; Community Services Administration, $2,000.

CISCO's records were examined by a team of auditors from the HEW Audit Agency. The team said its review of selected CISCO expenditures revealed that "$26,072 of unallowable and-or unallocable costs had been distributed to federal programs" operated by CISCO.

Sill said "unallocable costs" are expenses "that are not acceptable under federal regulations . . . the federal procurement regulation generally governs costs that are allocable or unallocable."

For example, $11,092 in federal grant money spent by CISCO for contractural services (hiring of teachers and consultants) was disallowed by the auditors because the money was spent without written contract with those who were paid the money or without evidence that the services were received, or was not spent in accordance with the terms of the federal grant.

Weaknesses were found in CISCO's accounting system, distribution of salaries and wages, equipment purchases, travel and telephone expenses, petty cash distribution, documentation of expenses, contracting controls and property management procedures, among other items.

CISCO in one instance spent $7,987—approximately 39 per cent of a $20,550 federal grant earmarked to establish a carpentry program—on supplies and administrative costs which the auditors said were not allowable.

Talking of investigative reporting in general, Atkins notes that "charities are the target of investigative reporters elsewhere—how they are collected, what expenses are, how much is spent." He himself rarely investigated charity organizations; he did, however, look into Open Door, an organization that helps people in trouble. He found its bookkeeping procedures "so lax that it was going into bankruptcy, not knowing why." After his story, the organization got additional money from United Way and is being managed better.

Not all of Atkins's investigations led to stories. He spent two weeks looking at the personal-expense vouchers of all local public officials. He found the documentation uneven, but the amounts were small and no wrongdoing emerged. In another instance, a tip did not work out. Atkins was told that the Corvallis chief of detectives was a major stockholder in the burglar-alarm system just then being set up to connect the homes of subscribers to the system with the central police station. Additional investigation revealed that both the chief of police and city manager knew about the situation and that the system was the best one available.

Now away from his investigative reporting duties, Atkins has had time to reflect on the subject.

"To begin with, you have to have a premise before you start," he says. "You may not have a lead, but if there's an aspect of a story that appears to require a deeper look than the beat reporter will have time for, the investigative reporter takes over. I've stayed away from fishing expeditions like 'Let's look at the real-estate industry.'

"In investigative reporting, you have to develop inside sources. Leads are provided by sources, not the city editor. The other thing in investigative reporting is that you have to have a full understanding of public records—how to use them, how to spring loose information through cross-referencing and tie together two bits of information otherwise disassociated.

"Another skill you need is more than a nodding acquaintance with statistics and how to use them to develop investigative pieces. Instead of being a pundit, you've got to support your stories with factual data. The biggest problem is the investment of time required for this kind of reporting. It does take away the production time of however many staff members you put on a story. That kind of decision has to be understood by management.

"One has to be careful in the context of investigative stories not to jeopardize the reputations and careers of those who may be merely bystanders, unless they've been duped monumentally.

"When you get started, you have to know when to let go, drop the subject, and know when a story isn't there. If you're out poking around, you keep wanting to go one step further. You've got to step back and take another look and see how much more effort will be required. The closer you get to the Mafia, criminal activity, graft, and violations of the public trust, the more worthwhile it is."

Although investigative features are most associated in the public mind with uncovering the bad, they do not have to be so. An investigative feature can be written on any subject: new legislation affecting large numbers of people, trends in the way men and women live, changes in societal behavior, and historical events as they relate to today.

Inside investigative reporting

If your mother says she loves you, check it out.

Norm Udevitz, investigative reporter, *Denver Post*

It's like climbing a mountain pocked with traps. When you get to the top, the applause is brief. You're faced with spurious lawsuits, embarrassed publishers, advertiser boycotts, loss of friends, threats of prison. Occasionally, you are assassinated.

Bob Greene, investigative reporter, *Newsday*

Investigative Reporters and Editors, Inc. (IRE) is a nonprofit corporation; it was organized in 1975 to provide educational services to reporters, editors, and others interested in investigative journalism. The organization is best known for its sponsorship of the Arizona Project, a team of reporters brought together to probe a number of stories in Phoenix, Arizona, that were being worked on by Don Bolles, an investigative reporter for the *Arizona Republic* who was killed before he could complete his work. The stories written by the team reached the newspapers in 1977.

IRE holds an annual national meeting on the subject of investigative reporting. In February, 1978, it held a regional workshop in Eugene, Oregon. Highlights of some of the sessions of that workshop follow as an adjunct to the section of this chapter on investigative reporting. These tips on investigative reporting come from the various panel discussions at that meeting:

Public records

There is little difference between the public-records laws of the various states. Everyone has the right to inspect every public record unless prohibited by law from doing so. Very few records are exempt from public inspection. Exemptions may apply to such things as personal and medical records. In these instances, the person wanting to inspect the information must prove a need to do so.

1. "Police blotter" information is always available to the press unless its revelation would jeopardize law enforcement.
2. Some business and government information is exempt from public disclosure: for example, reports of deposits to banking commissions that might reveal a bank was in trouble and cause a run on its assets by

frightened depositors. Trade secrets of various businesses are also kept from disclosure.

3. The federal Freedom of Information Act allows access to all records where, in the words of one IRE panelist, "anything somebody in government puts on paper" can be requested. The important point here is for the reporter to be able to identify the information desired. Sometimes the copying charges are excessive. Employees of various agencies may invoke the federal Privacy Act to prevent disclosure. Reporters should always ask them where such disclosure is prevented in the Freedom of Information Act.

Local government

The remoteness of federal and state government activities from most reporters makes local government an obvious area of reporter scrutiny. Officials at this level do more things that affect citizens, but what they do is often overlooked. A number of subject areas may lead to fraud, conflict of interest, and ethical violations:

1. *Planning.* Do only a few people in town control it?

2. *Total land use.* What parts of town have been set aside?

3. *Roadways and parkways.* Who profits, where are the exits?

4. *Zoning.* Who profits from the location of apartments and shopping centers?

5. *Variances.* When were they granted and to whom?

6. *Contracts.* Are specifications written in such a way that only one person can meet them and thus be awarded the contract?

7. *Personal service contracts.* Who gets them and whom do they know?

8. *Building codes.* Do the politically favored get away with using inadequate materials and have fewer official inspections?

9. *Basic payrolls.* Do phantom jobs exist?

10. *Tax assessment.* Do the relatives of those in government get favorable treatment?

11. *Courts.* Do the decisions of judges correlate with the property they hold and with their investments? Was the money paid in any victim-restitution program?

12. *District attorney.* Did the attorneys who contributed to his or her campaign have such records as their drunk-driving records eliminated?

13. *City audit.* Is the city getting lower interest than the county on its deposited funds? Is the county's interest lower than the city's?

14. *Travel and entertainment.* Are people on the payroll taking winter vacations at public expense? "Check the suntans in January," said one IRE panelist. Who has the telephone credit cards and how are they used? Are city officials cashing in first-class airline tickets and pocketing the money?

15. *Bond issues.* Who is the city bond counsel, and what commission does he or she receive?

Real estate

Land fraud is a billion-dollar business and touches most states. Because the business revolves around records kept on paper, reporters can sometimes track down fraud by following what an IRE panelist called the paper trail.

1. A good first step is to establish a chronology of what happened in a real-estate transaction, paying attention to dates and to how one thing relates to another.

2. Reporters should look next for patterns, for people involved in land deals in one state who turn up in another one.

3. Another thing to watch out for is union pension funds that are being funneled into real estate.

Investigative reporting in general

1. Reporters should keep copies of everything for use in future stories because events and people have a way of reappearing time after time; if someone keeps reappearing in fraud after fraud, scheme after scheme, the development of a pattern can be determined.

2. In this and all other kinds of investigative reporting, reporters should make friends with sources at all levels.

Preparing and Writing the Feature

The first consideration in preparing a feature story is the choice of a subject. Is the subject worthy of feature treatment? Is the person, place, or thing of interest to the general reader beyond any connection to a news event? For a sidebar feature, can the story legitimately be divided into several small stories? For a news feature, what is there to be found out and conveyed to readers about someone connected with a news event that can't be included in a simple story? For a short feature, is the subject funny, sad, or ironic? Once these questions have been answered satisfactorily, the reporter may begin to gather material for the feature.

Because feature stories are largely descriptive, feature writers look for material that goes beyond that gathered for a news story: What does the person look like, what does the room look like, how is the person dressed, how does the person speak—fast, slow, with an accent? A people feature, more than any other, succeeds or fails on good quotes; and reporters must search for these as the essence of a good story.

"Features are much more descriptive," says Dennis Stern, metropolitan editor of the *Washington Star*. "For example, in a crime follow-up, we use quotes and are much more liberal with attribution. Instead of saying something happened 'according to police,' we'd do this: 'Charley Jones was not having a good day. First, his wife and daughter moved out. Then, his German shepherd was run over. Finally, he was laid off.' Then we would get into the story.

"The same story with attribution: 'Charley Jones did such and such, according to police. First, his wife and daughter moved out, according to neighbors. Then he was laid off, according to a source at work.' The story moves much more quickly without the attribution.

"Even in a feature, however, you've got to tell what it's all about by the third or fourth graf."

One of the *Star's* reporters, Diane Brockett, adds, "To write a feature where I capture someone, like a member of Congress, I try to find out everything I can by reading material on the person from the library. I look at *Congressional Quarterly* and anything that says what the person is, who he is. I talk to their staff members about them, in the case of a member of Congress, and to other congressmen. I spend some time with the subject and go to his or her home district.

"I can't hope to explain all about any one person, so I usually pick out a theme, but not in advance. You pay attention to questions, the tone of voice, what they look like, an incident that captures what this person is about. You try to make it as fun and interesting as possible. You make the person seem as valid as possible. Hopefully, you would watch the subject in situations other than talking to you, usually not one-on-one but by observing him or her elsewhere."

When the writing process begins, it is the same as that used in writing a regular news story. The feature story must have a lead, a transition sentence, and a body. But it needs a better-than-average lead and a theme that will carry readers through to the end.

Straight news leads are out of place in features, and so is the inverted-pyramid structure. Perhaps that is why so many reporters enjoy writing features: It frees them from the strictures of conventional newswriting. Nothing is more pleasant to a reporter who has been covering a beat filled with night meetings than to be assigned to write a feature.

The writing in a feature is more colorful than in a news story, can use more adjectives, more vivid and vigorous words to describe the person or event, more variety in figures of speech and thought. To Diane Brockett, Forest Haven is both "a squalid symbol" and a "bleak, sprawling collection of . . . buildings, looking like a decaying college campus from the 1920s." Its residents were "profoundly retarded" and its staff "demoralized." John Atkins has Flo, the supermarket checker, "grinning," "admitting," "chuckling," and talking to her customers "in sympathy."

None of these descriptions would have been appropriate in an inverted-pyramid news story, but they are just right for a feature to set the tone and to make readers feel they are there standing alongside reporters. One caution: Reporters should not be so carried away by the freedom allowed by features that they forget the danger of editorializing. Although the selection of the adjectives and other descriptive words of the feature is inevitably based upon personal opinion, reporters need to resist the temptation of taking this to extremes.

Features also afford many opportunities for the use of quotations, which, if good, can greatly enhance the value of the story, sometimes almost tell the story for the reporters writing it: if bad, they can also ruin it.

Because the feature story is freer in form than the news story, a helpful structuring device is to link the end of the story with the beginning, bringing things full circle, tying it up in a package for readers. Bill Monroe's story "Larry," presented earlier in this chapter, is one of several that use the device successfully.

Monroe's story is a good example of both of the foregoing techniques. The quotes from the law officer and the boy's mother set the scene ("He's got every right to be a juvenile delinquent" and "I wanted him to get caught"), and then Monroe details the boy's background by offering a narrative of what happened to him. As he tells the story, he uses quotes from the mother at various points to heighten the interest ("I told him he had to go" and "We didn't want him home again"). Near the end, he brings readers into the mother's house ("a nice home, well-kept") and describes a prayer on the wall to end the piece. Then he goes back to the "Say goodbye to Larry" approach of the lead in closing, "Goodbye, Larry."

Summary

Feature stories are different from news stories. They are less timely, often longer, more vivid, and written in a less structured way. There are five kinds of features: news, which is based on a news event but treats the event in an interesting and relaxed way; sidebar, which is a story (or stories) that breaks up a major story into manageable (and reportable) portions; short, which makes people laugh or cry by the manner in which it is written; people, which describes the personalities, thoughts, and lives of people others will want to read about; and investigative, which uncovers wrongdoing or explains a subject to readers.

Suggested Exercises

1. Research and bring to class examples of each kind of feature story noted in this chapter. Clip them out and mount them on separate sheets of paper, indicating the characteristics that made you designate them as news, sidebar, short, people, or investigative features.

2. Select a news story from a newspaper and featurize it, rewriting the lead, strengthening the verbs, adding adjectives, and making better use of quotes.

3. Write a short feature with a sad, humorous, or ironic twist.

4. Gather the material for and write a news feature.

5. Gather the material for and write a people feature.

6. Select a recent large news story on campus or in town and gather the material and write at least two sidebar features to go with the main news story.

7. Gather the material and write a 2,000-word investigative feature.

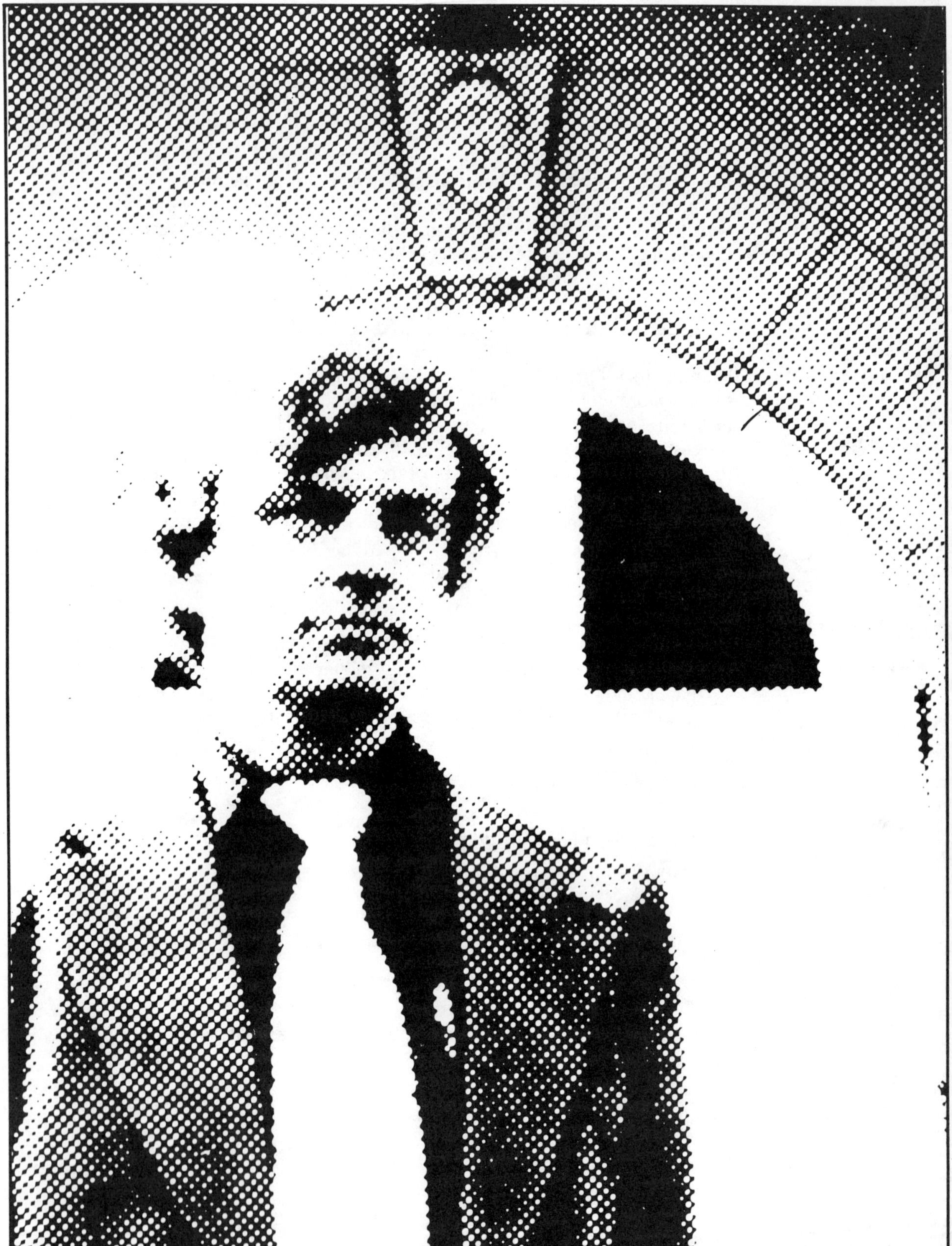

THREE

Preparing for the Unexpected

"I hope if we get sued, it's not for the wrong reason, that we haven't made an error that only a novice would make. If we are sued and have been truthful and courageous, we can hold our heads up high."

Rod Deckert, City Editor,
Corvallis Gazette-Times

"People are always charging you're biased. It's something that gnaws at you. You worry about whether it's true."

Mike Hall, Reporter,
Topeka Capital-Journal

14

Ethics

Codes of Ethics
Ethical Problems

"To me, ethics means keeping reins on your own biases," says Rod Deckert, city editor of the *Corvallis Gazette-Times*. "Some people you'd like to skewer, and you just resist the urge. Sometimes your biases get in the way, like holding a grudge. We sit here in the newsroom with somebody really taking shots at us, unmercifully criticizing us, and think, 'Boy, wait until that turkey needs us.' But when he comes around with that news release or speaks up at a public meeting, we quote him, we don't ignore him. Because of the nature of the business, you're going to get criticized. You've got to guard against vindictiveness, holding grudges. Reporters are, by and large, ethical, honest, and decent sorts. We worry more about ethics than most professionals do."

"I can't overestimate ethics," adds *Gazette-Times* reporter John Atkins. "It's something you just don't submit to in a newsroom handbook; a good reporter always has ethical considerations in mind in working on stories."

"I worry about being fair," says Diane Brockett of the *Washington Star*. "Most of what I write is negative. I've cost two people their jobs. The loss of jobs is very real. I worry about looking too much for the negative. But nobody is going to read us if we print only good news. Since I deal with that, I wonder if we sometimes lose our perceptions about ethics."

Codes of Ethics

Journalism has had various codes of ethics for years but none has ever been binding or formalized. The American Society of Newspaper Editors adopted such a code in 1923. In 1926, the Society of Professional Journalists, Sigma Delta Chi, developed a code, revised in 1973. The revised code is the one reproduced on pages 282–285. It deals with acceptable conduct for everyone working in journalism in matters of responsibility, freedom of the press, ethics, accuracy and objectivity, and fair play. These codes, and many others adopted by state newspaper organizations and broadcasters, are commendable in their collective goal of achieving the ideal in journalism.

Code of Ethics, of The Society of Professional Journalists, Sigma Delta Chi

The Society of Professional Journalists, Sigma Delta Chi believes the duty of journalists is to serve the truth.

We believe the agencies of mass communication are carriers of public discussion and information, acting on their Constitutional mandate and freedom to learn and report the facts.

We believe in public enlightenment as the forerunner of justice, and in our Constitutional role to seek the truth as part of the public's right to know the truth.

We believe those responsibilities carry obligations that require journalists to perform with intelligence, objectivity, accuracy and fairness.

To these ends, we declare acceptance of the standards of practice here set forth:

Responsibility:
The public's right to know of events of public importance and interest is the overriding mission of the mass media. The purpose of distributing news and enlightened opinion is to serve the general welfare. Journalists who use their professional status as representatives of the public for selfish or other unworthy motives violate a high trust.

Freedom of the press:
Freedom of the press is to be guarded as an inalienable right of people in a free society. It carries with it the freedom and the responsibility to discuss, question and challenge actions and utterances of our government and of our public and private institutions. Journalists uphold the right to speak unpopular opinions and the privilege to agree with the majority.

Ethics:
Journalists must be free of obligation to any interest other than the public's right to know the truth.

1. Gifts, favors, free travel, special treatment or privileges can compromise the integrity of journalists and their employers. Nothing of value should be accepted.

2. Secondary employment, political involvement, holding public office and service in community organizations should be avoided if it compromises the integrity of journalists and their employers. Journalists and their employers should conduct their personal lives in a manner which protects them from conflict of interest, real or apparent. Their responsibilities to the public are paramount. That is the nature of their profession.

3. So-called news communications from private sources should not be published or broadcast without substantiation of their claims to news value.

4. Journalists will seek news that serves the public interest, despite the obstacles. They will make constant efforts to assure that the public's

business is conducted in public and that public records are open to public inspection.

5. Journalists acknowledge the newsman's ethic of protecting confidential sources of information.

Accuracy and objectivity:
Good faith with the public is the foundation of all worthy journalism.

1. Truth is our ultimate goal.

2. Objectivity in reporting the news is another goal, which serves as the mark of an experienced professional. It is a standard of performance toward which we strive. We honor those who achieve it.

3. There is no excuse for inaccuracies or lack of thoroughness.

4. Newspaper headlines should be fully warranted by the contents of the articles they accompany. Photographs and telecasts should give an accurate picture of an event and not highlight a minor incident out of context.

5. Sound practice makes clear distinction between news reports and expressions of opinion. News reports should be free of opinion or bias and represent all sides of an issue.

6. Partisanship in editorial comment which knowingly departs from the truth violates the spirit of American journalism.

7. Journalists recognize their responsibility for offering informed analysis, comment and editorial opinion on public events and issues. They accept the obligation to present such material by individuals whose competence, experience and judgment qualify them for it.

8. Special articles or presentations devoted to advocacy or the writer's own conclusions and interpretations should be labeled as such.

Fair play:
Journalists at all times will show respect for the dignity, privacy, rights and well-being of people encountered in the course of gathering and presenting the news.

1. The news media should not communicate unofficial charges affecting reputation or moral character without giving the accused a chance to reply.

2. The news media must guard against invading a person's right to privacy.

3. The media should not pander to morbid curiosity about details of vice and crime.

4. It is the duty of news media to make prompt and complete correction of their errors.

5. Journalists should be accountable to the public for their reports and the public should be encouraged to voice its grievances against the media. Open dialogue with our readers, viewers and listeners should be fostered.

Pledge:

Journalists should actively censure and try to prevent violations of these standards, and they should encourage their observance by all newspeople. Adherence to this code of ethics is intended to preserve the bond of mutual trust and respect between American journalists and the American people.

Reprinted with the permission of The Society of Professional Journalists, Sigma Delta Chi. Code adopted 1926, revised 1973.

What are some of the ethical problems suggested by such codes? Implicit in such codes is the notion that—even as it is a function of journalism to question the ethics of others—so it must guard against the ethical hazards inherent in news reporting itself. Acceptance of travel expenses to the Caribbean, paid by a large company that opens a resort there, of discounts on new cars or clothes, or even of free groceries or of a bottle of whiskey offered by a news source as a Christmas gift—all of these compromise a journalist's integrity, especially if that journalist later writes, or chooses not to write, a story about the source of the gift.

In such cases, journalistic codes of ethics exert a great deal of moral force; indeed, they are often framed and hung on the walls of many newspaper offices, where they hold a kind of silent vigil over all that goes on in front of them. They carry a certain moral suasion that prevails almost subliminally in all matters journalistic.

The principles they espouse, then, set high ethical standards. But that is all they do—set them.

Unlike the professions of medicine and law, journalism has never had a formal and binding code of ethics that punished those who violated it. People who violate ethical principles in their journalistic work are not required to appear before a grand tribunal of black-robed editors and reporters who pass judgment on misdeeds. Lawyers, on the other hand, can be disbarred if they are unethical; doctors can be prevented from practicing if they transgress accepted medical practice. The action against a doctor or a lawyer comes from a formal body of peers, which investigates the particular allegation and takes decisive action if necessary.

The move for the press to police itself has been slow in coming. Editors and reporters always seemed to feel above reproach. They could write stories questioning the ethics of others but saw scant need to trouble themselves about their own. Since the exposure of the Watergate scandals, however, ethics has been on the minds of editors and reporters a great deal. If they were going to call attention to the wrongdoing of others, journalists felt the need to put their own house in order.

As the 1970s saw still further revelations of lapses in the ethics of government, big business, the military, and in many other areas of national life, the press moved to redefine and tighten its own standards. Because the profession is composed of thousands of news organizations large and small, however, the move was done piecemeal, publication by publication.

Many have issued their own rigorous codes of ethics to govern the conduct of their staffs. Others have fired reporters who do unethical things while on the job. Although somewhat late in making these moves, journalism as a profession has done as much as any area of national life to make the people working within its ranks as free from taint and temptation as possible.

Furthermore, if someone constantly violates the code, the grapevine that functions in journalism eventually works against him or her. A reputation for lack of ethics will gradually catch up with the person, if not on the first job, no doubt by the second or third. Eventually, an editor will call a past employer to ask about the ethics of someone being interviewed, and the truth will be revealed.

Ethical Problems

The new standards were aimed primarily at situations in which newspapers and magazines and their staffs are placed in compromising and tempting positions by a number of practices that used to be widespread.

Freebies

A gift to a reporter or editor had long been viewed as harmless. The company officials who gave the liquor or free dinners or pen sets or furs or perfume were trying to build good will among members of the press. An occasion like Christmas was usually the excuse, and the reporter or editor was not asked to provide anything in return. But how could a reporter write a negative story about a company that gave him or her cheese, wine, and liquor? Wouldn't that be rude? The temptation to water down a criticism or bury a piece of bad news was great. Many did so, but newspapers soon decided that it was wrong to place such temptations in their way at all.

Interestingly enough, the Watergate era has all but eliminated the problem of reporter gifts in Washington. "Christmas comes and goes with no cases of liquor," says Dennis Stern, metropolitan editor of the *Washington Star*. "Reporters know they can put lunch with sources on their expense accounts. They never let themselves be taken out for lunch. They don't want any kind of an impression they can be bought. We don't dwell on it." One of his reporters, Diane Brockett, adds, "I always pay for everything; that's big-city newspaper."

Brockett herself does encounter problems of freebies now and then. When she was doing a recent series on pornography in Washington, she discovered that the Mafia was moving into that field. During her reporting, the owner of a large liquor-wholesaling company said he would give her free liquor for a party if she wouldn't mention the name of his company in the story. He also talked vaguely of giving the Star a six-month advertising contract. She ignored both offers. "It was done very subtly," she says. "But he let me know the liquor would be there."

Also of concern to many in the press is a less obvious type of freebie, the allotment of office space and other facilities in government buildings to reporters who regularly cover state and federal agencies. The question is, Are reporters who cover these agencies influenced by the official help they receive? The solution, however difficult the details, is for the press and government officials to determine jointly a fair charge for desk space in a large pressroom or a seat in the visitors' gallery, making these facilities open to all members of the press equally.

Junkets

Participation by a reporter or editor in a trip in which all expenses are paid is another practice that used to have wide acceptance. It is difficult for television editors to turn down free trips to Hollywood to view new network programs or travel editors to refuse to go to China without paying for the trip if that is the only way they are going to be able to go. Yet acceptance of such trips leaves the reporters and their publications open to criticism. Some newspapers have solved the problem in recent years by allowing reporters to accept such junkets, provided, of course, that they deal with legitimate news events within the scope of the reporter's job, on the condition that the newspaper pay a share of the expenses. Smaller publications, however, whose budgets are limited, accept junkets without that condition.

Memberships in organizations, personal relationships

Holding an office or being a member of a club, committee, board, or other organization can be compromising to a journalist. How can the editor be fair in editing and placing the story? How can the reporter be objective in writing the story? Church membership excepted, many newspapers do not allow their staff to join any organization. "You have to be the kind of person who doesn't want to be a joiner or a doer," says *Gazette-Times* editor Tom Jenks. "As soon as you get involved, you set the stage for compromise."

Personal relationships, too, may be a source of compromise. In beat coverage especially, reporters often build friendships with the people they deal with every day. Indeed, they could not cover their beats adequately without good sources. At times, this leads to conflict of interest if information uncovered on the beat jeopardizes friendships with sources. Such personal considerations should not get in the way of good reporting. Reporters should make it clear from the start that their commitment to journalism comes before their friendships on the beat.

Objectivity

Bias or prejudice in news reporting is the most difficult ethical problem to overcome. "I always give people the chance to respond," says Diane Brockett. "One of the reasons I work such long hours is, I try to be fair. On lots of things, there are certain levels you can go. You can look at one day's material or three days' material. I take the three-day approach."

"You have to ask yourself," says Atkins of the *Gazette-Times,* " 'Is this an accurate, fair, and faithful job of capturing the story without misleading anyone? Have I done the best I could with the time I've had?' That's the kind of ethics—a working ethics."

And city editor, Rod Deckert: "Joe Blow makes a charge against Sam Smith. We've just got to get Smith's reaction. Occasionally a reporter will leave it out for lack of time, but he shouldn't leave it out because he hates the opposition or the one doing the accusing. Some papers don't stress it, we do. Early on, a reporter learns that you just don't have accusation stories without allowing for reaction."

Misrepresentation to sources

Are there times when it is acceptable for a reporter to hide his or her identity? George Wisner and Diane Brockett find that it is necessary to do so, when a difficult subject and source require it.

"My own code may be different, but I will masquerade myself," says Wisner. "I would willingly wear a disguise and do anything I thought was warranted. But that is based entirely on the situation. Usually, I would establish what I was doing, so there was no misunderstanding, when I started to write it down, that it would appear in the paper. I view ethics in terms of conscience, a feeling for the business, what you're doing as a reporter, and the people involved."

Diane Brockett sometimes fails to identify herself over the telephone, but she shares Wisner's reservations; any misrepresentation can be carried too far, and the direct, open approach is best, and sufficient, most of the time. "I have called on the telephone and acted like a citizen," she says. "I still think I get much farther by being open and honest, however."

Checkbook journalism

In recent years some large news organizations, especially television networks, have paid large sums to newsworthy people for the right to interview them. Former president Richard Nixon was paid over $1 million by TV personality David Frost for a series of interviews, his first since resigning as president. Former Nixon aide H. R. Haldeman was reportedly paid $50,000 for a CBS interview with Mike Wallace. Newspapers and magazines offer large sums for the exclusive right to print excerpts from forthcoming books.

The trend to pay for news material is a prevalent one today. Most newspapers cannot afford this practice. It also raises ethical questions. Doesn't the reporter or the news organization become a kind of captive of the person being interviewed? Should legitimate news have to be bought and paid for? These and other questions make the practice of checkbook journalism questionable and unethical much of the time. It should be avoided.

Withholding information at official request

At times, police and other government officials may ask reporters to withhold information because its revelation would disrupt an investigation or harm the welfare of the nation. President John Kennedy requested that the *New York Times* keep advance knowledge of the Bay of Pigs invasion out of its pages. He later said he wished he had let the paper print what it had, so that the invasion would have been called off. Former CIA director William Colby requested that several news organizations withhold their knowledge of the efforts to raise a sunken Soviet nuclear submarine. Police officials often request that reporters and editors keep quiet about negotiations to free a kidnap victim or details about hostages.

Such requests create ethical concerns for reporters and editors. Each instance should be judged individually, and the information withheld if its revelation would, in the opinion of the reporters and editors, harm individuals or the nation. No journalist would knowingly do that. If the request to halt a story is a smoke screen to cover official error or incompetence, however, it should not be granted.

New journalism

The techniques of the new journalism raise special ethical questions. This approach, which uses detailed description and narrative, applies the techniques of fiction writing to newswriting. Tom Wolfe was a pioneer in this field, in articles in *New York* and *Esquire* magazines in the 1960s. Truman Capote used it successfully in his book-length account of multiple murders in Kansas, *In Cold Blood,* in 1965. Many other magazine journalists have written in this style, which is interesting to read.

A question occurs to many readers, however, and to journalists as well: Is it really possible to use the detailed approach of the new journalism without, as a novelist does, resorting to fabrication? What people are thinking, how they talk, how they look, what their houses look like—all these details and more appear in articles using this approach. There have been

290   *Preparing for the Unexpected*

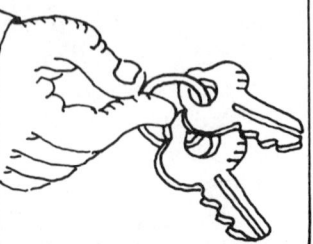

Ethics 291

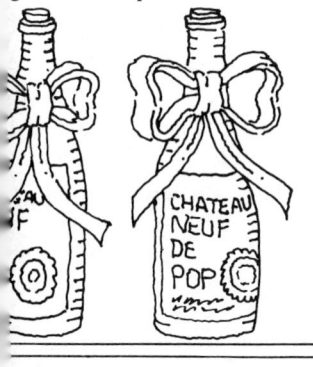

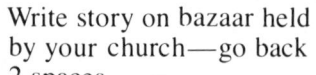

occasional lapses in ethics by magazine writers following this approach; they have sometimes cut corners and given the technique a bad name by making up quotations and using composite characters based on real people.

The new journalism has never been a style that newspaper editors were comfortable in using, and even on magazines its use seems to be on the decline now that the novelty has worn off. "There is no place for such advocacy journalism except on page 4, the editorial page," says Tom Jenks. Most newspaper editors would agree with him, although they can admire the good writing that went along with the new journalism. As Dennis Stern puts it: "The term is outdated, but what it stood for is still with us. . . . [The aspect] I dislike is a reporter posing as someone. But new journalism as it stood for better writing and better ways to do a story is still alive. Longer, magazine-like pieces I do encourage. . . . We spend more time on them, and they are better."

Newspapers today regularly prepare their own ethical codes as a guide to their editors and reporters in dealing with the kinds of ethical problems treated in this chapter. The ethical code of the *Corvallis Gazette-Times* is reproduced on this page, as a representative example, to be considered in the light of the foregoing discussion. It was prepared by editor Tom Jenks, who found that the national codes were not specific enough for his reporters' needs; it is designed, he says, to instill in reporters "what you can't do, why you can't say it."

Corvallis Gazette-Times, **Newsroom Code of Ethics**

Newsroom staffers should not at any time do anything which could reflect adversely on the integrity or credibility of the Gazette-Times.

1. *Elective office.* No newsroom staffer may seek elective office, or work for a candidate for elective office, either for money or voluntarily.

2. *Appointive office.* No newsroom staffer may accept appointment to any board, commission or other body that may be in any manner associated with the function of a government body or agency. This includes ad hoc groups formed to study and make recommendations to a government body or agency.

3. *Memberships.* Memberships and an active role in nongovernmental agencies or groups are encouraged. These could include a hospital board, Boy Scouts, Red Cross, United Way, Parent-Teacher Association, volunteer fire departments. (But not on the board which has direct

dealings with agencies of government.) It should be made clear to other members of the group or organization, however, that a G-T staffer will not serve in any kind of news dissemination role for the group, including coverage or presenting requests for coverage to the newspaper.

Active participation in a partisan or cause-promoting organization or group is discouraged.

4. *Public identification with causes.* Staffers may not display partisan or cause-promoting bumper stickers, lapel pins, buttons or other devices that publicly identify them with controversial or potentially controversial positions.

5. *Objectivity.* News stories are to be written objectively—fairly, if you find "objective" a philosophical impossibility.

Materials other than news stories—reviews, comment, analysis—are to be flagged by the editors with the appropriate slug so the reader clearly knows what he is reading.

There will be no advocacy journalism in the Gazette-Times news columns. Opinions of the paper or of its staff members belong on the editorial pages.

There is to be no personal involvement by a reporter—as a member of the audience—at an event being covered. The reporter is an observer, not a participant. When practical, questions are to be saved until intermission or after the event.

6. *Favors and gifts.* A newsroom staffer shall accept no favors or gifts, or discounts offered because of his association with the newspaper.

Free tickets for events being covered—political speeches, athletic events, plays for review purposes—are acceptable. But a staffer may not accept free tickets to an event he is not covering. The exception to this is tickets purchased by the Gazette-Times for distribution to employes.

A staffer is expected to pay for his own lunch or drinks when visiting or interviewing a source. Reimbursement will be made by the paper.

Junkets offered by a governmental agency are acceptable, but those offered by non-governmental agencies require the approval of the editor before a commitment is made.

7. *Outside or supplemental employment.* A staffer may not hold a job outside of the paper that will or could compromise it. He may not be a correspondent for a competing paper or medium, or hold a job that will or could conflict with his regular duties for the paper.

Stringing for the wire services is permissible, as is freelance work for a non-competing paper or medium. See the editor if there are questions about what is a competing publication.

8. *Radio and television.* Generally, avoid appearances on a competing commercial medium. See the editor before making a commitment.

9. *Petitions.* Newsroom employes are not to circulate petitions, nor are petitions from any person or group to be circulated in the newsroom. Because petitions are by definition issue- or cause-oriented, and because they are public documents, the signing of petitions by newsroom personnel is discouraged. Strictly personal interest petitions—seeking a go-slow sign on your street, making a neighborhood intersection a four-way stop—may be signed. If you have any questions, see the editor before signing.

10. *Other.* A reporter has an obligation to protect confidential sources of information. The newspaper will stand behind him in this regard.

    Charges of misconduct shall not be printed without giving the accused the opportunity to reply.

11. *Corrections.* The G-T will run corrections when presented with evidence that it or a source was in error. Requests for corrections having to do with story interpretation are to be referred to the city editor.

Questions about the ethics code or activity that may conflict with its intent are to be referred to the editor.

Once the codes have been carefully considered and ethical problems evaluated, ethics is, in the final analysis, an individual thing. If reporters and editors take it seriously, they will seldom have problems.

"Ethics are important," says Bill Monroe of the *Gazette-Times*. "I don't stop and think, This is in violation of the Oregon ethics code. I have a strong religious background. I rely on that more. I don't accept free things. Sometimes you can't avoid taking things to avoid insulting the giver. I consider myself an ethical person by nature. I don't stop and think about it; it just comes naturally."

His colleague George Wisner continues: "You have to have a sense of what is right. A lot of times you could write and make people look like idiots when you're being straightforward. I don't agree with those who say it's OK to go to the extent of breaking and entering. But there are certain circumstances where you tread a fine line between the ethical and the unethical and violate the law to prove a higher point."

The worry is always there: "People are always charging you're biased," concludes Mike Hall of the *Topeka Capital-Journal*. "It's something that gnaws at you. You worry about whether it's true."

Summary

Unlike the professions of medicine and law, journalism has never had a formal and binding code of ethics that punished those who violated it. Codes do exist but have no enforcement mechanism. They do exert a great moral force, however, and people who continually violate their principles will eventually not be able to work; the word of their unethical standards will have spread about. The revelations of Watergate have caused journalists to devote more attention to ethics. Such problem areas as freebies, junkets, memberships in organizations, objectivity, misrepresentation to sources, checkbook journalism, personal relationships with sources, and withholding information at official request are being handled more carefully by editors and reporters now than ever before. The technique of the new journalism—writing facts of stories in such a way that they read like fiction—also poses problems if reporters augment the facts with doctored quotes or composite characters.

Suggested Exercises

1. Interview a local reporter and ask him or her the policy on the newspaper regarding freebies, junkets, memberships, and some of the other ethical problems detailed in this chapter. Has the reporter's ethics ever been compromised? Report your findings to the class.

2. Interview a government official or other local news source, with a view to determining that person's opinions on the journalistic ethics of the local newspaper. Report your findings to the class.

3. Read an issue of the local newspaper and look for any apparent ethical violations in headlines, story placement, writing. Report your findings to the class.

4. Write a research paper on the topic "The American press is ethical (or unethical)." Cite examples from current news coverage.

5. Write a research report on the new journalism, detailing its past and present and dealing with its ethical aspects.

"Libel is a big worry to new reporters. I personally give them a forty-five-minute talk stressing the importance of having an understanding of the law without becoming panicky when someone says, 'I'm going to sue you.'"

Dennis Stern, Metropolitan Editor,
the *Washington Star*

15

Libel, Privacy, Contempt, and Other Legal Concerns of the Press

Libel
Invasion of Privacy
Obscenity
Contempt and Confidentiality
Access to Official Information

Libel

Everyone in a newsroom needs to think about libel. From the newest reporter on the most mundane beat to the top investigative reporter covering sensitive subjects to the editor who has the ultimate responsibility, libel has to be on many minds during a newspaper's day.

"I worry about libel constantly," says George Wisner, reporter for the *Corvallis Gazette-Times*. . . . "You make sure everything is true to start with, and you don't go out with the intent to get anyone. If you want someone out of office, you don't let them know. You make sure what you write is true and don't go off half-cocked, out on a limb. If sticking your neck out is based on a gut feeling—and I've done this—you think, I hope I'm right, and wait for the lawyer to walk through the door. You use common sense. If you know everything is correct, the chances of anyone suing are small. Win or lose, it's an expensive proposition."

His colleague Bill Monroe: "Libel is something the editor worries about. I worry about accuracy; that solves the libel. It's something you think about all the time but not as libel. You think about being correct more. You don't specifically think of it when writing a sentence, Is this libelous? but, Is this correct? Should I sit on a city desk, I'd change real quick."

Rod Deckert, city editor of the *Gazette-Times:* "I hope if we get sued, it's not for the wrong reason, that we haven't made an error that only a novice would make. If we are sued and have been truthful and courageous, we can hold our heads up high. I have a specific response to looking at stories that might be sensitive, touchy, or troublesome. I don't figure out if we are going to run it. The editor and I sit down and see if we will have an adequate defense if we run it. The best defense is truth."

Tom Jenks, *Gazette-Times* editor: "I tend to be supersafe in areas of libel, not because I've been stung. I do know what it costs to fight and to win and I'm willing to do it for the story that is worth it. I'm not willing to do it for something not that important. . . . I've pulled stories, some for reasons of taste or because we didn't really have a story. I've killed six stories in my years here. . . . I killed a story on a rape trial. The reporter did it as a slice of life, and it didn't come off. There was no way to justify the language in the testimony. It was explicit. It was not on the problems of rape victims. It was a sensational story."

Diane Brockett, reporter for the *Washington Star:* "On a story when you're saying someone has done something crooked, you make absolutely certain you're willing to stake your career on each word. You try to be as specific as possible. You don't suggest more than you have. If you build up a reputation of being careful and accurate, the desk will take things from you they won't take from other people. Your reputation with your bosses is very important."

Mike Hall, reporter for the *Topeka Capital-Journal:* "Libel is a big concern around here. We're too cautious on libel. I'm reasonably up-to-date. Our paper is deadly afraid of a libel suit. One of my great disappointments happened on a feature I wrote on a rock-and-roll disk jockey which didn't run. The excuse was that it was libelous. He was a controversial figure and made fun of political figures on the air. I didn't include anything he didn't use on his program."

Libel defined

What is libel? The *Random House* Dictionary defines it as "a defamation by written or printed words, pictures, or in any form other than by spoken words or gestures . . . the crime of publishing it . . . anything that is defamatory or that maliciously or damagingly misrepresents."

Everyone in the newsroom is liable for libel if they have handled any part of the story in question: reporter, editor, even news source. Most people realize, however, that reporters and editors don't make much money, so that the news organization itself is the ultimate target and has the final responsibility.

Publications must be careful in what they print about people. No matter what the original intention of the article was, the question is the effect upon those who read it.

Because people in journalism deal in words, it is some of these words that are likely to be libelous: *kidnapper, abortionist, bigamist, liar, cheat, degenerate, dope fiend, crazy, prostitute, bankrupt, deadbeat.* All of these words and many more tend to imply criminality or to question morals, sanity, or financial stability.

There are two kinds of libel: civil and criminal. Most libel cases are in the civil category; that is, a story that constitutes a printed defamation. If the publisher, editor, and reporter lose any lawsuit that results from publication of an alleged libel, they have to pay damages to the person who filed suit against them, called the plaintiff.

There are three kinds of damages:

Compensatory, or general damages are awarded to the plaintiff in a libel case who is harmed by published material; the plaintiff need not prove actual injury.

Special damages are awarded to a plaintiff in a libel case who can show evidence of particular loss to reputation, well being, or profession. This kind of damages may be given in addition to general.

Punitive damages are awarded as a punishment and an example because the offending publication showed malice in printing the alleged libel. The plaintiff must show proof of this malice, however.

Criminal libel, while rare in the United States, results when something written in a newspaper leads to a breach of the peace; for example, a riot or other disturbance that causes personal injury or property damage.

Lack of care causes most lawsuits for libel. Only fools risk their reputations—and that of their newspapers—and invite stiff fines by writing something that is false, inaccurate, or a lie.

Because of the potentially controversial nature of police-beat news and the outcome of court cases, a great many libel cases begin in these two areas.

Reporters can avoid many difficulties by being careful to verify the names and addresses of people in a story, especially those involved in police-beat news. Because police records are not always right, reporters must use telephone books and city directories to verify names and addresses. The proper spelling of names is especially important. For example, if John A. Browne, the leading citizen of a town, were misidentified as John R. Browne, an escaped murderer, he would not be happy and might sue. He might also collect. Reporters should also use the word *alleged* in crime stories to describe the actions of the people being reported.

At other times, people may think that they have been libeled just because their names were used at all, if this brought them to public notice against their wishes. The courts would probably think otherwise if the person in question were involved in a legitimate news event; but sometimes a reporter may well decide to leave out the name to protect a person from such publicity.

In nonlocal stories it is also important to identify a person's hometown correctly. This can be verified by calling directory assistance or by using the telephone book of the town in question.

Defenses

Truth. A reporter's best defense to a charge of libel is to prove in court that what was published is true. In making this defense, the reporter will ideally have saved relevant notes and tape recordings. It might not be sufficient, however, to prove simply the accuracy of the reporting—for example, that a quote was reported accurately—if the veracity of the story itself is not proved.

Fair comment and criticism. Critics, editorial writers, and sports editors are allowed to make "fair comment" on the performance of actors, players, government officials, and others provided that this comment is without malice. The critics and other commentators must restrict their writing to a person's work and not be malicious.

Privilege. Certain kinds of material can be used in stories by reporters as a means to ensure full and complete reporting. This material is thus "privileged" and immune to libel action: statements by judges, lawyers, and witnesses in court as long as the court is in session; debates in Congress and state legislatures; public documents. If something has been stricken from the public record or uttered by a judge or district attorney outside of official business, it is not privileged and might be libelous if used.

Supreme Court rulings as defenses

A series of First Amendment Supreme Court rulings has had a decisive effect on libel law but has made that law unpredictable for the reporters and editors who have to live under its provisions.

In *New York Times* v. *Sullivan,* 1964, the Court ruled that public officials cannot collect libel damages from their journalistic critics unless they are able to prove that what was written about them was a malicious and deliberate lie and in reckless disregard of the truth.

"Debate on public issues should be uninhibited, robust, and wide open," wrote Justice William Brennan in his majority opinion. "It may well include vehement, caustic, and sometimes unpleasant sharp attacks on government officials." If such public officials could collect libel damages from critics without proving that the criticism was a deliberate and malicious lie, the press might be so much intimidated in its reporting of public affairs that the right of free speech would be threatened.

The *Times* case resulted from the newspaper's running of an advertisement appealing for contributions to a defense fund for Martin Luther King. In the advertisement some unkind things were said about the police in Montgomery, Alabama. Although the newspaper conceded that there were inaccuracies in the advertisement, the Supreme Court found the *Times* innocent of malice in accepting it for publication.

This decision was a vital victory for the press, removing, at least for the time being, the anxiety that went with honest and accurate coverage of public officials. The so-called *New York Times* rule stemmed from this decision. As long as the journalists reported upon public officials and public people fairly and without malice, this unofficial rule would protect them.

In *Rosenbloom* v. *Metromedia,* 1971, the Supreme Court broadened the constitutional protection of the press against libel suits by private individuals. Stated simply, this case extended the protection of the *New York Times* rule to private individuals engaged in matters of general interest.

Justice Brennan wrote, "We honor the commitment to robust debate on public issues, which is embodied in the First Amendment, by extending constitutional protection to all discussion and communication involving matters of public or general concern, without regard to whether the persons involved are famous or anonymous."

This case involved a $275,000 libel judgment awarded by a lower court to George A. Rosenbloom, a distributor of nudist magazines. The defendant, Metromedia, Inc., which owns radio station WIP in Philadelphia, had reported Rosenbloom's arrest on charges of selling obscene material. The

Court rejected his argument that as a private citizen he enjoyed more protection of his reputation than did a public figure.

Once again, the press had won a victory, its libel worries eased, it appeared, even in instances where it was reporting upon newsworthy private individuals. The court again required, of course, that the reporting be fair and without malice.

In *Gertz* v. *Robert Welch, Inc.,* 1974, the Supreme Court began to draw back slightly from its earlier protection of the press in libel cases. In *Gertz,* the justices held that the press does not enjoy the same constitutional insulation from libel suits filed by private citizens as it does in cases brought by public figures. The Court held that private individuals can recover actual damages for what it called "defamatory falsehoods" without having to prove the sort of reckless disregard public figures must prove. The justices limited their finding to cases where the "defamatory potential" of the material is apparent to a "reasonably prudent editor or broadcaster."

The Supreme Court did not reverse its decisions in *New York Times* or *Rosenbloom*. "We think that these decisions are correct," it said. It noted, however, that there are legitimate reasons for imposing a higher standard of proof on public officials. Justice Lewis Powell said in his majority opinion that private citizens should not have to prove as much as public officials, such officials having readier access to communications channels that permit them to "counteract false statements." Moreover, individuals who decide to seek public office or prominence do so with the knowledge that they are inviting greater attention and, in turn, greater risk of "defamatory falsehoods."

The private individual does not fit into either category. Such citizens, said Justice Powell, "are therefore more vulnerable to injury and the state interest in protecting them is correspondingly greater."

The case arose in the aftermath of a fatal shooting of a youth by a Chicago policeman in 1968. The boy's family retained Elmer Gertz to represent it in a civil suit against the policeman. In March, 1969, *American Opinion,* a publication of the John Birch Society, published an article that the justices said portrayed Gertz as a "Communist fronter" and as a participant in a "Communist campaign against the police."

The Supreme Court said the article contained "serious inaccuracies" in its references to Gertz. Gertz had won $50,000 in damages in a suit against Robert Welch, Inc., but a federal judge overruled that decision, saying that Gertz had not met the "reckless disregard" standard of the *New York Times* v. *Sullivan* ruling. The U.S. Court of Appeals affirmed that ruling, but the Supreme Court overrode both courts.

In *Firestone* v. *Time,* 1976, the ruling of the Supreme Court broadened the category of individuals who can bring libel actions as private citizens rather than public figures. Like the *Gertz* decision, it is also important because private citizens are not required to prove as much as public figures to collect damages for the publication of defamatory falsehoods.

The dispute arose when *Time* magazine published an item about the divorce of Mary Alice Sullivan Firestone, the former wife of the tire-company heir. The item said the divorce was granted on the basis of "extreme cruelty and adultery." Mrs. Firestone brought a libel and defamation suit alleging that *Time* had falsely reported that the divorce had been granted on grounds of adultery. She won a $100,000 judgment, which was ultimately upheld by the Florida Supreme Court.

The Florida Supreme Court said it found ample support for earlier court findings that the item was incorrect in reporting adultery as one of the grounds for divorce. But the U.S. Supreme Court said *Time* could not be held liable unless its reporting was negligent, and it sent the case back for further consideration. It nevertheless rejected *Time*'s defense that the magazine could not be held liable unless it were proved to have published the item with "actual malice."

Most significant was the Court's ruling that Mrs. Firestone was a private citizen rather than a public figure. Although she was a well-known socialite, the court said, she "didn't assume any role of especial prominence in the affairs of society . . . and she did not thrust herself to the forefront of any particular public controversy in order to influence the resolution of the issues involved in it." The court based its conclusion on a narrow interpretation of the 1974 *Gertz* decision. In future libel cases, it indicated the court would require substantial persuasion before defining a plaintiff as a public figure.

A 1979 Supreme Court ruling further strengthened the rights of public figures in libel cases at the expense of the press. Voting 6 to 3, the Court ruled that journalists accused of libel may be forced to answer questions about their "state of mind" when they were preparing the story, including conversations they had with colleagues in the newsroom during the editorial process of getting the story into print or on the air.

The case involved a former Army colonel who had accused his superiors of covering up atrocities in Vietnam. After the story was presented on the CBS television program, "60 Minutes," Lt. Col. Anthony Herbert charged that he had been falsely portrayed as a liar and filed a multi-million dollar libel suit against CBS. The Court decision did not deal with that libel action but whether attorneys in the case could ask pre-trial questions of the defendants in the case, including newsman Mike Wallace, producer Barry Lando, and editors of the *Atlantic Monthly*, which ran an article using similar material.

The Court found that the federal appeals court in New York had extended greater protection than the First Amendment requires to defendants in a libel suit. In his majority opinion, Justice White said that under past Supreme Court rulings a public figure or a public official can't recover damages for a defamatory falsehood unless he can show it was made with "actual malice." Those decisions "made it essential to proving liability that plantiffs focus on the conduct and state of mind of the defendant," the justice wrote. "Inevitably, unless liability is to be completely foreclosed, the thoughts and editorial processes of the alleged defamer would be open to examination."

This ruling chipped away further the press's newly gained protection against libel suits. Once again the press must worry about libel as a potential legal problem. Reporters and editors should familiarize themselves with these five decisions and their impact. Otherwise, they could be inviting costly, if not ruinous, lawsuits.

Eliminating the risks Precision in reporting can eliminate libel as a problem for journalists. The speed required to meet deadlines often works against exactness. Reporters should fight the tendency to take shortcuts that sacrifice accuracy. They should get stories right, rather than get them first regardless of the consequences.

As a final safeguard in the event of later legal action, reporters should save the notes and tapes of interviews on potentially controversial and troublesome subjects for at least a year.

In any significant news story, says *Gazette-Times* editor Tom Jenks, there is always a risk of libel: "If a news event is all that significant, you take a chance." But such risks should never be courted, he says. "We have libel insurance, but it's silly to stick our neck out; we don't run something just because we're a newspaper and we can do what we want."

Dennis Stern, metropolitan editor of the *Washington Star,* adds: "Libel is a big worry to new reporters. I personally give them a forty-five-minute talk stressing the importance of having an understanding of the law without becoming panicky when someone says, 'I'm going to sue you.'

"Reporters avoid making phone calls to persons [involved in a controversial story]; for example, a doctor involved in a malpractice suit. I tell them to get him to talk about it. Most people are reluctant to talk to people . . . they are writing about in this way. The reporters say, 'Oh, they'll hang up.' At least a third of the time they say, 'No comment,' or 'Go fly a kite.' " But Stern says that more often than not they respond, giving the reporter their side of the story.

Stern lets the managing editor read all sensitive stories. About once every two months, he gives a story to the newspaper's attorney to read. "We get sued once every four months, almost every one a nuisance suit," he says. "We recently lost a libel suit and paid one dollar in damages."

Often, the reasons for the suits border on the ridiculous. "In a recent story about traffic accidents over a certain period," Stern says, "we said a two-car collision was caused when one guy 'darted' into the path of another car. The guy took offense to this description of his driving, and we wrote a correction."

Invasion of Privacy

The police-beat item being no different from countless others he had gathered on the job, Bill Monroe handled it routinely.

"A girl filed a report with the police that she'd been raped," he recalls. "At the police chief's desk I wrote down the facts. I took them back to the paper and wrote an 'On the Record' item. I asked the desk editor, should I use her name? He said yes."

His fellow reporter John Atkins was working the desk that morning, a Saturday in June. At the time, the newspaper had never spelled out a policy in such instances, so that Atkins used his judgment and put the name in, as was the rule in all such police news. Within a few weeks, the woman in question filed suit against the *Corvallis Gazette-Times* and the Corvallis police, pressing for damages of $400,000.

"This is an action for damages by the victim of a rape for invasion of her right of privacy against Corvallis police officials who 'revealed' her name and address and against a Corvallis newspaper which published 'the facts' of the crime, including her name and address," read the final Oregon Supreme Court decision in the case.

In framing their arguments in the case, lawyers for the newspaper and the police department said that the story appeared before the state law prohibiting disclosure of names in such cases had been enacted, a matter of a week later. Therefore, they said, the police and the newspaper were not in violation of the law in releasing information about and in writing the story. The Oregon Supreme Court agreed.

"There is no state law on privacy in Oregon," says editor Tom Jenks. "Your instincts tell you, be careful. But this does not preclude civil action. The [Oregon] Supreme Court did not address the issue. Our legal counsel pursued the matter to get us out of trouble. Instead of arguing that we had every right to print, he argued that at the time the printing of the story occurred, Oregon did not have a law that restricted access to police or criminal records. As long as there was no law against it, we could do it. It cost us $10,000 to win. The supreme court called it a careless error as opposed to making a more definite legal point."

The *Gazette-Times* won, but for the wrong reason. No clear-cut ruling resulted, only a technicality that saved the paper but provided no precedent for handling similar cases in the future.

Since the law went into effect, the newspaper does not use the names and addresses of rape victims, just as it does not use the names and addresses of juvenile offenders. It now proceeds with more caution in such areas.

There is a thin line between a reporter's coverage of legitimate news and an invasion of privacy. On the one hand, the person being reported upon quite often regards the news coverage as an intrusion, particularly if that person does not want to be interviewed. On the other, reporters are taught from their earliest days not to take no for an answer. These two positions often bring reporter and news source into conflict.

Privacy is an area of journalism with few legal precedents, however. The subject is not so well defined as libel. It is an ambiguous area filled with perils for journalists. Indeed, the mere absence of definitive law could invite aggrieved sources and ambitious lawyers to fill the void with lawsuits.

Time v. *Hill*

The Supreme Court has had few opportunities to issue opinions in this area. Its ruling in *Time* v. *Hill* in 1967 is still cited most often in this regard. Interestingly enough, the court went back to the *New York Times* rule for precedent in its finding. If the publication is false or fictitious, said the court, it must be judged by the *Times* rule, testing whether the falsehood was intentional and calculated.

The case involved the Hill family of Pennsylvania, who had been held captive for nineteen hours in 1952 by three escaped convicts. Members of the family had been treated courteously and nonviolently during that time. In his novel *The Desperate Hours,* however, which was based upon the experiences of the Hills, Joseph Hayes portrayed the convicts as beating the father and son and sexually molesting the daughter. None of this had occurred. Then *The Desperate Hours* became a play, and *Life* magazine took the actors to the house to depict events for a feature article. The Hills had moved out by this time.

Hill sued *Life* and its parent company, Time, Inc., after the article appeared. Using a New York State privacy statute, the family's attorney said that the article had given the impression that the play was a true account of their experiences, something *Life* knew was "false and untrue."

In his majority opinion, Justice Brennan rejected the argument that liability for this kind of invasion of privacy could ever be imposed, even for false statements, "unless actual malice—knowledge that the statements are false or in reckless disregard of the truth—is alleged and proved."

The Court has continued to follow the approach established in the *Hill* case, especially in cases involving well-known persons. Observers think there is some doubt, however, that it will be strictly applied when the person is not famous or well known. The test here is whether the activities of the reporter in pursuing the person suddenly made newsworthy are "offensive to the reasonable man." Although people who are suddenly thrust into the news by their chance involvement in accidents, assaults, fires, or riots might not want publicity, the courts have been upholding the rights of reporters to do their jobs.

Cantrell v. Forest City Publishing Company

A question of misrepresentation by a reporter to a source was precisely the problem in *Cantrell v. Forest City Publishing Company,* 1974. At issue was a family's accusation that a Cleveland *Plain-Dealer* reporter had portrayed it "in a false light through knowing or reckless untruths." The feature story in question described the family of a man who was killed when a bridge collapsed. Mrs. Margaret Mae Cantrell, the man's widow, said the story created the impression that she had been interviewed. Instead, the reporter had talked only to her children.

The Supreme Court upheld a verdict from an Ohio court that had awarded her $60,000 in damages. Justice Potter Stewart, in writing his majority opinion, applied the *New York Times* rule of calculated falsehood; the reporter had implied that Mrs. Cantrell had been interviewed, and the article contained what the court called "significant misrepresentations." Justice Stewart hinted, however, that the rule might not be applied routinely in all privacy cases.

Cox Broadcasting v. Martin Cohn

In *Cox Broadcasting v. Martin Cohn,* 1975, the Supreme Court upheld the press in a case involving use of the kind of information whose publication had led to the suit against the *Gazette-Times* in 1973—the publication of the name of a rape victim. Had its case come up after 1975, the *Gazette-Times* would have won for the right reason.

In this case the right of private persons to keep their personal affairs from public disclosure was at issue. The father of a young woman who had been raped and killed by a teenage gang sued an Atlanta television station for using his daughter's name. In its decision, the Supreme Court nullified a Georgia law making it a misdemeanor to use the name of a rape victim in print or broadcast.

The ruling supported the right of the press to carry news stories about open records used in open-court hearings. The decision also praised the press as a conduit for information to citizens about the conduct of their government. "The commission of crimes, prosecutions resulting therefrom, and judicial proceedings arising from the prosecutions," said the majority opinion, "are events of legitimate concern to the public and consequently fall within the press's responsibility to report the operations of government."

In the key opinion, however, Justice Byron White seemed to sound a warning in the area of privacy: "Powerful arguments can be made, and have been made, that however it may be ultimately defined, there is a zone of privacy surrounding every individual, a zone within which the state may protect him from intrusion by the press, with all its attendant publicity."

Further difficulties   Even when famous people are involved, the press must be careful; they have a right to privacy too. Although courts have historically ruled that for people so prominent as to be recognized wherever they go, privacy does not exist, such rulings *are not inevitable*.

There are few people so well known as Jacqueline Kennedy Onassis, widow of both a president of the United States and one of the world's richest men; her name is a household word. In 1972, a federal judge in New York ordered a photographer, who had been making a living from taking pictures of Mrs. Onassis, to stay at least 50 yards away from her, 75 yards away from her two children, and 100 yards away from the family's home and schools. And he was restrained from communicating with them in any way.

In his decision the judge found that individual privacy, while not specified in the Constitution, is protected by the First Amendment right of freedom of assembly and the Fourth Amendment restrictions on search and seizure. The question not settled in this case, however, was whether the right of privacy overrides the First Amendment rights of the press.

A major difficulty with the right to privacy is that it is based upon English common law and derives its authority from local precedent; unlike libel laws, it is not statutory, and it may vary from place to place. This vagueness leaves a large gray area for the press. Various local laws on privacy—yet to be tested in the Supreme Court—deal directly with the protection of individuals. Many of them involve matters of criminal justice and require the destruction of misdemeanor records, for example, or the withholding of information about arrests that do not result in conviction. Although many of them are well-intended laws, for the protection of people accused, but not convicted, of crimes, they do limit the press's ability to scrutinize and to report.

Dennis Stern of the *Washington Star* says the subject of privacy has to be handled more carefully now than in the past. "This is especially true if we are dealing with a nonsuspecting member of the public," he says. "Forty-five percent of them talk about invasion of privacy. They are catching on. They call in and say, 'Invasion of privacy.' This kind of thing is easier to control than libel. You can call a reporter off a story if there is no legitimate reason, no compelling need to run it. If the people involved are in public, there is no problem. If we knock on their door for a story, there might be."

Obscenity

When is printed material obscene?

In *Roth* v. *United States* in 1957, the Supreme Court ruled that obscenity is not protected by the First Amendment. The opinion went on to define obscenity as something the average person, relying on "contemporary community standards," would consider to be appealing only to the "prurient interest." That impression had to be gained as the "dominant theme of the material taken as a whole." The standards so determined should be enforceable nationwide.

In 1964, the *Jacobellis* decision added the requirement that to be judged obscene, material must be shown to be "utterly without redeeming social importance." Subsequent rulings formalized the *Roth* and *Jacobellis* decisions.

The *Miller* decision of 1973 modified the Supreme Court's view of obscenity, setting more definite guidelines to isolate hard-core pornography from expression protected by the First Amendment. Only explicit portrayal of sexual conduct was banned, however. Writing containing such a portrayal would be exempted only if it had "serious literary, artistic, political, or scientific value," or "social importance." Missing was the *Roth* decision's insistence that the community standards be nationwide. Controls on obscenity could thus be placed locally.

Since this decision, a number of district attorneys in cities around the country have used it to prosecute the publishers of magazines like *Hustler* and *Screw*, and several films. The average reporter on a newspaper, however, seldom encounters obscenity as a legal problem. When it becomes an issue, the best approach is to take these Supreme Court rulings and local attitudes into consideration before running a story likely to offend people in a community and be judged obscene.

Contempt and Confidentiality

Since the difficulties arose between the Nixon administration and the press, contempt has loomed as a problem for reporters. A reporter could always be held in contempt (and fined or jailed or both) by a judge for disobeying a court order, disturbing the court process, or attempting to influence a judge's decision or witnesses' testimony. After the Nixon days, however, the charge of contempt was also used increasingly to compel reporters to disclose the names of sources and turn over their notes to government agencies.

Sources

The relationship between a reporter and a source is basic to the practice of journalism. No element of the press, print or electronic, could exist without the sources for the news printed in its pages or broadcast over the airwaves.

Although it is preferable to include the name of a source in a story, a reporter may legitimately omit it if the source can offer a good reason for this. Sometimes the source does not want his or her name used for fear of reprisal because of the information given to the reporter. In these cases, the person can instead be called a "source," an "observer," or, somewhat melodramatically, an "informant."

If courts can compel reporters to reveal the names of their sources, it will become difficult to get people to provide information for stories. If all the sources dried up, there would soon be little news to report.

Notes

As sacred as the confidentiality of sources, is the right of reporters to keep their notes private. A reporter will often mark in notes any information that is to be used for background only and not in print, and also record names, addresses, and telephone numbers of sources there, even confidential ones. In short, a reporter's notes are personal property, not to be looked at or used by anyone else, least of all by officials of government agencies that have their own investigative resources. Otherwise, reporters lose their independence and become arms of the government, something never envisaged by the framers of the First Amendment.

The *Caldwell*, *Branzburg*, and *Pappas* cases

In its decision in the *Caldwell, Branzburg,* and *Pappas* cases in 1972, the Supreme Court went against long-accepted practice when it declined to give journalists the right to keep confidential the names of sources of information used in published or broadcast stories. In the process, it struck a blow at the ability of the press to protect notes and source names. The three cases were of a similar nature and were linked on appeal to the Supreme Court. (At the time, the decision was known as *Caldwell;* more recently, it has been called *Branzburg.*) By a 5 to 4 vote, the justices ruled that journalists can be called before grand juries and compelled to divulge the names of their news sources and answer any questions a jury deems relevant to the matter under investigation.

United States v. *Caldwell* involved Earl Caldwell, then a *New York Times* reporter in San Francisco. He had written a series of articles about the Black Panther party after gaining the confidence of sources in that organization. A federal grand jury subpoenaed him to testify "concerning the aims, purposes, and activities of that organization." It wanted his notes and tape-recorded interviews as well. Caldwell refused, arguing that his very appearance at closed hearings would destroy his relationship with his sources. He lost his case in district court but won in the Court of Appeals, which ruled that the First Amendment did provide a qualified privilege to news reporters, and that Caldwell had a right to refuse to appear. The Supreme Court disagreed and overturned the appeals court.

The *Pappas* case again concerned the Black Panthers. As a reporter for WTEV-TV in New Bedford, Massachusetts, Paul Pappas had gained access to party headquarters by agreeing to protect his sources there. The Bristol County, Massachusetts, grand jury demanded to know who and what he had seen. He refused to tell them and his case went to the Massachusetts Supreme Court, which ruled in favor of the grand jury.

Paul Branzburg, a reporter for the *Louisville Courier-Journal,* was involved in two cases, *Branzburg* v. *Hayes* and *Branzburg* v. *Meigs*. He had been permitted to interview and photograph two men synthesizing hashish from marijuana on the condition that he would keep their identities confidential. Subpoenaed by the local prosecutor, Branzburg said he was protected under the Kentucky reporter-privilege statute. A state court disagreed, as did the state supreme court. In the second case, Branzburg spent two weeks in Frankfort, Kentucky, interviewing and observing drug users and wrote about them. The Franklin County grand jury wanted his testimony; he refused to give it, and again lost in court. The difference between this case and the *Caldwell* and *Pappas* cases it was linked with in appeal is that Branzburg, unlike the other reporters, actually observed the commission of a crime.

"We do not question the significance of free speech, press, or assembly to the country's welfare," wrote Justice Byron White in the majority opinion. "Nor is it suggested that newsgathering does not qualify for First Amendment protection; without some protection for seeking out the news, freedom of the press could be eviscerated. But this case involves no intrusions upon speech or assembly, no prior restraint or restriction on what the press may publish, and no expressed or implied command that the press publish what it prefers to withhold. . . . The use of confidential sources by the press is not forbidden or restricted; reporters remain free to seek news from any source by means within the law. No attempt is made to require the press to publish its sources of information or indiscriminately to disclose them on request.

"The sole issue before us is the obligation of reporters to respond to grand jury subpoenas as other citizens do and to answer questions relevant to an investigation into the commission of crime. Citizens generally are not constitutionally immune from grand jury subpoenas. . . . The claim is, however, that reporters are exempt from these obligations because if forced to respond to subpoenas and identify their sources or disclose other confidences, their informants will refuse or be reluctant to furnish newsworthy information in the future."

In its decision, the Court rejected the claim that reporters were immune from grand jury's subpoenas. The ruling is also notable for recognizing, for the first time, a form of constitutional protection for the newsgathering process and for refusing to concede that that process depends on confidentiality. It also was the first appearance of a Supreme Court theme recurring in later decisions; namely, that members of the press are not in any way different from other citizens in their obligation to cooperate with courts and law-enforcement officials. In other words, although the Court affirmed the reporters' rights to First Amendment protection, it gave them no special privileges.

Repeatedly, the White opinion poses a conflict between supposedly purely private interests of the press and the public interests of the criminal-justice system. "Private restraints on the flow of information," he wrote, "are insufficient to override public interests."

In a strong dissent, Justice Potter Stewart wrote that "the court's crabbed view of the First Amendment reflects a disturbing insensitivity to the critical role of an independent press in our society."

The White opinion closed with the assurance that "official harassment of the press undertaken not for purpose of law enforcement but to disrupt a reporter's relationship with his news sources would have no justification."

Almost immediately after the *Branzburg* decision, judges, lawyers, and grand juries around the country began to subpoena news people. More than thirty-five reporters who refused to disclose the names of sources and give up notes were served with contempt citations in the first year after the ruling. A few were jailed as well.

Things eased on the federal level, however, with the issuance of guidelines for federal grand juries; the guidelines state that the press is not an investigative arm of the government.

Shield laws

In 1973, alarmed by the various contempt citations and jailings of reporters at the time of the *Branzburg* decision, senators and members of Congress introduced bills to protect journalists and their sources. Because they are designed to protect reporters from interference in the way they do their work, these proposed laws were called shield laws.

Reporters testifying in the congressional hearings that followed *Branzburg* pressed for a law that would give them absolute protection from subpoenas of confidential material at the federal and local levels. Such an approach was taken by Representative John Moss of California. His proposed law read, in part, "No person shall be required to disclose to any grand jury, or court in the United States, or to the Congress, or to any agency, the source from or through which such persons received information in their capacity as a newsperson."

Such absolute protection was opposed by other representatives and some reporters as unconstitutional; it would violate the Fifth and Sixth Amendments as they apply to the rights of defendants in trials.

Other proposals took a qualified shield-law approach, protecting the press within carefully prescribed limits. On this view, reporters would receive immunity unless they had actual personal knowledge which proved or disproved the commission of a crime charged or under investigation.

The move toward a federal shield law gradually slowed, however. No such law was ever enacted. The national threat eased as the Nixon administration backed off from its earlier confrontation with the press. When the president was forced to resign, the threat all but vanished on the national level.

It has been a different situation locally, however. The issuance of subpoenas and the jailing of reporters have continued unabated. For this reason, twenty-six states eventually passed shield laws.

An early—and typical—law was the one enacted in Oregon in 1973. It limits the power of the grand jury, legislature, court, or public official to require reporters and editors to disclose "the source of any published or unpublished information" obtained in reporting or "any unpublished information obtained or prepared . . . in the course of gathering, receiving or processing information." Shield laws in other states vary in some details.

Even in states with shield laws, however, there is still argument in differentiating between civil and criminal issues. A reporter can still go to jail for refusing to disclose information to a court, as *New York Times* reporter Myron Farber found out in 1978.

News People as Witnesses: Shield Law of Oregon
44.510 Definition:

(1) "Information" has its ordinary meaning and includes, but is not limited to, any written, oral, pictorial or electronically recorded news or other data.

(2) "Medium of communication" has its ordinary meaning and includes, but is not limited to, any newspaper, magazine or other periodical, book, pamphlet, news service, wire service, news or feature syndicate, broadcast station or network, or cable television system. Any information which is a portion of a governmental utterance made by an official or employe of government within the scope of his or her governmental function, or any political publication subject to ORS 260.502 to 260.532, is not included within the meaning of "medium of communication."

(3) "Processing" has its ordinary meaning and includes, but is not limited to, the compiling, storing and editing of information.

(4) "Published information" means any information disseminated to the public.

(5) "Unpublished information" means any information not disseminated to the public, whether or not related information has been disseminated. "Unpublished information" includes, but is not limited to, all notes, outtakes, photographs, tapes or other data of whatever sort not themselves disseminated to the public through a medium of communication, whether or not published information based upon or related to such material has been disseminated.

44.520 No person connected with, employed by or engaged in any medium of communication to the public shall be required by a legislative, executive or judicial officer or body, or any other authority having power to compel testimony or the production of evidence, to disclose:

(1) The source of any published or unpublished information obtained by him in the course of gathering, receiving or processing information for any medium of communication to the public; or

(2) Any unpublished information obtained or prepared by him in the course of gathering, receiving or processing information for any medium of communication to the public.

44.530 (1) ORS 44.520 applies regardless of whether a person has disclosed elsewhere any of the information or source thereof, or any of the related information.

(2) ORS 44.520 continues to apply in relation to any of the information, or source thereof, or any related information, even in the event of subsequent termination of a person's connection with, employment by or engagement in any medium of communication to the public.

44.535 ORS 44.520 does not apply with respect to the content or source of allegedly defamatory information, in civil action for defamation wherein the defendant asserts a defense based on the content or source of such information.

44.540 If the informant offers himself as a witness, it is deemed a consent to the examination also of a person described in ORS 44.520 on the same subject.

The *Farber* case

Farber was jailed by a judge in New Jersey—a state with a shield law—for refusing to surrender notes gathered in writing articles about thirteen mysterious deaths in a hospital in that state. His articles caused officials to reopen the case and eventually to charge a doctor for murder.

When Farber was called to testify in the trial, he refused to answer questions he thought would compromise his sources. The doctor's lawyer then subpoenaed his notes, and he refused to give them up. The judge then said he would review them to see whether the material was pertinent to the case. The reporter and the newspaper again declined and were cited for contempt of court. After several temporary delays, Farber was jailed and fined $2,000. The *Times* eventually paid $285,000 in fines and over $200,000 in legal fees. When the doctor was found not guilty by a jury, Farber was released after spending 40 days in jail.

In the meantime the case had progressed to the New Jersey Supreme Court, which upheld the reporter's conviction and the fines against the *Times*. A month after Farber's release the U.S. Supreme Court refused, without comment, to review the case, thus letting the earlier court verdicts stand.

In addition to its bearing on the protection of sources and notes, the case illuminates the clear clash between the First Amendment's guarantee of a free press and the Sixth Amendment's right to a fair trial. The doctor's lawyer contended that he needed the notes to prove his client's case. This argument was supported by the judge, despite Farber's insistence that he did not witness a crime or have anything in his notes to establish the defendant's guilt or innocence. The surrender of his notes, he said, would make him an investigative arm of the government, a role never intended for the press.

The shield law in this case was interpreted in different ways by the press and the judiciary. Farber and the *Times* thought it should protect them, and the lower court and the judge seemed to ignore it. The New Jersey Supreme Court decided that the shield law "must yield" to the defendant's Sixth Amendment rights to a fair trial.

Before the *Farber* case journalists in states with shield laws felt safer than those in states without. This case makes it an open question what protection is afforded by shield laws. Nevertheless, it is probably just as well that the U.S. Supreme Court declined to become involved in this vital area. In view of the antipress orientation of its recent decisions, a *Farber* decision might have gone against the press. The issue remains one to be dealt with case by case, state by state.

Most reporters and people planning to become reporters would like to think that they would willingly go to jail to protect the names of sources and the confidentiality of notes, as Farber did. Beyond romantic notions of martyrdom, there is a sound reason to do so: The rights being protected are basic to the successful practice of journalism.

This willingness should not be taken lightly. The jailing of a reporter, while still rare in this country, has widespread repercussions for the jailer as well as the jailed. If it occurs, it should be for the right reason—to protect sources in need of protection and not to rescue shoddy reporting.

In the section on libel, readers were advised to save their notes for at least a year. That advice must now be qualified: Reporters who conduct interviews with sources who need protection might best destroy all notes and tapes to safeguard both themselves and their sources. This is especially true since the Supreme Court ruling in the *Stanford Daily* case.

The *Stanford Daily* case

A new element concerning contempt problems for the press appeared in the 1978 *Zurcher* v. *The Stanford Daily* decision. Voting 5 to 3 to overturn a lower court's ruling, the justices held that police officers may obtain a warrant to conduct unannounced searches of newsrooms for evidence of a crime, even though they do not suspect anyone connected with the newspaper of wrongdoing. Previously the police had to obtain a subpoena for the material they wanted. A subpoena can be contested in court and takes longer to obtain than a search warrant.

The case resulted from a 1971 sit-in during which demonstrators seized part of the Stanford University Hospital. The *Daily* covered the event. In the resulting violence, nine policemen were injured. Three days later police obtained a search warrant and arrived at the offices of the *Daily* looking for other photographs of the clash than those already published by the newspaper. Only two of the assailants had been identified at the scene, and the police hoped to find out about others in any unpublished photographs found in the offices. They uncovered no new photographs in their search of the newspaper.

The *Stanford Daily* filed suit against the policemen making the search, the chief of police, the district attorney, one of his deputies, and the judge who had issued the search warrant, on the grounds that the paper's rights under the First and Fourth Amendments had been violated. (The Fourth Amendment protects against unreasonable search and seizure.)

Two lower courts found that the newspaper's constitutional rights had been violated and ordered police to pay attorney's fees. The Supreme Court majority rejected the lower courts' contention that a search warrant should be issued in such situations only if there is a "clear showing" that a subpoena ordering the newspaper to give up the material would result in the destruction of the material.

"Properly administered," wrote Justice White, "the preconditions for a warrant—probable cause, specificity with respect to the place to be searched and the things to be seized, and overall reasonableness—should afford sufficient protection against the harms that are assertedly threatened by warrants for searching newspaper offices.

"Valid warrants may be issued to search *any* property . . . at which there is probable cause to believe that fruits, instrumentalities or evidence of a crime will be found. . . . The critical element in a reasonable search isn't that the owner of the property is suspected of a crime but that there is reasonable cause to believe that the specific things to be searched for and seized are located on the property."

The varying definitions of such a "reasonable search" are what worries editors and reporters. What seems reasonable to police might not seem so to journalists. Editors and reporters all over the United States immediately raised the specter of heavy-handed policemen breaking down the doors of newspapers and pilfering files in their search for evidence.

Justice Stewart raised another problem in his dissent to the majority opinion. He attacked the court's "facile conclusion" that police searches of news organizations would not seriously burden the "constitutionally protected function of the press to gather news." He argued that if police can search a newsroom, "including, presumably, every file in the office," confidential sources might refuse to talk to the press if they think their statements might fall into official hands. This fear could dry up sources and inhibit the coverage of news.

Editors and reporters immediately pointed out that the *Stanford Daily* decision might have prevented stories about the Pentagon Papers and various aspects of the Watergate scandal. In contrast, others felt that although it might have a telling effect on small, local, independent, and socially dissident publications, the national press would probably be protected from abuses by its own access to the public.

Some government officials and politicians called for laws that would put strict limits on police searches of newsrooms. Some journalists countered that such new rules might be an admission that the First Amendment itself does not provide adequate protection to the press. In the end, most journalists agreed that full reporting of every infringement of press freedom was the best way to avoid police excesses.

Gag orders

Another part of the contempt problem is the practice by judges of issuing rules that prevent any coverage of trials because they fear the effect of publicity on the outcome. Because they halt all coverage, such rulings are called gag orders. In 1976 one found its way to the Supreme Court. During the trial of a man for mass murder in Nebraska, a judge issued such an order against coverage. The state press association filed suit, and the case reached the Supreme Court.

The Court's decision in *Nebraska Press Association* v. *Stuart* overturned the order of the Nebraska judge banning press publication of information obtained in open court, calling it prior restraint and a violation of the constitutional guarantee of freedom of the press. Although Chief Justice Warren Burger cautioned the press on its duty to "protect the rights of an accused to a fair trial by unbiased jurors," his decision in the case allows the press to perform that duty at its own discretion. Even while rejecting the notion that the First Amendment is an "absolute" ban on all court orders against prejudicial publicity, the Burger opinion leaves very little room for such orders.

Basically, the decision requires judges to explore all other possibilities before even considering attempts at direct control of the press. The ruling also casts doubt on the effectiveness of such controls and discourages their use.

Access to Official Information

Open meetings laws and public records laws

Many states have enacted open meetings laws and public records laws to aid reporters in covering governmental agencies. Those of Oregon are typical. The Oregon Public Records Law provides for "expanded citizen awareness and participation in the conduct of the public business by public bodies and broadened access to the records of the various public agencies."

The Oregon Public Meetings Law applies to any meeting of a state or local governmental board, commission, council committee, or subcommittee consisting of two or more members created to deliberate public matters. The law applies also to formal or informal advisory groups, but not to staff meetings where a vote is taken. The law expressly forbids private meetings of a quorum for the purpose of deciding something but does not prohibit "chance or social meetings of a quorum of a governing body." Public notice must also be given of the time and place of meetings.

Kansas has a similar law, and *Topeka Capital-Journal* reporter Mike Hall carries a copy of it in his briefcase at all times. "It outlines the procedures to be followed in closing a meeting," he says. "If the members of the city council are discussing the buying of property, for example, I might agree that that is a legitimate thing to keep out of a story. As long as I am convinced a closed meeting is necessary, I will leave with the understanding that someone brief me later. At other times, when I wasn't convinced, I have refused to leave, and the meeting has ended right then."

As Hall's experience with the city council illustrates, reporters still have no guarantee of easy, automatic access to government information. Nevertheless, open meetings laws and public records laws, where they exist, have opened up government at all levels. In states that lack such regulations it can often be difficult for reporters to do their jobs.

Freedom of Information Act

At the federal level the Freedom of Information Act is the governing law for the disclosure of information. Although its provisions are complicated and filled with exceptions, the act has succeeded in opening up areas of federal agencies previously allowed to operate in total secrecy.

The various parts of the act are too long to reproduce here. In brief, it sets up a procedure to follow in seeking information. The act establishes that any person can request information, the press having no more rights than the average citizen. Reporters and publications have made the greatest number of requests, however.

As a first step, the person making the request should "reasonably describe" the information wanted. This person does not have to know the specific document or docket number but must be specific enough to permit a government employee to identify the information. In general, reporters should call the agency, identify themselves as reporters, and request the information. If turned down on the telephone, they should next try the press officer, whose job it is to be understanding of reporters' problems.

The act contains a provision declaring an "arbitrary" or "capricious" denial of information sought under the act can subject the government employee concerned to administrative penalties by the Civil Service Commission, including the loss of salary. The Reporters Committee for Freedom of the Press says that the mention of this provision frequently causes lower-level employees to release the information or to pass the decision on to the next level of authority. The committee urges reporters to tell any agency officials they talk to that they intend to make a formal request; they should appeal any denial and then file a lawsuit.

One loophole in the act has been the fees for document reproduction and the time taken to provide the information. Individual agencies set the fees, and if an agency charges eight dollars a page for longer documents, for example, the cost might be prohibitive. Also, delays in the search process are sometimes hard to prove.

State open meetings and public records laws and the federal freedom of information legislation have aided the press. Reporters and editors should be familiar with their provisions and use them as often as necessary.

Summary

Legal problems confront reporters every day. Libel is their most frequent worry, although a series of defenses are possible to guard against it: truth, fair comment and criticism, privilege, and four Supreme Court decisions. The latter demonstrate the changeability of libel law. In *New York Times* v. *Sullivan* (1964) the court ruled that public figures cannot sue reporters and publications unless they can prove that what was written about them was a malicious and deliberate lie. In *Rosenbloom* v. *Metromedia* (1971) the court applied the same rule to private people when they are involved in matters of

320 Preparing for the Unexpected

Legal Concerns of the Press

public interest. In *Gertz* v. *Robert Welch, Inc.* (1974), however, the court said the press does not enjoy the same protection from libel suits by private citizens as it does in cases filed by public figures. *Firestone* v. *Time* (1976) broadened the category of those who can bring libel actions as private citizens rather than public figures.

Invasion of privacy is another legal concern for the press but its legal precedents are less clear-cut than those for libel. In general, the press must be more careful in reporting about private citizens than about public figures. Contempt and confidentiality of a reporter's notes and sources are an area of increasing concern. Since the *Branzburg* decision in 1972, when the Supreme Court ruled that journalists can be compelled to reveal names of sources to grand juries, the press has become more vulnerable. The 1978 decision in the *Stanford Daily* case created an even bigger problem. Because it sanctions police searches of newsrooms if the police have warrants, this Supreme Court decision jeopardizes both note and source confidentiality. Other legal concerns of the press include obscenity and access to official information.

Suggested Exercises

1. Write a research paper analyzing a Supreme Court libel ruling.
2. Research the libel laws of the state.
3. Research the privacy situation in the state, including any recent cases.
4. Research the situation in the state involving privilege and contempt. Does the state have a shield law?
5. Research the obscenity situation in the state, including any recent cases.
6. Research the Supreme Court decision in the *Stanford Daily* case and predict its likely effect on the press.
7. Does the state have a freedom of information act or an open meetings law? Find out and write a paper on the subject.
8. Research the changing libel situation for reporters. How serious a threat is libel now as compared with five years ago?

Appendix: Stylebook, Copy-Editing Marks, and Copy Preparation*

Stylebook

Abbreviations

1. Abbreviate the following titles before a full name: *Dr., Gov., Lt. Gov., Mr., Mrs., Rep., the Rev., Sen.,* and military titles like *Gen., Col., Capt., 1st Lt., Sgt., Pfc., Adm., Cmdr.,* and *Lt. j.g.* Spell out all except *Dr., Mr.,* and *Mrs.* when using them before a surname alone.

2. After an individual name, abbreviate *Junior* or *Senior.* Abbreviate *Company, Corporation, Incorporated,* and *Limited* after the name of a firm or corporation.

3. With dates or numerals, use the abbreviations *A.D., B.C., a.m., p.m., No.* Do not use them without numbers.

4. When a month is used with a specific date, abbreviate only *Jan., Feb., Aug., Sept., Oct., Nov.,* and *Dec.* Spell them out when using them alone or with a year alone.

5. In numbered addresses, abbreviate *Avenue, Boulevard,* and *Street.* Spell them out if they are used alone. Abbreviate the names of states or nations with a city or town in datelines, with a city or town in text, or in short-form listings of party affiliation (*R-Ore.*).

6. Spell out the names of the fifty states when they stand alone in text material. Never abbreviate *Alaska, Hawaii, Idaho, Iowa, Maine, Ohio, Texas,* and *Utah.* Abbreviate the other states as follows:

Ala.	Fla.	Md.	Neb.	N.D.	Tenn.
Ariz.	Ga.	Mass.	Nev.	Okla.	Vt.
Ark.	Ill.	Mich.	N.H.	Ore.	Va.
Calif.	Ind.	Minn.	N.J.	Pa.	Wash.
Colo.	Kan.	Miss.	N.M.	R.I.	W. Va.
Conn.	Ky.	Mo.	N.Y.	S.C.	Wis.
Del.	La.	Mont.	N.C.	S.D.	Wyo.

*The stylebook is based upon the Associated Press Stylebook and Libel Manual *(New York: The Associated Press, 1977).*

Capitalization

"In general," says the *Associated Press Stylebook,* "avoid unnecessary capitals. Use a capital letter only if you can justify it by one of the principles listed here."

1. Capitalize proper nouns, that is, nouns that constitute the special identification of an individual person, place, or thing (*John, America*).

2. Capitalize common nouns like *party* and *river* if they are used as part of a full name (*Republican Party, Columbia River*). Use lowercase (small) letters when they stand alone.

3. Capitalize popular names like *South Side of Chicago* and the *Badlands*.

4. Capitalize words derived from a proper noun and still depending on it for meaning (*American, Christian*).

5. Capitalize the first words in a statement that stands as a sentence.

6. Capitalize the principal words in the names of books, movies, plays, operas, songs, radio and television programs, works of art.

7. Capitalize formal titles when using them immediately before a name. Put them in lower case when using them alone in sentences where they are set off from the name by commas. Use lower case at all times for terms that are job descriptions rather than formal titles.

Numerals

1. Use letters *I, V, X, L, C, D,* and *M* for roman numerals; but use the arabic forms 1, 2, 3, 4, 5, 6, 7, 8, 9, 0 unless roman numerals are specifically required. The figures 1, 2, 3, and so on, and the corresponding words *one, two, three,* are called cardinal numbers; *1st, 2nd, 3rd,* and *first, second, third,* are ordinal numbers.

2. Spell out whole numbers of less than 10, use figures for numbers of 10 and more.

3. When large numbers are spelled out, use a hyphen to connect words ending in *y* to another word (*thirty-one*); do not use commas between other separate words that are part of one number (*one thousand one hundred fifty-five*).

4. Spell out a numeral at the start of a sentence, or if necessary, rewrite the sentence. A numeral that identifies a calendar year is an exception; never spell it out.

5. Spell out fractional amounts of less than one, using hyphens between words (*two-thirds*). Use figures for precise fractional amounts larger than one, converting to decimals when practical.

6. Spell out *first* through *ninth* when they indicate sequence in time or location (*first base*). Starting with 10th, use figures.

7. Use *1st, 10th,* and so forth when ordinals have been assigned in forming names (*7th Fleet*).

8. Use words or numerals according to an organization's practice (20th Century Fox, Big Ten).

Names

"In general," says the *Associated Press Stylebook,* "people are entitled to be known however they want to be known, as long as their identities are clear. When an individual elects to change the name by which he has been known . . . , provide both names in stories until the new name is known by the public. After that, use only the new name unless there is a specific reason for including the earlier identification."

1. Abbreviate *Junior* as *Jr.* and *Senior* as *Sr.* only with the full name of persons and do not precede by a comma. Use *II* or *2nd* after a person's name if the person desires it, although these are not the equivalent of *Junior*.

2. Use the middle initials; they are part of a person's name. Particular care is needed to use them when they help identify a specific individual in crime stories or on casualty lists.

3. A nickname should be used in place of a person's given name only when it is the way that person wants to be known (*Jimmy Carter*). When a nickname is used in addition to the full name it should be set off with quotation marks. In sports stories and sports columns, commonly used nicknames may be substituted without the use of quotation marks (*Bear Bryant, Catfish Hunter*); if the given name is used, the nickname must be set off in quotation marks (*Paul "Bear" Bryant*).

Punctuation

"Think of [punctuation] as a courtesy to your readers, designed to help them understand a story," says the *Associated Press Stylebook.* "Inevitably, a mandate of this scope involves gray areas. For this reason, the punctuation . . . entries [are] guidelines rather than rules. Guidelines should not be treated casually, however."

Apostrophe This mark shows possession (*John's,* dogs'). It also may indicate letters that have been omitted (*don't, rock 'n' roll*), figures that have been left out (*class of '70*), or the plural of a single letter (*three R's*).

Colon This mark is used most frequently at the end of a sentence to introduce lists. Capitalize the first word after a colon only if it is a proper noun or the start of a complete sentence. The colon can also be effective in giving emphasis ("One word described her day: hectic"), and it is used in expressing time of day and time elapsed (1:31:07.2), in biblical and legal citations, in dialogue, and for question and answer interviews. Whereas a comma is sufficient to introduce a direct quotation of one sentence, a colon can be used to introduce longer quotations within a paragraph and to end all paragraphs that introduce a paragraph of quoted material. The colon belongs outside quotation marks unless it is part of the quotation.

Comma This mark serves many purposes. It can be used to separate elements in a series but not before the conjunction in a simple series, to separate adjectives of equal rank, with nonessential clauses and phrases, with introductory clauses and phrases, with conjunctions, to introduce direct quotes, before attribution, with hometowns and ages, with party affiliations and academic degrees, with names of states and nations used with city names, with yes and no in a sentence, in direct address, and in large figures higher than 999. Commas belong inside quotation marks.

Dash This mark indicates an abrupt change in sentence structure, sets off a series within a phrase, and is used before an attribution, after a deadline, and to introduce items on a list. Put a space on both sides of a dash except at the start of a paragraph or sports summary set in small type.

Ellipsis This should be treated as a three-letter word, constructed with three periods (. . .) and two spaces. A regular period should be added before the ellipsis if the sentence ends. Use an ellipsis to indicate the omission of one or more words in condensing quotes, texts, and documents. Be careful to avoid omissions that distort the meaning of the material being quoted.

Exclamation mark This mark can be used for emphatic expression like a high degree of surprise or strong emotion. Its use should be avoided most of the time. If it is a part of a quotation, it should be placed inside the quotation marks, outside if it is not.

Hyphen This mark is what the AP calls a "joiner." It should be used to avoid ambiguity, with compound modifiers (two or more words expressing a single concept), two-thought compounds (socio-economic), compound proper nouns and adjectives. A suspensive hyphenation is done this way: "He received a 10- to 20-year sentence in prison."

Parentheses These should be used around abbreviations (AP, UPI) but otherwise used sparingly because they are jarring to the reader. At times, they can be used to insert necessary background material in stories or quotes. If something is inserted with a proper name, use parentheses (The Huntsville (Ala.) Times); use commas if the phrase is not a proper name (The Selma, Ala., group).

Period This mark indicates the end of a declarative sentence, of a mildly imperative sentence, of some rhetorical questions, and of an indirect question. It is used with many abbreviations, with initials, and in enumerations ("1. eat, 2. drink"). Periods always go inside quotation marks.

Question mark This mark is used at the end of a direct question, a question used inside another sentence, and in multiple questions. The mark goes inside or outside quotation marks, depending on meaning. The question mark supersedes the comma that is normally used when supplying attribution for a quotation (" 'Who is there?' she asked").

Quotation marks These twin marks surround the exact words of the speaker or writer in a story. If the quotation is more than one paragraph long, do not close the quotation marks at the end of the paragraph. Do open them again at the beginning of subsequent paragraphs until the quoted material has ended, followed by quotation marks. In dialogue each person's words, no matter how brief, are in quotation marks. Quotation marks should also be used around titles of books, movies, plays, operas, poems, songs, lectures, speeches, artwork and television programs, around nicknames, and around ironic or unfamiliar terms. They do not belong in question-and-answer formats or full texts, nor should they be used on brief quotations that consist of no more than a few unremarkable words or a commonplace phrase. For quotations within quotations, use single quotation marks. The period and comma always go within quotation marks, but the dash, colon, semicolon, question mark, and exclamation point go within the quotation marks only when they belong to the quoted material. They go outside when they apply to the whole sentence.

Semicolon This mark serves to indicate a more emphatic pause in thought than a comma can convey, but less than the pause indicated by a period. It also serves to separate elements in a series when those elements contain material set off by commas or to link independent clauses when they lack a coordinating conjunction like *as, and, but*. The semicolon is placed outside quotation marks.

Copy-Editing Marks

Copy-editing marks help reporters and editors. Without them, they would have to type their copy over and over until it was error free. With the marks, made neatly with a well-sharpened pencil, minor changes can be added quickly and easily. The cursor on the video-display terminal is rapidly replacing the pencil and the marks. But these marks are important for any basic knowledge of journalistic editing. They are still needed on rough drafts and on newspapers and magazines that do not yet have VDTs or other electronic equipment.

Paragraph Two marks suffice here, but they should never be used at the same time.

```
¶Now is the time for all good men to come to the aid of their

  country.  |Now is the time for all good men to come to the aid

of their country.
```

Capitalization Three lines under the letter or words to be capitalized is how this is done.

```
                    now is the time for
                    ===
```

Lowercase A slanted line drawn through the offending capital letter makes it lowercase.

```
              Now is the time for all good men
                             /
```

Abbreviations A spelled-out word can be abbreviated and an abbreviated word can be spelled out by drawing a circle around it.

```
(November) 5, 1978 was the date set for all good men to come to

  the aid

  Good men will come to the aid of their country in (Nov.)
```

Numbers Arabic figures can be changed to words and vice versa by drawing a circle around them.

```
      (7) good men came to the aid of their country

    The committee picked (twenty) men to come to the aid
```

Transposing   The transposing sign that surrounds the transposed letters or words puts them in their proper order.

  Now is (hte) time for all (men good) to come to the aid of their country.

Inserting   A bracket can be used to insert letters or words left out in typing.

  Nw is the time for good men to come to the aid of their country.

Space   A short curved line both above and below the open space indicates that it is to be closed up.

  Now is the ti me for all goo d men to come to the aid of their coun try.

No space   A vertical line drawn between closed-up letters adds space between them.

  Now is the time for all good men to come to the aid of their country.

Punctuation   Omitted punctuation marks can be added by enclosing the mark in a caret sign, V-shaped if the punctuation belongs above the line, an inverted V if it belongs on the line. It is best to add a period by putting an X in a circle, however.

  We wont be able to come at all even though it is to the aid of our country he said.

No paragraph, large deletion A line, possibly with an arrow on the end, indicates that material has been removed, leading on to that which is to be used.

```
Now is the time, to come to the aid of their party, said one
man to all the other good men around. Now is the time for
all good men to come to the aid of their country.
```

Deletion A deleted word is crossed through with a horizontal line, a single letter with a diagonal line. The close-up sign is also used; the mark on the top and bottom means close up completely, the mark on the top only, means close up leaving one space.

```
Now is the timme for all good men to come to the the aid of
their country.
```

Copy Preparation

On newspapers not using video-display terminals or in newswriting classes, copy should be prepared in the following manner:

1. In the upper left corner of the page, about one inch from the top, type your first and last name. The left margin should be one inch too.

2. Two spaces below that should be the "slug line," consisting of a word or phrase that identifies the story for those who read it after it is turned in. Reporters do not write headlines, so that it is an empty exercise to waste much time on this line. Put the date two spaces below the slug.

3. The story should begin about four or five inches below the date, to leave room for instructions to the typesetter or for rewriting of the lead if necessary.

4. All newspaper copy should be double-spaced, so that changes to it can be written in easily.

5. If the story runs more than one page, the word *more,* set off by hyphens (*-more-*) should be placed at the bottom so that the typesetter knows there are more pages to the story.

6. At the top of the next and succeeding pages, the name of the reporter, the slug line, and *p. 2* or *222222222* can be used.

7. At the end of the story comes the end mark (#), or *-30-* or *end*.

8. Reporters should not strike over letters and words that are in error. That will only obscure their meaning. It is best to make such changes after the typing is complete, using a pencil and not a ballpoint pen. A pen mark is too permanent and will have to be crossed out if an error is made; a pencil mark can be erased.

9. After reporters have edited their stories, they should verify the spelling of names and then box them to alert editors that this has been done.

The correct way to type a news story.

```
Ron Lovell

Election errors

Nov. 7, 1978
```

    There are many different issues, and two separate slates of candidates for voters to choose from during Tuesday's primary election, but officials believe most voters will have one thing in common: confusion.

    And, say the officials, confused voters frequently negate their voice government by voting incorrectly.

    Voters can save themselves time and trouble by knowing before they get to the polling place for whom and for what they are going to vote.

    The easiest method is to list choices in advance and take the list to the polling place, say officials. Doing this can save time, a precinct workers' time and--most important--your vote.

-30-

Glossary

Advance A story that appears in the newspaper a day or so before a particular event to give readers early information about that event.

Advertising A means to sell products to potential buyers through use of printed or broadcast advertisements that stress advantages of the products and reasons to buy them.

Advertising manager The person responsible for selling that space in the newspaper in which companies, organizations, and individuals advertise their products and services.

Advertising side The part of a newspaper organization concerned with selling advertising space and preparing advertisements.

Anecdotal lead A lead that uses an anecdote to interest readers in a story.

AP Associated Press, one of the two major wire services.

Assignment Instructions to a reporter on what story to cover.

Attribution Identification of the source of a newspaper story, in or near the lead paragraph.

Background Information that helps a reporter write a story, but does not necessarily appear in the story.

Beat That part of the area covered by a newspaper regularly assigned to a reporter in gathering information for news and feature stories.

Body The main part of the story, following the lead paragraph.

Business editor The editor responsible for gathering material and for writing stories about business in the area covered by the newspaper.

By-line The name of the reporter writing the story, usually appearing at the beginning of the story.

Caption The short identification of the contents of photographs in a newspaper, usually placed under the photograph.

Circulation The number of a newspaper's subscribers; the department that sees that these people receive their copies of the paper.

Circulation manager The manager responsible for seeking out new readers for the newspaper and for making sure that current subscribers receive their copies.

City editor The editor responsible for coverage of the city and to whom reporters submit their stories for review and correction.

Civil libel Printed and published defamation of a person, written in a malicious and false manner, that subjects those responsible to damage payments.

Classified advertisements Small advertisements sold by the square inch to customers seeking or offering goods, services, housing, employment, and so forth.

Code of Ethics The accepted practice in journalism as outlined in several documents adopted by national organizations like the Society of Professional Journalists, Sigma Delta Chi.

Cold type Typesetting by computer or photographic means; used in offset printing.

Column The vertical arrangement of type on a newspaper page at varying widths.

Contempt Direct defiance of the rules of the court or orders of a judge by a reporter or editor that can result in a fine or a jail sentence.

Copy block A paragraph or two on a photo page, identifying the photos and the theme depicted in them.

Copydesk That place in the newsroom where editors edit reporters' copy to improve the writing and to correct errors of style.

Copy editor An editor who edits the copy of reporters and writes headlines to accompany them.

Coverage The gathering of material for, and writing of, news stories.

Criminal libel Printed and published defamation that results in a breach of the peace and fines and jail sentences for those responsible.

Cutline A caption appearing under a photograph to identify it.

Dateline The line at the start of a story giving point of origin and date it is filed; used most often in wire-service stories, never in local ones.

Deadline The time when a final version of a story is due; also the time when the press rolls. Newspapers have several deadlines and everything is geared to them.

Delayed lead   A lead (first) paragraph that delays or slightly obscures the meaning of the story until the second or third paragraphs to heighten reader interest.

Display advertisements   Newspapers advertisements designed to promote products by means of headlines, copy blocks, illustrations, and imaginative arrangement.

Dummy   A plan of the arrangement of a newspaper page.

Edition   One printed version of a newspaper appearing at a set time of the day, changes in content being possible in subsequent editions to keep up with the flow of news.

Editor/editor-in-chief   The chief editor on a newspaper, who supervises news content; the term *editor* is also used generally, of any person on the newspaper who edits stories.

Editorializing   Expressing opinion in a news or feature story, as opposed to doing so on the editorial page or in an article labeled "Opinion" or "Analysis"; a grievous sin in journalism.

Editorials   Essays written to express the point of view of the newspaper and its editors on subjects of the day.

Ethics   The accepted standards of behavior for journalists.

Exclusive   A story that only one reporter and his or her newspaper knows the facts of and writes about.

Fair comment and criticism   A principle that protects critics, editorial writers, and sports editors from libel action when they express their professional opinions.

Features   Stories oriented less to recording the news than toward evoking reader interest in special persons, places, or things.

File   Submitting a story to the newspaper from an outside location, usually by telephone or teletype; that place in a newspaper's computer where the stories of various reporters are stored for later use.

First Amendment   The First Amendment to the United States Constitution, which reads, "Congress shall make no law respecting an establishment of religion, or prohibiting the free exercise thereof; or abridging the freedom of speech, or of the press; or the right of the people to assemble, and to petition the Government for a redress of grievances."

Five Ws and H   Who, what, when, where, why, and how; one or more of these elements should be used in every summary lead.

Flag The name of the newspaper that appears in large letters on the front page; this is sometimes mistakenly called a masthead.

Follow-up A story that appears the day after a news event to tell readers what has happened since that event was first reported.

Freebies Gifts like food and liquor given to reporters and editors to influence their coverage of news.

Future book or **future file** The day-to-day and month-to-month record of events the newspaper needs to cover; usually kept by the city editor or metropolitan editor as a reminder of events which need to be covered.

Gag order A ruling issued by a judge to prevent the press from reporting a trial.

Galley proof The first printing of a story after it has been set into type.

General assignment The status of a reporter not assigned to a specific beat, free to carry out any assignment given by the editor.

General manager The person on the newspaper in charge of the business side.

Graf An abbreviated form of *paragraph*.

Handout A press release or other form of information submitted to reporters and editors for direct use in the newspaper or for background.

Hard-copy printer A machine that gives a printed version of a story set electronically on a VDT and stored in the computer; this version is not used for editing, but for later analysis of the writing and as a record for the reporter.

Hard news News that is topical, timely, and perishable; it must be included in the newspaper as soon as it happens, or it will not be "news."

Headline Large, bold words appearing over a news or feature story to attract the attention of readers by presenting a few key facts of the story.

Hot type Type set by Linotype or similar machine using molten metal to cast lines of type; used in letterpress printing.

Interview The two-way interchange between reporter and source, used to gain information for stories; ideally, reporters ask the questions, sources give the answers.

Inverted-pyramid style The most common way to write a news story; most important facts first, followed by all the other facts in the descending order of their importance.

Investigative reporting A careful and complete investigation of a subject by a reporter or team of reporters; the published story is usually longer than a normal news or feature story.

Journalism Reporting, writing, editing, photographing, or broadcasting news; used interchangeably with *press*.

Junkets Free trips given to reporters and editors to influence their coverage.

Lead The first paragraph of a story, important because it is the reporter's first opportunity to capture a reader's interest.

Letterpress A printing method in which the raised surface image is pressed directly against the paper.

Libel A malicious, false, and defamatory statement issued in printed form.

Linotype A machine that casts lines of type from hot lead; used in letterpress printing.

Magazine A publication usually issued weekly or monthly, bound in soft cover, printed on high-quality paper, and containing articles, stories, poems, photographs, illustrations, and advertisements.

Makeup The arrangement of all elements of a newspaper page: headlines, text, photographs, advertisements.

Masthead The list, usually on the editorial page, of a newspaper's staff, place of publication, ownership and mailing information. (See "Flag.")

Mat A cardboard or papier-mâché mold from which type is cast in letterpress printing.

Metropolitan editor The editor responsible for coverage of a large metropolitan area encompassing several cities and to whom reporters submit their stories for review and correction.

Morgue The files of past stories and newspaper issues, used by reporters and editors for reference.

Mug shot A photograph that shows only a person's head and shoulders and usually runs in a small size.

The new journalism The writing of news and feature stories in such detail that they read like fiction.

News features Feature stories with a close tie to the day's news.

News hole The space available for news after advertisements have been placed.

Newspaper A publication on newsprint appearing at a set interval and containing news, editorials, features, photographs, and advertisements.

News peg The reason a reporter's story is being published; the element in it that makes it newsworthy.

News release Another term for *press release*.

Newsroom The large room in the newspaper, where reporters, editors, and photographers work.

News side That part of the newspaper organization in which the nonadvertising content is prepared—reporters report, editors edit and write headlines, and photographers take pictures and develop film.

News source The person or persons who give reporters the information from which they write stories.

Not for attribution Information, gained in interviews, whose sources are not to be revealed by the reporter; the information itself can be used, however.

Obituary The written account of a person's death that appears in a newspaper.

Obscenity Printed material that is offensive to modesty or decency, is indecent or lewd, causing, or intending to cause, sexual excitement or lust.

Offset An indirect printing method based on the principle that grease and water do not mix; the image goes from plate to a rubber blanket to the paper.

Off the record Material, gained in an interview, that serves only as background for the reporter and cannot be used in print.

Open meetings laws State laws that ensure that a reporter can cover a meeting of a governmental or other organization without hindrance.

Paste-up The process of preparing a complete newspaper page; when the headlines, stories, and advertisements have been set into type, and the photographs prepared, they are attached, with wax, to a special measured sheet, ready to be photographed.

People features Feature stories that capture their subjects—people, and even places or things—through descriptive, vivid writing, and many direct quotes.

Personal lead A lead that uses "you" or an "implied you" approach to gain reader interest.

Photographer A person on the newspaper who takes photographs to accompany news and feature stories or to appear as separate photo essays.

Photojournalism Telling a story by means of photographs, with little or no text material.

Pica A printer's way of measuring line width (6 picas to an inch, 12 points to a pica).

Plate Metal from which something is printed; formed to fit the press.

Point A printer's way of measuring type size (72 points to an inch).

Press Printed publications and broadcast stations and their employees who gather and present news; used interchangeably with "journalism."

Press release A story written by an organization to give its point of view of an event; releases are sent to members of the press in the hope they will be used in the newspaper; many are not, however, because they are often thought biased and one-sided.

Privacy The public's right to be let alone; the reporter's right to cover people involved in news events as long as they don't unnecessarily or carelessly invade their privacy.

Privileged material Material set aside as immune from prosecution under libel laws: court records, transcripts of congressional debates.

Production That part of the newspaper where stories and advertisements are set into type, pasted up, prepared for the press, and printed.

Production manager The manager responsible for seeing that stories and advertisements are set into type, pages pasted up, negatives and plates made, and the newspaper printed on the press.

Public relations The art and technique of promoting goodwill toward a company or other organization by printed and other means; also called PR.

Publisher The owner of the newspaper, or representative of the owner, who is ultimately responsible for all aspects of the newspaper's operation.

Question lead A lead paragraph that gains the interest of readers by asking a question.

Quotation lead A lead paragraph that begins with a quotation from a source to gain reader interest.

Quotes The actual words of an interview subject set off with quotation marks in the story and used to heighten reader interest and to give readers a good "feel" for the subject.

Reporter A person who gathers material and writes news and feature stories.

Reproduction proof A final, printed proof ready to be pasted down and photographed for final printing. Also called a repro proof.

Rewriting Editing and otherwise changing newspaper stories to improve them; this process is done by a reporter or editor.

Screening Processing photographs in order to build up a tiny dot-structure on them that will retain ink and enable them to be printed.

Second-day story Using a fresh angle on a story the day after it first becomes known.

Secondary sources Printed material, any source other than a person, used by a reporter to gather facts for a story.

Shield laws State laws to protect reporters from having to reveal names of sources and or content of notes.

Short features Brief stories that treat a subject in a humorous, sad, or ironic manner.

Sidebar features Stories that explore one aspect of a main news event; sidebars break the main subject into understandable and manageable units.

Slander A malicious, false, and defamatory statement or report by oral, rather than printed, means.

Soft news Stories that are interesting and informative, but not necessarily timely; features are soft news because they can appear at any time, whereas hard news must be in the newspaper as soon as possible.

Source The person who provides a reporter the information for a story, a very important part of the journalistic process.

Sports editor An editor who gathers material for and writes stories about sports events in the area covered by the newspaper.

Stereotyping The process, used in letterpress printing, of making a duplicate metal plate of a newspaper page from a mat; the duplicate plate is flat or curved to fit the press.

Style The conventions according to which a newspaper wants its stories to be written, determining such matters as abbreviation, spelling, capitalization.

Stylebook The details of a newspaper's style compiled in a book for easy access by reporters and editors.

Subhead A heading, in a smaller type size than the headline, used to break up a long story into easily read segments.

Summary lead A lead that summarizes the most important facts of a story, usually through the use of the five Ws and H.

Syndication The selling of material to a number of newspapers by companies called syndicates.

Transition The sentence that guides readers from the lead to the body of a story.

Type Printed letters and characters of various sizes and styles.

Updating The combining and rewriting of wire-service stories received over a period of several hours, which ensures that the published story is both up-to-date and complete.

UPI United Press International, one of the two major wire services.

VDT Video-display terminal, a kind of electronic typewriter consisting of a keyboard and video screen; reporters use the keyboard to type their stories, and an electronic "cursor" to make editorial changes.

Wire service A company that employs hundreds of reporters and editors around the country and the world to cover and prepare news and feature stories for member newspapers, magazines, and broadcasting stations; the material is sent to these clients by teletype machines.

Women's editor An editor responsible for gathering material and writing stories of interest to women and other members of the family.

Bibliography

History and press problems

Agee, Warren K., Edwin Emery, and Phillip H. Ault. *Introduction to Mass Communications*. 5th ed. New York: Dodd, Mead, 1975.

Emery, Edwin. *The Press and America*. 4th ed. Englewood Cliffs, N.J.: Prentice-Hall, 1978.

Emery, Michael C., and Ted Curtis Smythe. *Readings in Mass Communication*. 3rd ed. Dubuque, Iowa: Wm. C. Brown, 1977.

Fedler, Fred. *An Introduction to the Mass Media*. New York: Harcourt Brace Jovanovich, 1978.

Hiebert, Ray E., Donald F. Ungurait, and Thomas W. Bohn. *Mass Media: An Introduction to Modern Communication*. 2nd ed. New York: David McKay, 1979.

Lutz, William D. *The Age of Communication*. Pacific Palisades, Calif.: Goodyear Publishing, 1974.

Pember, Don R. *Mass Media in America*. 2nd ed. Palo Alto, Calif.: Science Research Associates, 1977.

Sandman, Peter M., David M. Rubin, and David B. Sachsman. *Media*. 2nd ed. Englewood Cliffs, N.J.: Prentice-Hall, 1976.

Snyder, Louis L., and Richard B. Morris, eds. *A Treasury of Great Reporting*. New York: Simon and Schuster, 1962.

Tebbel, John. *The Media in America*. New York: Mentor, 1974.

Voelker, Francis H., and Ludmila A. Voelker, eds. *Mass Media*. 3rd ed. New York: Harcourt Brace Jovanovich, 1978.

Whetmore, Edward Jay. *Mediamerica: Form, Content, and Consequence of Mass Communication*. Belmont, Calif.: Wadsworth Publishing Co., 1979.

Whitney, Frederick C. *Mass Media and Mass Communications in Society*. Dubuque, Iowa: Wm. C. Brown, 1975.

News writing

Bernstein, Carl, and Bob Woodward. *All the President's Men*. New York: Simon and Schuster, 1974.

Burken, Judith L. *Introduction to Reporting*. Dubuque, Iowa: Wm. C. Brown, 1976.

Charnley, Mitchell V. and Blair Charnley. *Reporting*. 4th ed. New York: Holt, Rinehart and Winston, 1979.

Fedler, Fred. *Reporting for the Print Media*. 2nd ed. New York: Harcourt Brace Jovanovich, 1979.

Harriss, Julian, Kelly Leiter, and Stanley Johnson. *The Complete Reporter*. 3rd ed. New York: Macmillan, 1977.

Hill, Evan, and John L. Breen. *Reporting & Writing the News*. Boston: Little, Brown, 1977.

MacDougall, Curtis D. *Interpretative Reporting*. 7th ed. New York: Macmillan, 1977.

McCombs, Maxwell, Donald Lewis Shaw, and David Grey. *Handbook of Reporting Methods*. Boston: Houghton Mifflin, 1976.

Mencher, Melvin. *News Reporting and Writing*. Dubuque, Iowa: Wm. C. Brown, 1977.

Strunk, William, and E. B. White. *The Elements of Style*. New York: Macmillan, 1975.

Wicker, Tom. *On Press*. New York: Viking, 1978.

Fact finding and feature stories

Brady, John. *The Craft of Interviewing*. Cincinnati: Writer's Digest Books, 1976.

Metzler, Ken. *Creative Interviewing*. Englewood Cliffs, N.J.: Prentice-Hall, 1977.

Nelson, Roy Paul. *Articles and Features*. Boston: Houghton Mifflin, 1978.

Rivers, William L. *Finding Facts*. Englewood Cliffs, N.J.: Prentice-Hall, 1975.

Rivers, William L. *Free-Lancer and Staff Writer*. 2nd ed. Belmont, Calif.: Wadsworth, 1976.

Scanlon, Paul. *Reporting The Rolling Stone Style*. Garden City: Anchor Press/Doubleday, 1977.

The Washington Post. *Of the Press, by the Press, for the Press, and Others, Too*. Boston: Houghton Mifflin, 1976.

The Washington Post. *Writing in Style*. Boston: Houghton Mifflin, 1975.

Wolfe, Tom. *The New Journalism*. New York: Harper & Row, 1973.

Editing, makeup, and production

Arnold, Edmund. *Functional Newspaper Design*. New York: Harper & Row, 1969.

Click, J. W., and Russell N. Baird. *Magazine Editing and Production*. 2nd ed. Dubuque, Iowa: Wm. C. Brown, 1979.

Nelson, Roy Paul. *Publication Design*. Dubuque, Iowa: Wm. C. Brown, 1972.

Turnbull, Arthur T., and Russell N. Baird. *The Graphics of Communication*. 3rd ed. New York: Holt, Rinehart and Winston, 1975.

Westley, Bruce. *News Editing*. 2nd ed. Boston: Houghton Mifflin, 1972.

Advertising and public relations

Cutlip, Scott M., and Allen H. Center. *Effective Public Relations*. 5th ed. Englewood Cliffs, N.J.: Prentice-Hall, 1978.

Dunn, S. W., and A. M. Barban. *Advertising: Its Role in Modern Marketing*. 4th ed. Hinsdale, Ill.: Dryden Press, 1978.

Johnson, J. Douglas. *Advertising Today*. Chicago: Science Research Associates, Inc., 1978.

Kleppner, Otto. *Advertising Procedure*. 7th ed. Englewood Cliffs, N.J.: Prentice-Hall, 1979.

Nelson, Roy Paul. *The Design of Advertising*. 3rd ed. Dubuque, Iowa: Wm. C. Brown, 1977.

Newsom, Doug, and Alan Scott. *This Is PR: The Realities of Public Relations*. Belmont, Calif.: Wadsworth, 1976.

Weilbacher, William M. *Advertising*. New York: Macmillan, 1979.

Index

Abbreviations, 325
Access to official information, 318–19
Accidents, stories about, 17, 113–14
Accuracy, 119
   in code of ethics, 284
   and editor, 129
   need for, 113, 115, 116–17
Advertising, 47–49
   classified, 49
   local, 48–49
   national, 49
Advertising manager, 48
Agricultural editor, 137
Allbriton, Joe L., 9
American Newspaper Publishers Association, 7, 57
American Society of Newspaper Editors, 282
AMs, 8
Anecdotal lead, 146–47
Anniversary stories, 203
Appointments for interviews, 228
Associated Press, 10, 47, 131
Atkins, John
   on ethics, 282
   on feature stories, 276
   on interviewing, 226, 227, 228, 230, 232
   on invasion of privacy, 305
   on investigative features, 268–71
   on objectivity, 288

Atkins, John (continued)
   on people features, 254–56
   on reporters, 115, 118–19
   on speech stories, 206
Atlantic Monthly, 303
Attribution, 165–66
   in feature stories, 275
   in speech stories, 220–21

Bakke case, 248, 249
Barth, John, 215–17
Beat, 111, 112–14. *See also* City-hall beat; Police beat
Beat reporters, 98–99, 104–7, 110–14
   vs. investigative reporters, 268, 271
   personal relations with sources, 287–88
Bellows, James, 9
Bias, 280, 282, 288. *See also* Editorializing; Objectivity
Birthday stories, 202–4
Birth stories, 202
Bogart, John, 14
Bolles, Don, 272
Branzburg decision, 310–12
Brennan, Justice William, 301, 306
Brockett, Diane
   on editorializing, 171
   on ethics, 282, 288

Brockett, Diane (continued)
   on feature stories, 242–46, 260–67, 275–76
   on freebies, 287
   on interviewing, 227, 229, 230, 232, 233
   on libel, 298
   on misrepresentation to sources, 288
   on objectivity, 288
   as reporter, 111–12, 115, 117, 120–21
   on writing news stories, 162–64, 171
Bullets
   in feature stories, 242, 261
   as organizational device, 218–19
Burger, Chief Justice Warren, 317–18
Business editor, 46, 137
Business manager, 48
Business side of newspaper, 47–50
Butz, Earl, 234

Caldwell case, 310
Calendar page, 200–202
Cantrell v. Forest City Publishing, 307–8
Capitalization, 326
Capote, Truman, 289
Carriers, newspaper, 49

"CBS Evening News with Walter Cronkite," 12
Checkbook journalism, 288–89
Christian Science Monitor, 37
Circulation, 49
Circulation manager, 49
City editor, 44, 46, 137
　job of, 126–30, 256–59
　role in production, 63
City-hall beat, 106–7, 110–11, 114, 116
　stories based on, 156–62
Civil libel, 299
Civil War reporting, 143–44
Clarkson, Rich, 76, 78–79, 80
Classified advertisements, 49
Codes of ethics, 282–86, 292–94
Colby, William 289
Cold type, 57
　compared to hot type, 60
Colon, 177–78
Column, 57
Confidentiality, legal issues of, 309–18
Contempt of court, 309–18
Copydesk, 137, 179
Copy-editing marks, 329–32
Copy editor, 46–47, 126–27, 137
　in production, 62, 63
Copy preparation, 332–33
Corvallis Gazette-Times, 10, 37, 39, 59
　code of ethics of, 292–94
　editor of, 126–30
　front-page placement in, 37
　production technology at, 59–73
　reporters of, 47, 98–99, 104–7, 110
Court reporting, 300
Coverage, different kinds of
　meetings, 114
　police beat, 113
　unexpected events, 113–14
Cox Broadcasting v. Martin Cohn, 307

Crime stories, 17. *See also* Police beat
Criminal libel, 300

Damages in libel suits, 299
Deadlines, 118, 132, 133, 179
Deckert, Rod
　on being sued, 279
　career of, 136
　as city editor, 126–30, 136, 256–59
　on editors, 124, 132–33, 134, 136
　on ethics, 282, 288
　on libel, 298
　on meetings stories, 199–200
　on news, 17, 40
　on note-taking accuracy, 117
　on objectivity, 288
　on production technology, 52
　on reporters, 118
Defenses against libel suits
　fair comment and criticism, 300
　First Amendment Supreme Court decisions, 301–4
　privilege, 300
　truth, 300
Delayed lead, 147–48
　in feature stories, 241, 248
Dictationist, 179–80
Dummy, 57
Dummying, 63

Editor, 44, 137. *See also* Editors
Editorializing
　in feature stories, 249, 276
　in news stories, 169–71
　in speech stories, 219
Editorial-page editor, 46
Editor-in-chief, 137

Editors
　ability to edit stories, 133, 134
　assertiveness, 132
　characteristics needed in, 132–36
　as gatekeepers, 27–37, 40, 130
　kinds of, 44–47, 126–32, 137–38
　news sense, 132
　objectivity, 132–33
　as people managers, 133–34
　relations with reporters, 133–34
　rewriting by, 179–81
　role in offset production, 60, 62
　sense of layout and design, 134–35
　training and experience, 135–36
　use of VDT by, 128, 129, 130–31, 137
　work pressures on, 133
Engagement stories, 197–99
Ethics
　and checkbook journalism, 288–89
　codes of, 282–86, 292–94
　and freebies, 286–87
　historically, 285
　and junkets, 287
　and membership/personal relationships, 287–88
　and misrepresentation to sources, 288
　and new journalism, 289–92
　and objectivity, 288
　personal basis of, 294
　and photographers, 89
　problems of, 286–92
　in recent years, 285–86
　of withholding information at official request, 289
Executive editor, 137

Fairness, 282, 284–85. *See also* Bias; Objectivity
Fair trial, right to, and freedom of the press, 314–16

Farber case, 313, 314–16
Feature stories, 142
   interviewing for, 227, 230
   investigative, 259–71, 276
   news, 242–46, 275, 276–77
   people, 253–59, 275–76
   short, 248–53, 275
   sidebar, 246–48, 249, 275
   types of, 242–71
   writing of, 275–77
Fires, stories about, 113–14
Firestone v. Time, 302–3
Five W's and H, 142, 145–46, 151, 152, 154–55, 156–58
Flatbed press, 55
Folts, James (photos), 64–72, 100–103
Foreign editor, 137–38
Freebies, 286–87
Freedom of Information Act, 273, 318–19
Front-page placement, 27–37, 126–28
Frost, David, 288–89

Gag orders, 317–18
Galley proof, 57
Gatekeeper theory, 27, 130
   and front-page placement, 27–37
General-assignment reporter, 114
General manager, 48
Gertz v. Robert Welch, 302
Glossary
   of general terms, 335–43
   of printing terms, 57–59
Gobright, Lawrence, 144–45
Goldstein, Robert, 211–13
Gortner, Marjoe, 213–15
Government
   action of, as news element, 26
   investigative reporting on local, 268, 273–74.
   See also City-hall beat; Public records

Greene, Bob, 272
Gutenberg, Johann, 54

Haldeman, H. R., 289
Haley, Alex, 208–13
Hall, Mike
   on charge of news bias, 280
   on ethics, 294
   on interviewing, 224, 229
   on legal issues, 318
   on libel, 299
   on news, 16
   as reporter, 110–11, 116, 117, 118, 119, 120, 121
   on rewrite process, 180–81
   on writing news stories, 142, 159–62
Hard-copy printer, 58
Headlines, 63, 177
Herbert v. Lando, 303–4
Hot type, 58
   compared to cold type, 60

Interviewing
   after, 233–34
   interview itself, 228–31
   note-taking during, 231–32, 233–34
   preparation for, 227–29
   tape recorders for, 232–33
   telephone for, 233
Inverted-pyramid style, 142
   defined, 143
   derivation of, 143
   examples of, 151–64
   how to write, 143–45
   not used in feature stories, 276
Investigative features, 259–71, 276
Investigative reporters and editors, 272

Investigative reporting
   vs. beat reporting, 268, 271
   problems of, 268–71
   tips on, 272–74.
   See also Investigative features

Jacobellis decision, 309
Jefferson, Thomas, 3
Jenks, Tom
   career of, 136
   as editor, 126–28, 136
   on editors, 132, 133–34, 136
   on ethical problems, 287
   on invasion of privacy, 305
   on investigative features, 268
   on libel, 298, 304
   on meetings stories, 200
   on new journalism, 292
   on news, 16, 17
   on newspaper production, 42, 52
   on obituaries, 195
   on reporters, 118
   on service stories, 194–95
Johns, Chris, 80–90
   photos of, 18–25, 82–86
Johnson, Lyndon, 7, 217
Journalism
   history of, 6
   power of, 7
   social role of, 6–7
Junkets, 287

Kennedy, John F., 289
King, Dick
   career of, 135
   on news, 16, 17
   on service stories, 192, 194

Leads
   anecdotal, 146–47
   delayed, 147–48, 241, 248

Leads (continued)
   for feature stories, 238, 241, 242, 276
   personal, 149
   question, 148–49
   quotation, 150
   rewriting, 179
   for speech stories, 219–20
   summary, 145–46
   and transitional sentences, 167–69
Legal problems of the press
   access to official information, 318–19
   contempt and confidentiality, 309–18
   invasion of privacy, 305–8
   libel, 298–305
   obscenity, 309
Letterpress printing
   explained, 54, 58
   newspapers using, 57
   steps in, 54–56
Libel, 298–305
   causes of, 299–300
   civil, 299
   criminal, 299, 300
   damages in, 299
   defenses, 300–304
   defined, 299–300
   eliminating risks in, 304–5
Life, 9, 10–11, 79, 306
Lincoln assassination reporting, 144
Linotype, 55–56, 58
Lippmann, Walter, 4
Look, 10–11, 79

Magazines, 10–11, 12
Makeup, 58
Managing editor, 44, 137
Marshall, John
   on accuracy, 117
   on reporters, 118

Marshall, John (continued)
   on short features, 252–53
   on speech stories, 213–17
   on writing news stories, 142
Mat, 55, 58
Meeting announcement stories, 199–202
Meeting coverage, 114
Memberships in organizations, 287–88
Mergenthaler, Ottmar, 55–56
"Metro" beat, 111–12
Metropolitan editor, 44, 130–32, 137
Miller decision, 309
Misrepresentation to sources, 288
Monroe, Bill
   on editorializing, 170–71
   on ethics, 294
   on feature stories, 238–42, 246–48, 250–52, 256–59, 276–77
   on gathering news, 95, 96
   on interviewing, 228, 232, 233, 234
   on invasion of privacy, 305
   on libel, 298
   on news, 16, 17
   on note-taking, 114
   as reporter, 98–99, 104–7, 110, 115, 116–17, 118, 120
   on writing news stories, 142, 143, 151–59, 170–71
Moss, John, 312

Names, 327
Natural disasters, stories about, 17
Nebraska Press Association v. Stuart, 317–18
New journalism, 289–92
New photography, 79
News
   defined, 16–27

News (continued)
   and gatekeepers, 27
   knowing what it is, 37–40
   photo essay on, 18–25
   selection and placement of, for front page, 27–37
   on television and radio, 11–13
News editor, 62
News elements, 16–27
   and editorial policy, 37
   and front-page placement, 27–37
   and readership patterns, 37, 40
News feature, 242–46, 275, 276–77
News hole, 48
Newspaper organization, 44–50
Newspaper production, 50, 52–74
   at *Corvallis Gazette-Times,* 62–73
   letterpress printing, 54–56
   offset printing, 57, 59–73
   photo essay on, 64–72
Newspapers, 7–10
   advertising in, 47–49
   AMs, 8
   business side of, 8, 47–50
   circulation of, 7
   compared to magazines and television/radio, 12
   consolidation of ownership of, 8, 9–10, 44
   employment in, 8
   news side of, 44, 46–47
   number of, 7
   organization of, 44–50
   PMs, 8
   production side of, 50
News releases, rewriting, 182–87
News story, 150–64
   approach to, 150–51
   attribution in, 165–66
   editorializing in, 169–71
   inverted-pyramid structure of, 143–45
   leads in, 145–50
   parts of, 142

Index

News story (continued)
   placement of, in paper, 27–37, 126–28
   transitional sentences in, 167–69
   updating wire-service, 187–89
   writing, 142–71
New technology
   explained, 59
   impact of, 73
Newton, Wally, 59, 61–62, 73
New York Herald, 143
New York Times, 13, 195, 220, 313–15
New York Times rule, 301, 302, 306, 307
New York Tribune, 144
Nixon, Richard, 6, 7, 288, 309
Notes, 98, 114–15
   example of, 108–9
   for interviews, 231–32, 233–34
   need for accuracy in, 116–17
   protection of, 310, 315–16
   for speech stories, 217–18
Not for attribution, 231
Numerals, 326–27

Obituaries, 195–97
Objectivity, 288
   in codes of ethics, 284, 293
   vs. editorializing, 169–171
   required in editors, 132–33
Obscenity, 309
Offset printing
   at *Corvallis Gazette-Times,* 59–73
   explained, 57, 58
   steps in, 62–73
Off the record, 231
Onassis, Jacqueline Kennedy, 308
Open meetings laws, 320
Open records laws, 320
Oregon State University press releases, 184–85

Pappas case, 311
Paraphrasing, in speech stories, 220, 221–22
Paste-ups, 58, 63
People feature, 253–59, 275–76
Personal lead, 149
Personal relationships, 287–88
Photographers, 46, 79–90
   and ethics, 89
   interaction of, with editorial staff, 79–80
   photo essay on, 82–86
   typical day of, 80–81, 88–90
Photography. *See* Photojournalism
Photography editor, 46
Photojournalism, 78–90
Pica, 58
Plates, 58, 73
Playboy, 226
PMs, 8, 130–32
Point, 58
Police beat, 98–99, 104–5, 113, 116, 131–32
   format for stories based on, 142, 151–53
   and law suits, 113, 116, 300
   short feature stories based on, 252–53
Pornography, 260–67, 287
Powell, Justice Lewis, 302
Preparing copy, 332–33
Press releases, 128
   rewriting, 182–87
Printing terms, 57–59
Privacy Act, 273
Privacy, invasion of, 305–8
Production manager, 50, 58, 59–73
Production side of newspaper, 50, 54–73
Proofreaders, 62
Public records
   for investigative reports, 271, 272–73
   laws on access to, 318–19
Public relations people, 111

Public relations people (continued)
   rewriting press releases of, 182–87
Publisher, 44
Punctuation, 327–29

Question leads, 148–49
Questions, how to ask, 227, 229–30
Quotation leads, 150, 220
Quotations
   in feature stories, 276–77
   in speech stories, 221–22

Radio, 9, 10, 11–13
Reader's Digest, 11
Reagan, Ronald, 226
Real estate, investigative reports on, 274
Reporters
   characteristics of good, 115–20
   daily routine of, 100–103, 112–15
   deadlines of, 118
   defined, 47
   editorializing to be avoided by, 169–71
   as gatekeepers, 27, 40, 171
   reasons to become, 120–21
   relations with editors, 133–34
   types of, 98–112
   use of VDTs by, 60, 62, 104, 106, 178
Reporters' Committee for Freedom of the Press, 319
Reporter's Ethics Game, 290–91
Reporter's Legal Game, 320–21
Reproduction proof, 58, 62–63
Research
   for interviews, 227
   for speech stories, 217
Rewrite person, 179–80

Index

Rewriting
   in general, 179–81
   of press releases, 182–87
   of wire-service copy, 187–89
Richardson, Jim, 79
Robberies, stories about, 113–14
Rosenbloom v. Metromedia, 301–2
Roth v. United States, 309

Sales people, 48–49
Saturday Evening Post, 10–11
Semicolon, 178
Senefelder, Aloys, 57
Service stories
   anniversaries, 203
   birthdays, 202–4
   births, 202
   engagements, 197–99
   meetings, 199–202
   obituaries, 195–97
   weddings, 197–99
Shield laws, 312–14, 315
   defined, 312
   effect of Farber case on, 313, 314–16
   Oregon's, as example of, 313–14
Short feature, 248–53, 275
Sidebar feature, 246–48, 249, 275
Sigma Delta Chi, code of ethics of, 282–86
"60 Minutes," 303–4
Society of Professional Journalists, code of ethics of, 282–86
Sources
   attribution of, 165–66
   checking copy with, 234
   importance of, 111, 113, 114, 115
   interviewing, 228–34
   in investigative reporting, 272–73, 274
   misrepresentation to, 288
   off the record comments of, 231

Sources (continued)
   protection of, as legal issue, 113, 309–10, 315–16
Specialty editors, 137–38
Speech stories
   examples of, 208–17
   how to report, 217–18
   how to write, 218–22
Spelling, importance of correct, 178
Sports, stories about, 27
Sports editor, 46, 137
Sports Illustrated, 9, 117
Spot news, 114
Stanford Daily case, 316–17
Stereotyping, 54–55, 58
Stern, Dennis
   career of, 135
   as editor, 130–32, 133, 135
   on editors, 133, 134, 135
   on feature stories, 236, 275
   on freebies, 286–87
   on invasion of privacy, 308
   on investigative stories, 260
   on libel, 296, 304–5
   on new journalism, 292
   on news, 14, 16
   on writing news stories, 146–47
Stewart, Justice Potter, 307, 312, 317
Stylebook, 104, 178–79, 325–29
Summary lead, 145–46
Supreme Court, U.S.
   on contempt and confidentiality, 310–12, 316–18
   on invasion of privacy, 306–8
   on libel, 301–4
   on obscenity, 309

Tape recorders
   for interviews, 232–33
   for speech stories, 218
Telephone
   for interviews, 233
   and rewrite process, 179–80

Television, 9, 10, 11–13
Thompson, Hunter, 228
Time, 9, 78
Time v. Hill, 306–7
Times v. Sullivan, 301
Topeka Capital-Journal, 9, 32–37, 38
   front-page placement in, 32, 36–37
   photography in, 78–90
   reporters on, 47, 110–11
Trade publications, 11
Transitional sentences, 167–69
Type, 59

Udevitz, Norm, 272
Unexpected events coverage, 113
United Press International, 10, 47, 131
Updating, 187–89
Urban-affairs editor, 137
U.S. News and World Report, 226

VDT. *See* Video-display terminal
Video-display terminal, 59, 61–63, 73
   editor's use of, 128, 129, 130–31, 137
   reporter's use of, 60, 62, 104, 106, 178
Vietnam War, 6, 7, 258
Villard, Henry, 143–44

Wallace, Mike, 289, 303
War, stories about, 26
Warrants, search, 316–17
Washington Post, 9, 130, 146, 260
Washington Star, 9, 28–35
   editor's job on, 130–32

Washington Star (continued)
   front-page placement in, 28–32
   reporters on, 47, 111–12
Watergate, 7, 260
Weather, stories about, 27
Wedding stories, 197–99
White, Justice Byron, 304, 307–8, 311–12, 316–17
Whitman, Alden, 195
Wire editor, 47, 126–27
   and updating, 187
Wire services, 10, 47, 131
   rewriting stories from, 187–89

Wisner, George
   on ethics, 294
   on interviewing, 227, 228, 230, 231
   on libel, 298
   on misrepresentation to sources, 288
   on news, 16
   on reporters, 112, 113, 116, 118
   on sidebar features, 248, 249
   on speech stories, 208–11, 218
   on writing news stories, 140–46

Withholding information at official request, 289
Wolfe, Tom, 289
Women's editor, 46, 137
Writing
   feature stories, 275–77
   general rules of, 176–79
   leads, 145–50
   news stories, 142–72
   obituaries, 195–97
   service stories, 194–205
   speech stories, 208–22.
   See also Rewriting.

PN
4775   Lovell, Ronald P.
.L6
         The newspaper

DATE DUE
